Inheritance Act Claims

With best wishes
Thoughts.
Paul Hewitt

Related titles available from Law Society Publishing:

Contentious Probate (due Autumn 2007)
Law and Practice
Brendan Hall

Probate Practitioner's Handbook (5th edn)
General Editor: Lesley King

Trust Practitioner's Handbook
Gill Steel (with contributions by Robert Mowbray and Charles Christian)

Will Draftsman's Handbook (8th edn)
Robin Riddett

All books from Law Society Publishing can be ordered from good bookshops. For more information or a catalogue, please email our editorial and marketing office: publishing@lawsociety.co.uk.

INHERITANCE ACT CLAIMS

A Practical Guide

Tracey Angus, Anna Clarke, Paul Hewitt and Penelope Reed

The Law Society

The authors have asserted the right under the Copyright, Designs and Patents Act 1988 to be identified as the authors of this work.

Crown copyright material is reproduced with the permission of the Controller of HMSO and the Queen's Printer for Scotland.

The material in Appendices C1 and C2 is reproduced with the kind permission of the Association of Contentious Trust and Probate Specialists.

© Tracey Angus, Anna Clarke, Paul Hewitt and Penelope Reed 2007

ISBN-10: 1–85328–553–6
ISBN-13: 978–1–85328–553–0

Published in 2007 by Law Society Publishing
113 Chancery Lane, London WC2A 1PL

Typeset by J&L Composition, Filey, North Yorkshire
Printed by MPG Books Ltd, Bodmin, Cornwall

Contents

Table of cases

ix

Table of statutes

Table of statutory instruments and European legislation

About the authors

Tracey Angus is a barrister at 5 Stone Buildings where she has a general Chancery practice with emphasis on professional negligence, equity and trusts, probate, land law and mortgages, family provision and the Court of Protection. She is a member of PNBA and ACTAPS.

Anna Clarke is a barrister at 5 Stone Buildings where she has a general Chancery practice with an emphasis on probate, administration of estates, equity and trusts and family provision. She is a member of ACTAPS.

Paul Hewitt is a principal solicitor in the Contentious Trust and Probate team at Withers LLP. He is a regular contributor to various legal publications and lectures on contentious trust and probate matters.

Penelope Reed is a barrister at 5 Stone Buildings where she has a wide Chancery practice with emphasis on trusts, wills, contentious probate, family provision claims, tax and property matters. She is a member of STEP, ACTAPS and the Revenue Bar Association. Penelope is also author of several trust and will books.

CHAPTER 1

Introduction

1.1 OVERVIEW

Many clients who are told that the court can interfere with what they put in their wills react with indignation. However, English law is relatively unusual in allowing complete testamentary freedom. Many jurisdictions have rules about forced heirship which are unknown in England and Wales. However, the law recognises the need for testators to make provision for those to whom they owe an obligation. Quite apart from anything else, there is a social reason for ensuring that those who die provide for those dependent on them and do not leave them to fall back onto the State for support.

The Inheritance (Family Provision) Act 1938 was fairly limited in form excluding many of the categories of applicants who can apply under the Inheritance (Provision for Family and Dependants) Act 1975 (the Act or 1975 Act). In 1974 the Law Commission produced *Family Law: Second Report on Family Property, Family Provision on Death* (Law Com. No. 62) which reviewed the law in this area and led to the enactment of the 1975 Act. That Act was hailed in some quarters as a 'mistresses' charter' in that dependants could for the first time apply for provision. The Act also allowed for the first time adult children to apply for provision which has over the years spawned a considerable amount of litigation. It also tied the provision made for a widow or widower in with the provision which they might have expected to receive on divorce – as it had been observed that divorcing wives were doing better in terms of provision than widows under the 1938 Act.

The Act has in many ways provided a barometer of social change. In 1995 the Law Reform (Succession) Act introduced a new category of applicant – the cohabitant. This new category was introduced in respect of deaths after 1 January 1996 and meant that applicants who had lived with the deceased for more than two years but might not be able to show dependency within the terms of the Act could still make an application. The change recognised the fact that many more couples were living together rather than marrying.

In 2004 the Civil Partnership Act was introduced which put registered civil partners on the same footing as spouses as far as the 1975 Act was concerned. It is fair to say that how such applications will fare under the Act is untested.

Those cohabiting as if they were civil partners are included in the class of applicants who can apply, as well as children treated as a child of the family where there was a civil partnership and former civil partners.

There is little doubt that this is an area of law where family and chancery law meet; where the chancery practitioner needs to understand family law concepts such as a child of the family and what provision might be expected on divorce, and the family practitioner needs to understand concepts of succession law such as the meaning of the net estate and the tax implications of any order made or compromise reached.

In approaching any claim under the Act, it is wise to adopt a step-by-step approach. The following chapters of this book take the reader through those steps in detail but the following is a summary of the questions which the practitioner needs to work through:

1. Did the deceased die domiciled in England and Wales? This may be self-evident in many cases but the world is now a much smaller place and people may live and work in a country which is not their country of domicile.
2. Does the potential claimant fall within one of the classes of applicant set out in s.1 of the Act? This can pose particular difficulties in the case of a dependant, for example, or a child where paternity is disputed.
3. If the claimant does qualify as an applicant, does the will fail to make reasonable financial provision for him or her having regard to the factors listed in s.3 of the Act? It is important to undertake this test first. There will be cases where, for example, the financial resources of the claimant will mean that it was reasonable for him or her to be completely excluded from benefit under a will or on intestacy.
4. If the will or the provision on intestacy do not make reasonable financial provision for the claimant, what is the appropriate provision for the claimant? It is likely that all that can be advised is a range of possible awards.
5. Both stages (3) and (4) require the practitioner to look at the size and nature of the net estate. This is a crucially important part of the overall picture. It is perhaps trite to point out that if the estate is small and there are a number of competing claims on it, the task of making adequate provision for a claimant may be a very difficult one. A large estate makes the task far easier and so a claimant who might not be able to succeed against a modest estate might have a better chance against a more substantial one. This is the point where the issue of whether there is joint property which has passed by survivorship needs to be considered. The question of property which is subject to a nomination arises less often. It also at this point needs to be decided whether any of the anti-avoidance provisions need to be addressed – can property of which the deceased disposed in his lifetime be recovered for the net estate?

6. If a claim is to be made then time limits need to be addressed and a standing search (not a caveat) entered at the Probate Registry to alert the practitioner to when a grant has been issued in any case.

It is important to stress that this jurisdiction is an objective one. The court cannot do what it thinks would be fair in the circumstances. Sometimes clients see the Act as a method of bringing into effect the unexecuted testamentary wishes of the deceased but the court cannot use it for that purpose. The question for the court is not was the deceased reasonable in failing to make provision for a particular applicant? The answer to that question might well be no because it seems unfair to the judge that, for example, a particularly deserving person has been omitted from the will. The issue is whether objectively it is reasonable having regard to the factors in s.3 of the Act that the will or the intestacy makes no provision for the deceased.

Assessing the likely quantum of awards is one of the most difficult tasks both for the practitioner and the court. In practice, lump sum awards are most frequently made although sometimes a claimant will, for example, be given a life interest in a fund or a property in which to live. In the case of all claimants except for spouses, civil partners and those whose relationship has been dissolved less than one year before the death and are treated as spouses or civil partners, it is a question of what is required for their maintenance. In the case of spouses, civil partners and those who have been treated as such, the provision is what would be reasonable in the circumstances and the court is required to cross-check the provision it is envisaging making against the provision which the court would have awarded if the relationship had been terminated by divorce or the dissolution of the civil partnership rather than death. It is therefore necessary in those cases to have regard to recent developments in ancillary relief applications – an exciting area of law at the present time.

This book is designed to take the reader through the step by step process with reference to the Act and the most important case law.

CHAPTER 2

Threshold of the jurisdiction

2.1 INTRODUCTION

Section 1 of the Inheritance (Provision for Family and Dependants) Act 1975 sets out the circumstances in which an application may be made to the court for an award under the Act. This section provides that where a person:

(a) has died after the commencement of the Act;
(b) is domiciled in England and Wales; and
(c) has been survived by one or more of the persons listed in s.1(1)(a)–(e) then

any of those persons listed may apply for an award under s.2.

The common law of England and Wales recognises the concept of complete testamentary freedom. The court's jurisdiction under the Act is the only exception to the principle that a person is free to dispose of his property as he chooses or to let the intestacy provisions apply to his estate.

2.2 ESTABLISHING THE DATE OF DEATH

The Act came into force on 1 April 1976.

In most cases no difficulty will arise in establishing that there has been a death after the commencement of the Act. The written evidence in support of the claim should have exhibited to it an official copy of the grant of representation (Civil Procedure Rules 1998 (CPR) rule 57.16(3)(a)). This will specify the date of death of the deceased and the court would not, ordinarily, look for any further proof of his death.

In rare cases the question of whether a person has died or not may be uncertain. In those cases it may be possible for a grant of representation to be extracted by the persons entitled under the presumed deceased person's will or intestacy making an application to the Probate Registry for leave to swear death (Non-Contentious Probate Rules 1987, SI 1987/2024, r.53). The application will need to be supported by evidence that the person presumed to be deceased has not been heard of for a considerable period of time or that he has disappeared in circumstances which point to either suicide or accidental death.

2.3 ESTABLISHING DOMICILE

The court can only make an award out of the estate of a person who was domiciled in England and Wales at the time of his death. Economic migration and the freedom of movement of persons within the European Union mean that practitioners are increasingly likely to come across estates where the deceased was either born outside the jurisdiction or has lived outside the jurisdiction for a significant part of his life and where domicile will be a potential issue in any claim under the Act.

The fact that 'the somewhat antiquated notion of domicile' should be a pre-requisite to the court's jurisdiction under the Act has been described as 'surprising' given that, in many family disputes, the court's jurisdiction is determined by reference to habitual residence (*per* Longmore LJ in *Agulian* v. *Cyganik* [2006] WTLR 565).

The burden of proving that the deceased died domiciled in England and Wales lies upon the claimant.

The grant of representation will usually contain a statement as to the deceased person's domicile. This will be based on the information provided in the oath sworn in support of the application for the grant. A statement of domicile contained in the grant of representation will not prevent the issue of domicile being put in issue in any proceedings under the Act concerning that estate; however, the person swearing the oath would be expected to explain any alteration in his position on this issue.

Similarly, the fact that Her Majesty's Revenue and Customs (HMRC) may have formed a view as to a deceased person's domicile for income or capital gains or inheritance tax purposes will not bind the court when it comes to determine the issue of domicile in proceedings under the Act (*Agulian* v. *Cyganik* (above)).

If domicile is put in issue in any proceedings under the Act, then it will usually be appropriate for that issue to be determined as a preliminary issue. As with any issue which goes to jurisdiction, the onus is upon the person disputing jurisdiction to raise it at the earliest possible stage and, if he does not do so, then this may result in an order that he pay any wasted costs which have resulted even in the event that he succeeds on the domicile issue.

In any proceedings under the Act, the question of domicile must be decided in accordance with the law of England and Wales. Under the law of England and Wales, at any given time, a person must have a domicile and can only have one domicile. His domicile must be one of the following:

(a)   his domicile of origin;
(b)   his domicile of choice;
(c)   his domicile of dependency.

An existing domicile is presumed to continue until it is proved that a new domicile has been acquired. The presumption is weakest in the case of the domicile of dependency and strongest where the domicile is one of origin.

2.4   DOMICILE OF ORIGIN

Every individual acquires at birth a domicile, known as domicile of origin. In the case of a legitimate child born during his father's lifetime, this will be the domicile of the father at the time of the child's birth. In the case of an illegitimate child or a legitimate child born after his father's death, the child's domicile will be the domicile of his mother at the time of his birth.

A domicile of origin may be altered as a result of adoption but not otherwise. On adoption, a child acquires a new domicile of origin, namely the domicile of origin he would have had had he been born to the adopters in wedlock.

A person's domicile of origin may be supplanted by his domicile of choice. However, the domicile of origin will prevail if a domicile of choice has never been acquired or if, having acquired a domicile of choice, a person then abandons that domicile of choice (see *Re Fuld (Deceased) (No. 3)* [1968] P 675 at 682D–E, approved in *Agulian* v. *Cyganik* [2006] WTLR 565).

A domicile of origin of a dependent person may also be displaced by a domicile of dependency. If a minor child acquires a domicile of dependency which is different from his domicile of origin and then, in later life, acquires a new domicile of choice, if and when that child abandons that domicile of choice, it will be his domicile of origin and not his domicile of dependency which revives.

2.5   DOMICILE OF CHOICE

A domicile of choice is acquired when a person voluntarily fixes his sole or chief residence in a particular place with a distinctive legal system with an intention of continuing to reside there permanently and indefinitely. The intention must be formed independently of external pressures.

If the deceased intended to return to his domicile of origin on the happening of a clearly foreseen and reasonably anticipated contingency (e.g. the termination of his employment), then the intention required to establish a domicile of choice will be absent. However, if he had in mind a return to his domicile of origin in an event which is only a vague possibility (e.g. winning the lottery) or some sentiment about dying in the land of his fathers, then he may have had an intention sufficient to acquire a domicile of choice (see *Re Fuld* (above) at 684F–685D, approved in *Agulian* v. *Cyganik* (above)).

However, even if the deceased has left the territory of his domicile of origin with the intention of never returning, his domicile of origin will adhere unless there is affirmative proof that he has formed an intention to reside permanently in another territory with a different legal system

The question of domicile will be determined on the particular facts of each individual case, upon the weight to be attached to the factors in the mind of the deceased and their importance to him, and his assessment of the likelihood of particular contingencies. Moreover, the question should not be addressed in stages; the court should consider the entirety of the deceased's life to determine whether he had acquired a domicile of choice at the date of his death and, if such an exercise is carried out, it is unlikely that one particular factor will be decisive (see *Agulian* v. *Cyganik* (above)).

The domicile of origin is not easily displaced by a domicile of choice. The court is not prepared to infer the acquisition of a domicile of choice lightly. It requires cogent and convincing proof of the necessary intention on the part of the deceased to make a different territory his permanent home. Oral or written declarations on the part of the deceased are unlikely to be conclusive.

A domicile of choice can be abandoned. If the deceased ceases to reside in the territory of the domicile of choice and has no intention of returning to it, then his domicile of choice will be abandoned. In such circumstances, his domicile of origin will revive unless and until he acquires a new domicile of choice (*Re Flynn* [1968] 1 All ER 49). The burden of proving abandonment of a domicile of choice is said to lie upon the person asserting it and, again, requires cogent proof (*Inland Revenue Commissioners* v. *Duchess of Portland* [1982] Ch 314; *Irvin* v. *Irvin* [2001] 1 FLR 178).

2.6 DOMICILE OF DEPENDENCY

Special rules determine the domicile of dependent persons. The class of dependent persons is restricted to unmarried children under the age of 16 (Domicile and Matrimonial Proceedings Act 1973, s.17(5)) and to persons suffering from a relevant mental disorder (see Lawrence Collins *et al.* (eds), *Dicey and Morris on the Conflict of Laws* ('*Dicey and Morris*'), 13th edn, Sweet & Maxwell, 2001: rule 16). Dependent persons are incapable of acquiring a domicile of choice. Thus, it is possible for dependent persons to be domiciled in countries where they do not have their permanent home.

The domicile of dependency of an unmarried legitimate child under the age of 16 is, during the lifetime of his father, the domicile of his father and will change with the domicile of his father (*Re Duleep Singh ex p. Cross* (1890) 6 TLR 385 (CA); *Henderson* v. *Henderson* [1967] P 77). It is thought that this rule would apply to a legitimated child from the date of his legitimation (*Dicey and Morris*, rule 15).

If the dependent child is illegitimate or if his father is dead, then, in general, his domicile will be the same as, and change with, the domicile of his mother. However, whether or not the child's domicile will alter with that of the mother depends on whether, in any given case, she has exercised her power to change the child's domicile with her own (see *Re Beaumont (Deceased)* (1980) 1 Ch 444 at 496–7).

The domicile of dependency of an unmarried adopted child under the age of 16 will be determined as if he was the legitimate child of his adopted parents.

However, the domicile of a legitimate or legitimated unmarried child aged under 16 whose parents are living apart, or were living apart at the date of death of the mother, is subject to different rules (see Domicile and Matrimonial Proceedings Act 1973, s.4). If the child has a home with his mother and no home with his father or if the child's last home was with his mother and he has not since had a home with his father, the child's domicile will be the same as, and change with, the domicile of his mother. Further, if at the time of death of his mother his domicile was that of his mother by virtue of the above rules, and he has not since had a home with his father, the domicile of the child will be the domicile his mother had at the date of her death. In any other case, the domicile of the child is the same as, and changes with, the domicile of the father. Thus if, since the parents have been living apart, the child has had no home with either parent (and has, for example, been living with his grandparents or foster parents), his domicile will be the same as, and change with, the domicile of his father.

A person who suffers from a mental disorder may be incapable of forming the necessary intention to acquire a domicile of choice. If he is incapable of forming such an intention, then he cannot change his domicile. If a person's disorder dates from birth or from a time when he was a dependent child, then his domicile will remain that of his dependency unless and until he recovers capacity. In all other cases, his domicile will remain the same as when the relevant disorder began.

On ceasing to be dependent, a person may continue to be domiciled in the country of his last domicile of dependency. However, he is now capable of changing his domicile.

9

2.7 RELATED MATTERS

In any claim under the 1975 Act where domicile is a potential issue, consideration should be given to the fiscal implications of either arguing for or against a particular domicile. For example, a finding that the deceased was domiciled in England and Wales may lead to an inheritance tax liability on property which would otherwise have been accepted by HMRC as being excluded property for inheritance tax purposes.

CHAPTER 3

Categories of applicant

3.1 INTRODUCTION

The classes of persons who may apply for provision under the Inheritance (Provision for Family and Dependants) Act 1975 are listed in s.1(1) of the Act as follows:

(a)   the spouse or civil partner of the deceased;

(b)   a former spouse or former civil partner of the deceased, but not one who has formed a subsequent marriage or civil partnership;

(ba) any person (not being a person included in paragraph (a) or (b) above) to whom subsection (1A) or (1B) applies;

(c)   a child of the deceased;

(d)   any person (not being a child of the deceased) who, in the case of any marriage or civil partnership to which the deceased was at any time a party, was treated by the deceased as a child of the family in relation to that marriage or civil partnership;

(e)   any person (not being a person included in the foregoing paragraphs of this subsection) who immediately before the death of the deceased was being maintained, either wholly or partly, by the deceased . . .

Section 1(1A) applies to a person if the deceased died on or after 1 January 1996 and:

. . . during the whole of the period of two years ending immediately before the date when the deceased died, the person was living –

(a)   in the same household as the deceased, and

(b)   as the husband or wife of the deceased.

Section (1B) of the Act applies to a person if:

. . . for the whole of the period of two years ending immediately before the date when the deceased died the person was living –

(a)   in the same household as the deceased, and

(b)   as the civil partner of the deceased.

The court has no jurisdiction to make provision for persons who do not fall within any of these classes. In every case, it is for the claimant to prove his or her standing to make a claim.

3.2 THE SURVIVING SPOUSE OF THE DECEASED

The relevant date for assessment of whether a claimant falls within one of the classes of persons listed in s.1(1)(a) of the Act is the date of the deceased's death.

Accordingly, if the claimant was the deceased spouse at the date of his death but has remarried since the deceased's death, the remarriage will not affect the claimant's standing to make a claim. However, clearly, the fact of the remarriage will be a matter the court will take into account when deciding if the disposition of the deceased's estate effected by his will or the law relating to intestacy has made reasonable financial provision for the claimant and also when deciding how it should exercise its discretion to make provision for the claimant.

In most cases there will be no difficulty establishing whether a claimant was the surviving spouse of the deceased. It is good practice for a surviving spouse who seeks provision under the Act to exhibit a copy of the marriage certificate with the evidence in support of the claim and, in the majority of cases, that will suffice as proof of standing.

However, in a minority of cases, an issue may arise as to whether there has been a marriage at all.

There may be doubt as to whether the ceremony of marriage which was entered into by the deceased and the claimant was sufficient to amount to a marriage recognised by the law of England and Wales (see *Ghandhi* v. *Patel* [2002] 1 FLR 603). If the ceremony takes place in England and Wales, it will only amount to a marriage recognised by the law of England and Wales if it meets the requirements of the Marriage Act 1949.

Under the private international law of England and Wales, a marriage which takes place outside the jurisdiction will be recognised as a marriage so long as the ceremony met the formal requirements of a marriage under the law of the territory where it took place. If the validity of a foreign marriage is put in issue, the court is likely to require expert evidence from a suitably qualified lawyer in the relevant jurisdiction before being satisfied that a marriage took place.

Section 25(4) of the Inheritance (Provision for Family and Dependants) Act 1975 provides as follows:

> For the purposes of this Act any reference to a spouse, wife or husband shall be treated as including a reference to a person who in good faith entered into a void marriage with the deceased unless either –

(a) the marriage of the deceased and that person was dissolved or annulled during the lifetime of the deceased and the dissolution or annulment is recognised by the law of England and Wales, or

(b) that person has during the lifetime of the deceased formed a subsequent marriage or civil partnership.

It is important to note that this subsection will not assist a person who has been party to a ceremony which, as a matter of the law of England and Wales, does not amount to a marriage at all. Such a ceremony is not a 'void marriage' but 'no sort of marriage at all, valid or void' (*per* Park J in *Gandhi* v. *Patel*, above; but contrast *Gereis* v. *Yagoub* [1997] 1 FLR 854). The concept of a 'void marriage' is recognised both by statute and by judicial authority as being something different from a non-marriage (see Marriage Act 1949, s.2; Matrimonial Causes Act 1973, s.11; *Gereis* v. *Yagoub* above; *A-M* v. *A-M* [2001] 2 FLR 6).

In some cases there may be an issue as to the capacity of one or both of the parties to marry. In *Sheffield City Council* v. *E and S* [2004] EWHC 2808 (Fam) at 68, Munby J summarised the authorities on capacity to marry as follows:

(i) It is not enough that someone appreciates that he or she is taking part in a marriage ceremony or understands its words.

(ii) He or she must understand the nature of the marriage contract.

(iii) This means that he or she must be mentally capable of understanding the duties and responsibilities that normally attach to marriage.

(iv) That said, the contract of marriage is in essence a simple one, which does not require a high degree of intelligence to comprehend. The contract of marriage can readily be understood by anyone of normal intelligence.

A marriage which is entered into by a party who lacks capacity to marry is not a 'void marriage' for the purposes of s.25(4) of the 1975 Act. In common law, a contract entered into by a party who lacked capacity to make that contract is voidable not void. Moreover, s.12 of the Matrimonial Causes Act 1973 provides that, in the case of any marriage celebrated after 31 July 1971, the marriage shall be voidable if, at the time of the marriage, either party did not validly consent to it in consequence of unsoundness of mind.

The following are void marriages:

1. A marriage which is invalid under any of the provisions of the Marriage Acts 1949–86 (i.e. where the parties are within the prohibited degrees of relationship; where either party is under the age of 16 or the parties have intermarried in disregard of certain requirements as to the formation of marriage).

2. A marriage which takes place at a time when either party to it was already married or a civil partner.

3. A marriage entered into by parties of the same gender.

4. A marriage entered into in a jurisdiction where polygamous marriage is permitted at a time where one or other of the parties is already married and where either party is domiciled in England and Wales. (If neither of the parties to such a marriage is married, the fact that the marriage is potentially polygamous and either of the parties to it is domiciled in England and Wales will not prevent it from being a valid marriage under the law of England and Wales.)

(See Matrimonial Causes Act 1973, s.11.)

For the purposes of the Inheritance (Provision for Family and Dependants) Act 1975, s.25(4), a claimant will have entered into a void marriage in good faith if he or she honestly believed that he or she was entering into a valid marriage at the time he or she entered into it (see *Gandhi* v. *Patel*, above at 629).

A claimant will qualify as a surviving spouse notwithstanding the fact that divorce proceedings between the claimant and the deceased had commenced prior to the deceased's death unless a decree absolute had actually been made prior to the death. If no decree absolute was made prior to the deceased's death, any ancillary relief order made prior to his death will have no effect (see *McMinn* v. *McMinn* [2003] 1 FLR 823); however, it may be possible for the terms of a consent order to be enforceable as a contract against the deceased's estate and this question should be considered before a claim is made under the Act.

If a decree of judicial separation was in force at the time of the deceased's death, then, subject to s.14 of the Act, the standard of reasonable financial provision made for the claimant will be the less generous standard which is available to applicants other than spouses (see s.1(2)(a) of the Act).

Section 14(1) of the Act provides:

(1) Where, within twelve months from the date on which a decree of divorce or nullity of marriage has been made absolute or a decree of judicial separation has been granted, a party to a marriage dies and –

   (a) an application for a financial provision order under section 23 of the Matrimonial Causes Act 1973 or a property adjustment order under section 24 of that Act has not been made by the other party to that marriage, or

   (b) such an application has been made but the proceedings thereon have not been determined at the time of death of the deceased,

   then, if an application for an order under section 2 of this Act is made by that other party, the court shall, notwithstanding anything in section 1 or section 3 of this Act, have power, if it thinks it just to do so, to treat that party for the purposes of that application as if the decree of divorce or nullity of marriage had not been made absolute or the decree of judicial separation had not been granted, as the case may be.

Thus, in cases where the financial affairs of the parties to the divorce proceedings have not been determined in ancillary relief proceedings prior to the deceased's death, the court has a discretion, even after a decree absolute has been made, to treat the claimant as if he or she remained a spouse of the deceased for the purposes of the Act.

3.3 CIVIL PARTNERS AND FORMER CIVIL PARTNERS

If the deceased died on or after 5 December 2005, a claim may be made for provision out of his estate under the Act by his civil partner.

The 1975 Act itself does not define what is meant by 'civil partner' in s.1(1)(a) and (b). However, the addition of civil partners to the classes of persons who may apply under the Act was effected by the Civil Partnership Act 2004 (the '2004 Act'). Under s.1(1) of the 2004 Act, a civil partnership is defined as a relationship between two people of the same sex ('civil partners') formed when they register as civil partners of each other in accordance with the 2004 Act, Parts 2, 3 or 4. The 2004 Act sets out the requirements for the creation of civil partnerships in England and Wales, Scotland, Northern Ireland and certain overseas territories.

Relationships between persons of the same sex which are of an indeterminate duration and which are registered in a country outside the United Kingdom may qualify as 'overseas relationships' within the meaning of s.212 of the 2004 Act. Section 215 of the 2004 Act provides that, in general, two people in an overseas relationship are to be treated as having formed a civil partnership if, under the relevant law, they had capacity to enter into the relationship and met all the requirements necessary to ensure the formal validity of the relationship. There are exceptions to this general rule, and reference should be made to Part 5, Chapter 2 of the 2004 Act in any particular case where the deceased was involved in a relationship which could potentially amount to an overseas relationship within the meaning of s.212 of the 2004 Act.

A civil partnership can only be brought to an end by dissolution, annulment or death. Dissolution and annulment both require an order of the court (2004 Act, ss.1(3) and 37).

Section 25(4A) of the 1975 Act provides that any reference to a civil partner shall include a person who, in good faith, entered into a void civil partnership with the deceased unless either the civil partnership between the deceased and that person was dissolved or annulled during the lifetime of the deceased in a manner recognised by the law of England and Wales or that person has, during the lifetime of the deceased, formed a subsequent civil partnership or marriage.

As is the case with spouses, it is thought that this section will not assist a person who, by reason of any procedural defect, was not the deceased's civil partner at all, but can only assist a person whose civil partnership with the deceased was of a nature which the 2004 Act expressly provides is void (2004 Act, ss.3(1) and 49).

Section 1(2) of the 1975 Act provides:

> (aa) in the case of an application made by virtue of subsection (1)(a) above by the civil partner of the deceased (except where, at the date of death, a separation order under Chapter 2 of Part 2 of the Civil Partnership Act 2004 was in force in relation to the civil partnership and the separation was continuing), means such financial provision as it would be reasonable in all the circumstances of the case for a civil partner to receive, whether or not that provision is required for his or her maintenance.

Thus, a civil partner may claim the more generous level of provision formerly only available to the deceased's surviving spouse.

Section 14A of the Act gives the court a power to treat a person as a surviving civil partner of the deceased in circumstances where the deceased has died within 12 months of the making of a dissolution order, a nullity order, a separation order or a presumption of death order under Part 2, Chapter 2 of the 2004 Act, in relation to their civil partnership but their financial affairs had not been determined under the 2004 Act, Sched.5, Parts 1 or 2 prior to the deceased's death.

3.4   FORMER SPOUSES AND FORMER CIVIL PARTNERS

A former spouse or civil partner of the deceased can make a claim for provision out of the estate of the deceased provided that, at the date of the deceased's death, he or she had not formed a subsequent marriage or civil partnership (Inheritance (Provision for Family and Dependants) Act 1975, s.1(1)(b)).

Section 25(1) of the Act defines 'former spouse' as a person whose marriage with the deceased was, during the lifetime of the deceased, either dissolved or annulled by decree of divorce granted under the law of the British Islands or dissolved or annulled under the law of any overseas territory which is recognised by the law of England and Wales. The same subsection defines 'former civil partner' as a person whose civil partnership with the deceased was, during the lifetime of the deceased, dissolved or annulled by an order made under the law of any part of the British Islands or in any overseas territory by a dissolution or annulment recognised by the law of England and Wales.

A former spouse or civil partner cannot make a claim if he or she has entered into a subsequent marriage or civil partnership by the time of the deceased's death. Section 25(5) of the Act makes clear that, for the purposes of s.1(1)(b), a subsequent marriage or civil partnership includes the formation of a marriage or civil partnership (as the case may be) which is either void or voidable. The distinction between a non-marriage and a void marriage has already been pointed out above. Sections 11 and 12 of the Matrimonial Causes Act 1973 set out the circumstances in which marriages celebrated after 31 July 1971 are void or voidable respectively. For the circumstances in which a civil partnership formed in England and Wales will be void, see s.49 of the 2004 Act.

In practice, in most cases, whether or not a particular person is a surviving former spouse or a former civil partner of the deceased within the meaning of s.1(1)(b) of the 1975 Act will be abundantly clear. However, in many cases, those persons will be unable to make a claim as a result of the family court having made an order during the deceased's lifetime under one or other of ss.15, 15ZA, 15A and 15B of the Act at the time the financial affairs of the parties to the marriage or civil partnership (as the case may be) were determined.

As mentioned above, in cases where the marriage has been determined in the 12 months leading up to the deceased's death without the financial affairs of the parties having been resolved, the court is able to treat the former spouse or civil partner as if he or she were a surviving spouse or civil partner (as the case may be) under one or other of ss.14 and 14A of the Act, thereby enabling the former spouse or civil partner to seek the more generous level of provision available to spouses or civil partners under the Act.

3.5 COHABITEES

If the deceased died on or after 1 January 1996, then a person who, during the whole of the period of two years ending immediately before the date when the deceased died, was living in the same household as the deceased as the husband or wife of the deceased may make a claim under the Act (Inheritance (Provision for Family and Dependants) Act 1975, s.1(1)(ba) and s.1(1A)).

In cases where the deceased died after 5 December 2005, a claim may also be made by a person who, during the whole of the period of two years ending immediately before the date when the deceased died, was living in the same household as the deceased as his or her civil partner (1975 Act, s.1(1B).

3.5.1 '. . . during the whole of the period of two years ending immediately before the death of the deceased . . .'

In order to make a claim under s.1(1A) or (1B) of the Act, the claimant must have cohabited with the deceased for the whole of the period of two years ending immediately before the deceased's death. It is not necessary for the claimant to establish that his or her cohabitation with the deceased was lawful (see *Witkowska* v. *Kaminski* [2006] WTLR 1293 at paras 44–51).

It is clear that absences of either of the parties resulting from hospital admissions or periods of respite care during the last two years of the deceased's life would not prevent this requirement being met (see *Re Watson* [1999] 1 FLR 878 at 882).

Moreover, if there is a temporary interruption in the cohabitation for other reasons during the two-year period leading up to the deceased's death, the claimant may still be able make a claim under the Act. In *Gully* v. *Dix* [2004] 1 FLR 918 the Court of Appeal held that, when considering whether the requirement for two years' cohabitation had been met, the court is not obliged to confine itself to looking only at the two-year period leading up to the deceased's death but should also consider the preceding period to see what the established relationship between the parties was. If that relationship ended before or during the two-year period, then the test will not be satisfied. However, if the relationship was merely temporarily suspended, perhaps for a period of reflection about the future of a relationship going through a difficult time, then the applicant can satisfy the test.

3.5.2 '. . . living in the same household as the deceased . . .'

For the claimant to fall within s.1(1A) or (1B) of the 1975 Act, the claimant and the deceased must have been sharing the same 'household' during the relevant period. The concept of a 'household' has been described as 'somewhat elusive of definition' (*per* Potter LJ in *Kotke* v. *Saffarini* [2005] 2 FLR 517). However, it involves both a physical connotation of a particular house (or houses – it is possible to have one household and two properties: see *Churchill* v. *Roach and Others* [2003] WTLR 779) as well as more abstract connotations of personal association.

It is possible for two persons to be 'living in the same household' even if they are temporarily separated, provided that they are still held together by a particular tie (*Santos* v. *Santos* [1972] Fam 247 at 262–3; *Gully* v. *Dix* (above)).

In *Churchill* v. *Roach and Others* (above) HHJ Norris QC pointed out that 'it is, of course, dangerous to try to define what "living in the same household" means'; however, he pointed out that cohabitation in the same household is likely to involve elements of permanence, frequency and intimacy of contact, mutual support, voluntary restraint upon personal freedom and community of resources.

3.5.3 '. . . living . . . as the husband or wife of the deceased'

To qualify under s.1(1A) of the 1975 Act, the claimant must have been living with the deceased as his or her husband or wife. Although s.1(1A) treats this as a separate requirement from the requirement that the claimant have shared a household with the deceased, it was pointed out in *Re Watson* [1999] 1 FLR

878 (at 883) that it is very unlikely that a person could have lived with the deceased as his or her husband or wife without sharing the same household as the deceased and the two requirements will merge to a certain degree.

In the same case, Neuberger J cautioned against indulging in 'too much over-analysis' of this requirement. He held that the court should ask itself whether, in the opinion of a reasonable person with normal perceptions, it could be said that the two people in question were living together as husband and wife.

Similar wording contained in the Fatal Accidents Act 1976, s.1(3) was considered by the Court of Appeal in *Kotke* v. *Saffarini* (above). In that case the Court of Appeal held that the following are 'signposts' which tend to indicate that two persons are living together in the same household as husband and wife: whether the parties live under the same roof, illness, holidays and work and other periodical absences apart; whether there is stability; whether there is financial support; whether there is a sexual relationship.

However, the absence of any one of those signposts (other than, possibly, the first) is unlikely to be conclusive in any particular case. As Neuberger J pointed out in *Re Watson* (above), the court cannot ignore 'the multifarious nature of marital relationships'. In that case, the absence of a sexual relationship between the claimant and the deceased did not prevent the claimant from qualifying under s.1(1A) of the 1975 Act in circumstances where the claimant and the deceased had had a relationship for over 30 years, had lived alone together for the last 10 years, were closer to each other than any other person, made joint contributions to the household outgoings on an informal basis and where there were particular incidents at the commencement and end of the cohabitation which demonstrated the concern and affection which the deceased felt towards the claimant.

It appears that s.1(1A) of the Act is capable of applying to same-sex cohabitees (see *Saunders* v. *Garrett* [2005] WTLR 749). It has been held that Article 8 of the European Convention on Human Rights – the right to private and family life and home – is capable of being engaged by that subsection and, thus, that Article 14 of the Convention – which calls for an absence of discrimination in the exercise of Convention rights – may also be engaged. In circumstances where those rights are engaged, s.3 of the Human Rights Act 1998 requires the court to interpret s.1(1A) of the Act in a manner which complies with the Convention in so far as is possible (see *Ghaidan* v. *Godin-Mendoza* [2004] 3 WLR 113) and this would result in a construction which brings single sex cohabitees within the ambit of the subsection.

However, it is thought, now that the Civil Partnership Act 2004 is in force, same-sex cohabitees who fell within the ambit of s.1(1A) of the 1975 Act are likely to apply under s.1(1B) of the Act instead. Section 1(1B) is concerned with claimants who, for whatever reason, did not in fact have a civil partnership with the deceased during the relevant two-year period but *who were living as if they were civil partners* during that period. It is thought that a cohabitee will not be outside the ambit of s.1(1B) purely because the deceased died before, or within two years of, the date when it first became possible to become a civil partner under the 2004 Act. If this view is correct, then there should be no need for single-sex cohabitees to apply under s.1(1A) of the 1975 Act in the future. (For a contrary view, see Andrew Francis, *Inheritance Act Claims*, looseleaf and CD-Rom, Jordans, update 5 at 4[45].)

3.5.4 '. . . living . . . as the civil partner of the deceased'

Section 1(1B) of the Inheritance (Provision for Family and Dependants) Act 1975 requires the claimant to have been living as the civil partner of the deceased during the specified period.

As mentioned above, the Act itself contains no definition of what is meant by 'civil partner' for the purposes of s.1(1A). Civil partnerships did not exist prior to the commencement of the Civil Partnership Act 2004 and, accordingly, the characteristics of a civil partnership must be ascertained (so far as is possible) from the 2004 Act itself.

Section 1(1) of the 2004 Act defines a civil partnership as 'a relationship between two people of the same sex . . . which is formed when they register as civil partners of each other . . .' in accordance with the requirements of the 2004 Act and which is not rendered void by the provisions of the 2004 Act. Thus the 2004 Act tells us that a civil partnership involves a 'relationship'; however, it does not stipulate any requirements as to the nature or quality of that relationship. (It is noteworthy that, in order for an overseas relationship to qualify as a civil partnership, it must be a relationship of indeterminate length.)

Presumably, the requirement that there be a 'relationship' between the two persons of the same sex referred to in s.1(1) of the 2004 Act does import a requirement that those two persons have some degree of personal knowledge of each other. However, it is unclear precisely what degree of familiarity is required. For example, there is no requirement that the relationship be a sexual one or that it be consummated.

However, in order to qualify as a claimant under s.1(1B) of the 1975 Act, the claimant must not only have been living as the deceased's civil partner, but must also have been *sharing the same household* as the deceased for a two-year period. As explained above, the authorities on s.1(1A) of the Act indicate that a shared household connotes an element of mutual support, of permanence, of frequency and intimacy of contact, of voluntary restraint upon personal freedom and of community of resources. Thus, a claimant who formed a civil partnership with the deceased solely for some fiscal advantage or to meet a visa requirement is unlikely to have standing to make a claim under s.1(1B). Moreover, even if such a claimant did have standing, the claimant's lack of intimacy with or support of the deceased is likely to be a matter which the court would take into account under s.3(1)(g) and (2A) of the Act when considering the substantive merits of the claim.

3.6 CHILDREN

A child of the deceased is able to make a claim for provision from the deceased's estate. Section 25(1) of the 1975 Act defines a child as including an illegitimate child and a child *en ventre sa mere* at the date of the deceased's death. An adopted child may only claim in respect of the estates of his adopted parents and not his natural parents (see Adoption Act 1976, s.39(2)).

It is important to note that it is not only minor children who may claim under this subsection, adult children also fall within the subsection and their claims should be approached in the same manner as that of any other applicant, i.e. by carrying out a balancing exercise in relation to all the factors in s.3 of the 1975 Act (*Re Hancock (Deceased)* [1998] 2 FLR 346).

3.7 PERSONS WHO IN THE CASE OF ANY MARRIAGE OR CIVIL PARTNERSHIP OF THE DECEASED WERE TREATED AS A CHILD OF THE FAMILY

In order for the claimant to fall within s.1(1)(d) of the 1975 Act, he must show that he was treated by the deceased as a child of the family in relation to a marriage or civil partnership between the deceased and another person. It follows that if the deceased has never been married or formed a civil partnership, the subsection cannot apply.

Again, it is important to note that adult claimants can fall within the ambit of s.1(1)(d) as well as minors.

Whether the claimant was treated as a child of the family in relation to a particular marriage or civil partnership of the deceased may not be easy to ascertain. The phrases 'child of the family' and 'treated . . . as the child of the family' are not defined in the Act. However, the Act clearly contemplates applications under s.1(1)(d) by persons who were not maintained by the deceased (1975 Act, s.3(3) and *Re Leach (Deceased)* [1986] Ch 226 at 231).

If at any time the claimant has been treated as a child of the family in relation to any marriage or civil partnership of the deceased, the fact that the claimant was not continuing to be so treated at the time of the deceased's death will not prevent him from falling within s.1(1)(d) (*Re Leach* (above) at 233). It is not necessary that the deceased should have treated the claimant as a dependent minor child at any time (*Re Callaghan* [1985] FLR 116 at 120, approved in *Re Leach (Deceased)* (above) at 236).

As it is only the deceased's treatment of the claimant which matters for the purpose of this subsection, conduct which preceded the marriage or civil partnership in question can be relevant provided that it stems from that marriage or civil partnership as the case may be (*Re Leach* (above) at 234).

The court has warned against attempting to define the conduct which amounts to treatment of a person as a child of the family (*D* v. *D* (*Child of the Family*) [1980] 2 FLR 93 at 98). Every case must stand on its own facts. However, it is clear that the hospitality, kindness and affection which any step-parent could reasonably be expected to show a step-child will not suffice (*Re Leach* (above) at 235).

The relevant question in any case is whether the deceased has, as wife or husband or civil partner under the relevant marriage or civil partnership, expressly or impliedly assumed the position of a parent towards the claimant, with the attendant responsibilities and privileges of that relationship (*Re Leach* (above) at 237). Factors such as whether the claimant lived with the deceased as a minor child, whether the deceased paid for the claimant when he or she was a minor child, whether the deceased exercised discipline over the claimant as a minor child, whether the deceased assumed the role of grandparent to an adult claimant's children, whether the deceased reposed confidence in the claimant as to his property and affairs, whether there was any dependency by the deceased upon the claimant for care during the deceased's later years, whether the deceased showed financial generosity towards the claimant and whether the deceased indicated an intention to confer testamentary benefit on the claimant are all of potential relevance (*Re Callaghan* (above) at 121; *Re Leach* (above) at 239).

3.8 DEPENDANTS

Section 1(1)(e) of the 1975 Act permits any person (not being a person included in any of the other paragraphs of s.1(1)) who immediately before the death of the deceased was being maintained, either wholly or partly, by the deceased to make a claim under the Act.

Section 1(3) provides that, for the purpose of s.1(1)(e), a person shall be treated as having been maintained by the deceased either wholly or partly, as the case may be, if the deceased, otherwise than for valuable consideration, was making a substantial contribution in money or money's worth towards the reasonable needs of that person.

When an application is made under s.1(1)(e), the court is directed to take into account the following under s.3(4) of the Act:

> ... the extent to which and the basis upon which the deceased assumed responsibility for the maintenance of the applicant, and to the length of time for which the deceased discharged that responsibility.

and it can reasonably be inferred from this subsection that, unless the claimant can show that there was such an assumption of responsibility, on the part of the deceased, the claimant will not fall within s.1(1)(e) at all.

The court has held that a patient of the Court of Protection, who was mentally incapable of assuming responsibility for another person's maintenance, could nonetheless assume responsibility for that person's maintenance provided that person had indirectly benefited through payments made from the patient's estate with the authority of the Court of Protection (*Re B* [2000] Ch 662). This generous interpretation of ss.1(1)(e) and 3(4) of the Act means that the 1975 Act is a potential method of addressing the unfairness which arises when a minor who is a patient of the Court of Protection dies intestate and, under the trusts arising on this, his estate passes to next of kin who have had little or no contact with the patient or have made little or no contribution to the patient's well being.

3.8.1 '. . . immediately before the death of the deceased . . .'

When deciding whether the claimant was being maintained immediately before the deceased's death, the court will not confine itself to considering the state of affairs in the instant before death. The court will consider whether, at the moment before death, there was a settled basis or arrangement of maintenance which subsisted at the date of the deceased's death, rather than focus on any particular fluctuation in the arrangement in the instant before death (*Re Beaumont (Deceased)* [1980] 1 Ch 444 at 451–2; *Jelly* v. *Iliffe* [1981] Fam 128 at 136, 141). Such an approach is consistent with the assumption of responsibility on the part of the deceased towards the claimant which s.3(4) of the Act envisages will be present whenever an application is made under s.1(1)(e).

3.8.2 '. . . was being maintained either wholly or partly by the deceased'

In order for a claimant to be regarded as having been maintained by the deceased, the deceased must have been making a substantial contribution in money or money's worth towards the reasonable needs of that person.

The court will consider the standard of living of the claimant in the relevant period prior to the deceased's death and ask itself whether the deceased was making a substantial contribution to the cost of meeting that standard of living.

In cases where there has been an interflow of benefits between the claimant and the deceased, the question of whether the deceased made a *substantial* contribution to the claimant's maintenance will be linked to the issue of whether the maintenance was provided in return for consideration provided by the claimant. Without using an accountant's pen, the court will ascertain whether there is an obvious imbalance in favour of the claimant

(*Jelley* v. *Iliffe* [1981] Fam 128 at 181; *Bishop* v. *Plumley* [1991] 1 WLR 582 at 587).

The requirement that the deceased's contribution be made otherwise than for valuable consideration can cause difficulties in cases where the claimant carried out domestic duties or provided care to the deceased. A too rigid approach to s.1(3) would result in the most deserving of claimants, namely those who provided benefits of a value commensurate to the financial bene-fits provided by the deceased, falling outside of s.1(1)(e). This difficulty has been partially resolved in relation to deaths after 1 January 1996 by the inclusion of cohabitees as a new class of potential claimants. However, a carer who did not live with the deceased as his or her husband or wife and who provided care services which were broadly commensurate with the maintenance provided by the deceased will be excluded from the classes of applicants who can claim under the Act, no matter how deserving.

CHAPTER 4

Matters which the court will take into account

4.1   INTRODUCTION

Section 3 of the Inheritance (Provision for Family and Dependants) Act 1975 sets out the factors which the court must take into account when assessing whether the will or intestacy has made reasonable financial provision for the applicant and then in deciding what provision to make. The factors are therefore important as part of a two-stage process. It is only if having regard to all the relevant factors the court decides that the disposition of the deceased's estate does not make reasonable financial provision for the applicant that it then looks at the factors to assess the quantum of the claim. The test of whether reasonable provision has been made, having regard to the factors in s.3 of the Act, is an objective one (*Moody* v. *Stevenson* [1992] Ch 486).

It is also important to note that the approach in deciding whether reasonable financial provision has been made differs depending on whether the applicant is the husband or wife or civil partner of the deceased or falls within one of the other categories. In s.1(2) of the Act 'reasonable financial provision' is defined as such provision as would 'be reasonable in all the circumstances of the case' for a husband or wife (s.1(2)(a)) or civil partner (s.1(2)(aa)) 'to receive, whether or not that provision is required for his or her maintenance'.

In the case of other applicants it is 'such financial provision as it would be reasonable in all the circumstances of the case for the applicant to receive for his maintenance' (s.1(2)(b)). This is a crucial difference in approach which has to be borne in mind at both stages of the two-stage process which the court undertakes.

Maintenance is not defined in the 1975 Act. However, in *Re Coventry (Deceased), sub nom: Coventry* v. *Coventry* [1980] Ch 461 at 485 the Court of Appeal approved the description which had been given in the Ontario case of *Re Duranceau* [1952] 3 DLR 714 of maintenance as being 'sufficient to enable the dependant to live neither luxuriously nor miserably, but decently and comfortably according to his or her station in life'. It is therefore not breadline subsistence which is in issue.

It might be thought that maintenance would extend to what is required by way of an income nature to contribute to a claimant's well being. However, it is clear that awards of a capital nature are entirely justified if they are in effect for the maintenance of the claimant. The provision which is frequently made to provide housing for an applicant falls within maintenance. In *Re Callaghan (Deceased)* [1985] Fam 1 the court awarded a sum so that the claimant could purchase her house under the right to buy legislation. In *Espinosa* v. *Bourke* [1999] 1 FLR 747 the court made an award which enabled the claimant to pay off business debts and in *Re Pearce (Deceased)* [1998] 2 FLR 705 a sum was awarded to enable the claimant to introduce capital into a business.

There are general factors which apply to every category of applicant and then specific factors to which s.3 requires the court to have regard in relation to particular types of applicant. The first part of this chapter looks at the general factors which are applicable to all cases before turning to the specific matters which the court must take into account when faced with an application by a particular claimant. There are then some general points made at the end in relation to the assessment of awards.

4.2 GENERAL FACTORS: A SUMMARY

In deciding whether the will or intestacy of the deceased makes reasonable financial provision for the applicant and in assessing the quantum of the claim the court must have regard to the following general matters (1975 Act, s.3):

(a) the financial resources and financial needs which the applicant has or is likely to have in the foreseeable future;

(b) the financial resources and financial needs which any other applicant for an order under section 2 of this Act has or is likely to have in the foreseeable future;

(c) the financial resources and financial needs which any beneficiary of the estate of the deceased has or is likely to have in the foreseeable future;

(d) any obligations and responsibilities which the deceased had towards any applicant for an order under the said section 2 or towards any beneficiary of the estate of the deceased;

(e) the size and nature of the net estate of the deceased;

(f) any physical or mental disability of any applicant for an order under the said section 2 or any beneficiary of the estate of the deceased;

(g) any other matter, including the conduct of the applicant or any other person, which in the circumstances of the case the court may consider relevant.

In looking at these factors the court has to take into account the facts as known to the court at the date of the hearing (1975 Act, s.1(6)). A striking example of this principle can be found *Re Hancock (Deceased)* [1998] 2 FLR 346 where by the date of the hearing a plot of land comprised in the estate had greatly increased in value. This emphasises the objective nature of the process in that the facts as might have been known by the deceased are irrelevant.

4.3 THE FINANCIAL NEEDS AND RESOURCES OF THE APPLICANT

In many if not all cases this is the factor which attains the greatest importance. Financial resources include the earning capacity of the applicant (1975 Act, s.1(6)) and financial needs take into account financial obligations and responsibilities. The standard approach is to list the outgoings of the claimant including expenditure on items such as entertainment and holidays. If the applicant has dependants, then the expenditure on them can also be included. **Appendix B4** contains a suggested schedule which can be adapted depending on the circumstances of the client. If there is a serious challenge to the amount of outgoings set out then they may need to be backed up with documentary evidence such as bills and bank statements.

The applicant may also have a need for housing and it can be helpful to the court to provide particulars of suitable properties on the market either to rent or to buy.

As far as resources are concerned, these may include actual earnings and of course earning capacity has to be taken into account. Social security benefits, pensions and income from investments all have to be taken into account as well as any capital which the claimant is in possession of, and any entitlement which the claimant may have to any gifts under the will or on intestacy.

4.4 THE FINANCIAL NEEDS AND RESOURCES OF ANY OTHER APPLICANT

This is a factor which will only apply if there is more than one claim made against the estate under the Act and that does not occur frequently. In essence the court will need to weigh in the balance the financial position of each of the claimants in deciding whether the disposition of the deceased's estate makes reasonable financial provision and then in assessing the claim.

4.5 THE FINANCIAL NEEDS AND RESOURCES OF BENEFICIARIES

The financial position of the beneficiaries of the estate has to be weighed in the balance. Sometimes beneficiaries are reluctant to disclose information about their needs and resources, in which case the court can simply assume that they are comfortably off and the factor will not weigh against the claim.

However, if beneficiaries give any evidence of their financial position they run the risk of having to make full disclosure of all documents on the subject and of being cross-examined on this area if the matter comes to trial.

4.6 THE OBLIGATIONS OF THE DECEASED TOWARDS ANY APPLICANTS OR BENEFICIARIES

In some cases the obligations of the deceased towards an applicant or beneficiary may be obvious: for example, the obligation of the deceased to his spouse or civil partner; the obligation of a parent to a minor child. In other cases the matter may not be so clear cut.

Claims concerning adult children have given rise to problems in this area. This is because a deceased's obligation to his spouse or civil partner or to someone with whom he cohabited for many years or to an infant child is often self-evident. However, the issue of whether or not the deceased had an obligation to an adult child can be more problematic. In *Re Coventry (Deceased), Coventry* v. *Coventry* [1980] Ch 461, it was held that an adult son capable of earning his own living had to demonstrate some additional factor such as a moral obligation on the part of the deceased to make provision for him before his claim could succeed. That decision led to an argument in *Re Hancock (Deceased)* [1998] 2 FLR 346 that in all cases of a claim by an adult child some sort of obligation had to be shown. The Court of Appeal rejected that argument and held all the factors set out in s.3 of the Act had to be weighed in the balance and that was the approach which that court adopted in *Espinosa* v. *Bourke* [1999] 1 FLR 747. In that case Butler-Sloss LJ stated:

> subsection 1(1)(d) refers to 'any obligations and responsibilities'. Plainly those obligations and responsibilities extend beyond legal obligations and that is why, in my view, the word moral has been used to underline and explain that the deceased's obligation and responsibilities are not to be narrowly construed as legal obligations but to be taken into account in a broad sense of obligation and responsibility.

It is therefore clear that this subsection does not refer only to legal obligations which the deceased had to any claimant. Indeed, some of the successful adult children cases provide some excellent examples of where the court has found an obligation which the deceased owed to the claimant which goes beyond any legal obligation. For example, see *Goodchild* v. *Goodchild* [1996] 1 WLR 694 (a son in necessitous circumstances who had been promised provision and whose mother had left her estate to his father on that basis); *Re Abram (Deceased)* [1996] 2 FLR 379 (a son who had worked in the family business for little remuneration for years in the expectation it would be left to him); *Re Pearce(Deceased)* [1998] 2 FLR 705 (a son who had done a great deal of work on the family farm in the expectation it would be his one day); *Re Hancock (Deceased)* [1999] 2 FLR 346 (a daughter in necessitous circumstances where the estate was large and promises had been made by the deceased to his wife that he would benefit her) and *Espinosa* v. *Bourke* [1999] 1 FLR 747 (a daughter who had cared for her father and had been promised provision and had no means of earning her own living).

It is clear that the failure of the deceased to meet obligations which he had to a child many years before his death will not create an obligation which will weigh in favour of an adult applicant. In *Re Jennings* [1994] Ch 286 the Court of Appeal rejected the claim by a well-off adult claimant whose father had failed to maintain him as a child or indeed to play any role in his life. The Court of Appeal held that obligations and responsibilities could not include obligations in the past.

4.7   THE SIZE AND NATURE OF THE NET ESTATE

There is no doubt that the size and nature of the net estate is a crucial factor. In cases such as *Re Myers* [2005] WTLR 851 (claim by an adult daughter against her father's estate) the substantial nature of the estate clearly weighed in favour of the claimant. Where the estate is small, the court may be less willing to make an award in favour of an applicant to whom the deceased did not owe legal obligations. What is more, the size of the net estate will obviously have crucial ramifications as far as the size of any award is concerned. In the case of a spouse or civil partner, the size of the estate has to be taken into account in looking at the award which might have been made on a divorce or dissolution of the partnership.

The net estate is defined in s.25(1) of the Act as follows:

'net estate', in relation to a deceased person, means –

(a)   all property of which the deceased had power to dispose by his will (otherwise than by virtue of a special power of appointment) less the amount of his funeral, testamentary and administration expenses, debts and liabilities, including any inheritance tax payable out of his estate on his death;

(b)   any property in respect of which the deceased held a general power of appointment (not being a power exercisable by will) which has not been exercised;

(c)   any sum of money or other property which is treated for the purposes of this Act as part of the net estate of the deceased by virtue of section 8(1) or (2) of this Act;

(d)   any property which is treated for the purposes of this Act as part of the net estate of the deceased by virtue of an order made under section 9 of the Act;

(e)   any sum of money or other property which is, by reason of a disposition or contract made by the deceased, ordered under section 10 or 11 of this Act to be provided for the purpose of the making of financial provision under this Act.

Therefore, the net estate comprises property which the deceased owned less liabilities of the estate including tax. There must also be taken into account property which he or she has nominated another should receive under s.8 of the Act. That section is fairly limited in extent and covers payments nominated under enactments. Benefits nominated within a private pension scheme were not within s.8(1) (see *Re Cairnes, sub nom: Howard* v. *Cairnes* (1983) 4 FLR 225). Similarly, property owned jointly by the deceased with another which passes by survivorship can also be treated as part of the net estate if the appropriate application is made. Cases where jointly owned property has been treated as part of the net estate include: *Kourkgy* v. *Lusher* (1983) 4 FLR 65; *Re Crawford (Deceased)* (1982) 4 FLR 273 (joint bank account); *Jessop* v. *Jessop* [1992] 2 FLR 591; *Powell* v. *Osborne* [1993] 1 FLR 1001 (property subject to a mortgage secured by an endowment policy); and see further **Chapter 5**. The net estate also includes property which is the subject of a court order under ss.10 and 11 of the Act (see **Chapter 6**).

The nature of the net estate is also important. The estate may be large but illiquid and it is always of concern to the court how any award should be met. To take a not uncommon example: the net estate is largely tied up in the modest matrimonial home of the deceased which his widow of many years occupies. His adult children make a claim for provision. The court will be reluctant in such a case, whatever the circumstances, to make an order which will mean the house will need to be sold. Other difficult cases may arise where the bulk of the estate is tied up in shares in the family business which may be difficult to realise.

Particular problems may arise where there are unquantified liabilities of an estate. For example, the deceased's lifetime tax affairs may not be in order, and there could be a large claim from HMRC for tax and penalties. In such circumstances it may take some time before the court can ascertain the size and nature of the net estate. Similar problems can arise if there is litigation pending against the estate or disputes as to the ownership of assets in the estate. In general terms the court needs to have these matters resolved before it can make any award under the Act.

Information as to the net estate must be provided in a written statement by the personal representative to the action in accordance with CPR rule 57.16 and the Practice Direction to CPR Part 57, para.16 (see **Chapter 8**).

4.8   MENTAL OR PHYSICAL DISABILITY OF ANY APPLICANT OR BENEFICIARY

Mental and physical disability is not defined by the Act itself. Certainly the sort of mental incapacity which would lead to a claimant being a patient under the Mental Health Act 1983 would be included as would someone who fell within the Disability Discrimination Act 1995 (a person has a disability for the purposes of this Act if he has a physical or mental impairment which has a substantial and long-term adverse effect on his ability to carry out normal day-to-day activities). It is questionable whether anything else would qualify. Certainly in *Robinson* v. *Bird* [2004] WTLR 257 where the claimant suffered from body dysmorphic syndrome necessitating plastic surgery the court did not treat this as a disability.

However, an illness falling short of a disability which prevented the claimant or beneficiary from working in the short or long term would be taken into account in assessing the needs and resources of the claimant or beneficiary.

4.9 ANY OTHER MATTER INCLUDING CONDUCT

This provision enables the court to take into account circumstances which do not otherwise fall within the other factors. Most frequently that will equate to conduct. It should be noted that it is the conduct of any person which the court can take into account and not just that of the applicant. It may be the conduct of the deceased which is relevant. Therefore, in *Marks* v. *Shafier* [2001] All ER (D) 193 the adult son of the deceased relied, albeit unsuccessfully on the facts, on the abusive conduct of the deceased towards him as a child as justifying the estrangement between them. In *Re Jennings* [1994] Ch 286 the Court of Appeal refused to place any weight on the conduct of a neglectful father where the conduct had occurred many years before and had no impact on the claimant's financial position at the date of the application.

In general terms, great care has to be taken in relying too heavily or at all on conduct. Courts often find it unhelpful and distracting to trawl through the rights and wrongs of events which may have happened many years before and may find it hard to make findings in respect of matters when they cannot hear the deceased's side of the story. In *Cunliffe* v. *Fielden* [2006] Ch 361, for example, a great deal of time at trial was taken on the subject of the conduct of the widow who had been the deceased's housekeeper and married him shortly after going to work for him. Reliance on conduct proved unsuccessful.

However, the court will inevitably make findings of fact in respect of the relationship between the deceased and the claimant and even in cases where conduct is not the main plank of the defence to the claim by the estate and beneficiaries. Therefore, conduct and other related circumstances frequently do play a part in the court's decision. However, it is a rare case where the conduct of the claimant who is otherwise in need of maintenance from the estate will defeat the claim. In *Espinosa* v. *Bourke* [1999] 1 FLR 747 the court at first instance rejected a claim by an adult daughter because of her conduct towards her father. The Court of Appeal held that the conduct on her part did not outweigh her need for provision for her maintenance. Conduct also clearly played a part in another claim by an adult child in *Re Myers* (above). In that case the daughter applicant was in her sixties and had suffered a difficult relationship with her deceased father. She was awarded provision and the court found that she had not behaved as badly to her father as he had seemed to believe.

Good behaviour on the part of the applicant can also strengthen a case. For example, in *Re Abram (Deceased)* [1996] 2 FLR 379 the court relied on the fact that a son had worked in the family business for little remuneration for years in the expectation that it would be left to him. In *Re Pearce (Deceased)* [1998] 2 FLR 705 a similar consideration was taken into account, namely that a son had done a great deal of work on the family farm in the expectation that it would be his one day.

4.10 SPOUSES

Applications by spouses (and from now on civil partners) have always been different from applications by other claimants. As stated above, in other cases it has to be shown that the provision is reasonable for the *maintenance* of the applicant, in the case of a spouse it is the more generous test of what is reasonable provision. In addition to the factors under s.3 of the Act which have to be taken into account, in respect of spouses the court has to consider:

- the age of the applicant and the duration of the marriage;
- the contribution made by the applicant to the welfare of the family of the deceased, including any contribution made by looking after the home or caring for the family;
- the provision which the applicant might reasonably have expected to receive if on the day on which the deceased died the marriage, instead of being terminated by death, had been terminated by divorce.

The age of the applicant can in practice make a great deal of difference to the award which the court will make. A middle-aged widow may need a far greater sum to meet her income needs than an elderly widow, for example. There is also a theory (see *Re Krubert (Deceased)* [1997] Ch 97) that an elderly widow does not really need substantial capital provision but should have her income needs met. In light of the discussion later about the provision which the applicant might have been able to obtain on divorce, this is possibly not at all correct.

The duration of the marriage is clearly important but perhaps not as important as in divorce cases. In *Cunliffe v. Fielden* [2006] Ch 361, a case involving an elderly disabled man who married his housekeeper after knowing her for six months and died within a year of the marriage, Wall LJ in the Court of Appeal accepted that the brevity of the marriage affected the housing needs of the claimant in that she could not expect to stay in a house which had been her matrimonial home for such a short time when she had not contributed to the family wealth in any significant way. He also used the brevity of the marriage to reject an argument by the claimant that she should be maintained to the extent of £50,000 per annum. However, he did emphasise that she had gone into the marriage not expecting it to be curtailed so early.

The contribution of a widow to the welfare of the family may be in terms of her financial contribution or in her assisting the deceased to create wealth or in running the household and bringing up children. This is clearly a factor which will be affected by the duration of the marriage.

The last factor – the provision on divorce – has always caused some difficulty, not least because sorting out the finances of a divorcing couple involves considering the needs of two living parties whereas there is only one party to the marriage whose needs the court has to consider in a claim under the Act. What is more, there had been some suggestion that what the spouse might receive on divorce was an overriding factor. However, *Re Krubert (Deceased)* [1997] Ch 97 made it clear that the provision which the court might make on divorce is only one of the factors which the court will take into account in deciding on the appropriate provision. However, as was made clear in that case, the award which might have been expected on divorce provides a useful cross-check when seeing whether the financial provision awarded is about right. The factor was in fact introduced by the Act to ensure that widows making a claim under the Act did at least as well as divorcing spouses.

Therefore, developments in the law of matrimonial finance such as *White* v. *White* [2001] AC 596 and *Miller* v. *Miller* [2006] 2 WLR 1283 inevitably have had an impact on the jurisdiction of the Act insofar as it deals with spouses. In essence *White*, which involved a couple who had been married for many years, provided that in seeking to achieve a fair outcome there was no place for discrimination between husband and wife and their respective roles. A judge should come to a tentative view having taken the statutory criteria into account and then should check it against the yardstick of equality of division. The House of Lords made it clear that it was not introducing any presumption of equal division, but stated that equality should be departed from only if, and to the extent that, there were good reasons for doing so. It also held that in the context of a clean break in a big money case there should be no rule that the available assets of one party became immaterial once the financial needs of the other were satisfied, such that any surplus belonged exclusively to the former. Where the husband and wife had jointly contributed to their total net worth, there was no justification for awarding the wife only what she reasonably required, whilst leaving the husband with a far larger share.

How this principle should be applied in the jurisdiction of the Act was explored by the Court of Appeal in *Cunliffe* v. *Fielden*. Prior to this case the principles had been applied in this jurisdiction at first instance in *Adams* v. *Lewis* [2001] WTLR 493 and *McNulty* v. *McNulty* [2002] WTLR 737. Those cases involved long marriages between parties where they had together built up wealth by a contribution to the family. *Cunliffe* involved a marriage of just

33

over a year, no children and no contribution to the wealth of the deceased by his widow. At first instance the judge awarded Mrs Cunliffe £800,000 from an estate of £1.4m in circumstances where she inherited joint assets of £225,000. The Court of Appeal substituted an award of £600,000 and Wall LJ discussed the impact of the matrimonial finance cases in this jurisdiction. He seemed to suggest that the divorce approach may not produce the right result in cases under the Act. However, he did not really say how great a role it will play. What he did seem to suggest is that where there is a short marriage as here terminated by death, the courts will not necessarily be as ungenerous with a widow as they would be with a wife.

The first really 'big money' application under the Act by a spouse was heard by Black J in *P* v. *G, P and P* [2006] 1 FLR 431. That case raised some interesting points. The court held that there was no need to undergo a theoretical ancillary relief application taking into account hypothetical tax and historical values. It was also argued that in big money cases the award which might be made on divorce should be a ceiling rather than a floor. No decision was in fact given on that point.

Since those cases the House of Lords has given judgment in the *Miller* appeal which was in effect an appeal from two big money divorce cases. *Miller*, which is perhaps of more importance in this area, concerned a short childless marriage. The wealth of the husband had increased significantly, by in excess of £15m, during the marriage of less than three years. The appeal in *Miller* was dismissed and the 'clean-break' award of £5m upheld. The concept of 'legitimate expectation' (which had played some part in *Cunliffe*) was rejected as was attributing blame to Mr Miller for the breakdown of the marriage. The Law Lords made it clear that they view marriage as a partnership of equals and that the principle of fairness in *White* v. *White* is of universal application, however long or short the marriage is. It can no longer be argued that in a short childless marriage a husband simply has to restore the wife to the position she was in before the marriage. In giving judgment, Lord Nicholls made it clear that a wife's entitlement does not only accrue over time and that the *White* approach should not be confined to long marriages. To do that would introduce the sort of discrimination that *White* was intended to negate – discrimination between the breadwinner and homemaker and that each party is entitled to a fair share of the matrimonial assets. To achieve fairness, the Law Lords identified three main strands to which the court has to give consideration: financial needs; compensation; and equal sharing (unless there is a good reason to the contrary).

In essence, therefore, the award which a spouse will obtain on divorce is important when looking at spouse applications under the Act but may not automatically provide the answer. It would seem that in cases where the marriage was short a widow will not find herself so penalised as a divorcing spouse. What is more, if the estate is not substantial the widow may warrant a far greater share of the estate than the provision which might be made for her on divorce would suggest.

4.11 CIVIL PARTNERS

The additional factors which the court has to take into account on an application by a surviving civil partner correspond with those which apply to a widow or widower:

- the age of the applicant and the duration of the civil partnership;
- the contribution made by the applicant to the welfare of the family of the deceased, including any contribution made by looking after the home or caring for the family;
- the provision which the applicant might reasonably have expected to receive if on the day on which the deceased died the civil partnership, instead of being terminated by death, had been terminated by a dissolution order.

As yet there is no case law as to the sort of provision which the courts will award on the dissolution of a civil partnership but the statutory criteria applicable are similar to those on divorce and therefore it is reasonable to assume that the courts will adopt a similar approach. Therefore, the factors referred to above in respect of claims by widows and widowers will be relevant in respect of claims by surviving civil partners.

4.12 FORMER SPOUSES AND CIVIL PARTNERS

In the case of an application by a former spouse or civil partner of the deceased, the age of the applicant and the duration of the marriage or partnership are particular factors to be taken into account and the contribution made by the applicant to the welfare of the family of the deceased, including any contribution made by looking after the home or caring for the family.

As far as a former spouse is concerned, it has been said that exceptional circumstances must be shown before provision will be made (see *Re Fullard (Deceased)* [1982] Fam 42 and *Barass* v. *Harding* [2001] 1 FLR 138); particularly in the case where there has been a clean break and that principle will apply even where there is an intestacy and the estate of the deceased will go *bona vacantia* (see *Cameron* v. *Treasury Solicitor* [1996] 2 FLR 716).

However, it is important to note the provisions of s.14(1) of the Act where death takes place within 12 months of a decree of divorce or nullity. This provides that where, within 12 months from the date on which a divorce order or separation order has been made under the Family Law Act 1996 in relation to a marriage or a decree of nullity of marriage has been made absolute, a party to the marriage dies and an application for a financial provision order or a property adjustment order has not been made by the other party to that marriage, or such an application has been made but the proceedings have not been determined at the time of the death of the deceased, then, if an application is made by that other party under the 1975 Act, the court has power, if it thinks it just to do so, to treat that party for the purposes of that application as if the divorce order or separation order had not been made or the decree of nullity had not been made absolute. There is a similar provision contained in s.14A in respect of former civil partners. This is an extremely important provision because of the more generous basis on which spouses and civil partners are treated. There is little guidance in the reported cases as to the circumstances in which the courts will exercise this power, but experience suggests that in all cases where the financial affairs of the divorcing parties have not been dealt with by the court, that the more generous approach accorded to spouses will be adopted.

4.13 COHABITANTS

In the case of an applicant whose application is made under s.1(1)(ba) of the 1975 Act as someone who has lived in the same household as the husband or wife or civil partner of the deceased for at least a two-year period, the court will look at the age of the applicant and the length of the period during which the applicant lived as the husband or wife or civil partner of the deceased and in the same household as the deceased and the contribution made by the applicant to the welfare of the family of the deceased, including any contribution made by looking after the home or caring for the family.

The length of the relationship is a factor which the court will take into account (see *Re Watson* [1999] 1 FLR 878 where Neuberger J took into account the fact that the applicant had lived with the deceased for 10 years which was five times the statutory minimum). This is interesting in light of the fact that the duration of a marriage is becoming less important in divorce cases.

4.14 CHILDREN

The additional factor to which the court must have regard in relation to a child is to the manner in which the applicant was being or in which he might expect to be educated or trained. This is a factor which in general will apply only to minor children, although a child who has reached his majority but is in full-time education can also rely upon it.

In the case of a claim by a minor child, any school fees which might be expected to be incurred might well form a very important part of the claim. In the case of a very young child, it can be difficult to predict with certainty how they might be educated.

As far as adult children are concerned, there are no specific factors to which the court is required to have regard, but many of the cases have turned on the issue of the obligation of the deceased towards them, which is discussed above.

4.15   CHILD OF THE FAMILY

The first special factors with regard to such an applicant is the manner in which the applicant was being or in which he might expect to be educated or trained, the same factor which applies in respect of a child. This will, of course, have more application in respect of an application by a minor child. However, as set out above, a person treated as a child of the family can already be an adult when they become a step-child.

The additional factors which the court must take into account are whether the deceased had assumed any responsibility for the applicant's maintenance and, if so, the extent to which and the basis upon which the deceased assumed that responsibility and to the length of time for which the deceased discharged that responsibility. Also, whether in assuming and discharging that responsibility, the deceased did so knowing that the applicant was not his own child.

Although the assumption of responsibility for a child of the family's maintenance is a factor which has to be taken into account, it is not fatal to a claim that the deceased never did in fact assume such responsibility, perhaps because the child was an adult when they became a step-child (*Re Leach (Deceased), sub nom: Leach v. Linderman* [1986] Ch 226 and *Re Callaghan (Deceased)* [1985] Fam 1).

There is no guidance in the reported cases in respect of the knowledge which the deceased has that the child he was supporting was not his own. It might perhaps be the case that if the deceased supported a child believing him to be his own when in fact he was not, that his assumption of responsibility was less weighty as it was based on a false premise. However, this seems unduly harsh on a child who has been supported by someone who turns out not to be his parent.

4.16   DEPENDANTS

In the case of a claim by a dependant, the court will additionally take into account the extent to which and the basis upon which the deceased assumed responsibility for the maintenance of the applicant, and to the length of time for which the deceased discharged that responsibility.

It is, of course, part of the threshold requirement to apply under s.1(1)(e) of the Act that the applicant was being maintained by the deceased and the difference between this additional requirement and the requirement in respect of a child of the family was noted in *Re B* [2000] Ch 662. This was an unusual case which involved the mother of a mentally disabled child applying for provision from her estate on the basis that funds under the control of the Court of Protection had been used to maintain her.

In practical terms, the court will be more inclined to be generous to a dependant who has depended on the deceased for a long period of time. The extent of the dependency is also crucial. How much has the deceased in fact contributed on an annual basis to the needs of the applicant? This may form the basis for the court ascertaining a lump sum figure based, for example, on the Duxbury tables.

In *Witkowska* v. *Kaminski* [2006] WTLR 1293 an award was made on the basis of the needs of the claimant if she went back to live in Poland even though she had continued to live in England after the death of her partner, although possibly illegally. That did not entirely reflect the level of maintenance she had received during the lifetime of the deceased who had sent money to her when she was staying in Poland and had maintained her fully when she was living with him in England. However, it was regarded as right in all the circumstances including the size of the net estate.

4.17 ASSESSING AWARDS

Assessing the size of an award under the Act is one of the most difficult aspects of the jurisdiction. One of the problems is that each case will turn very much on its own facts and the result in one reported decision will rarely be helpful in ascertaining what the court is likely to do in another.

In cases where the test is what is reasonable for the maintenance of the applicant (the meaning of which is discussed at **4.1**), a good starting point has to be the reasonable needs and resources of the applicant. Is there an income shortfall? Can that shortfall be satisfied by a lump sum award calculated by reference to a table? For this purpose the Duxbury tables are most frequently used whereby a sum needed to produce a particular income for an applicant of that gender and age is shown on the basis that the capital will be reduced to nil by their expected date of death. All this needs to be looked at in light of the current and future expected earning capacity of the applicant.

The next question might be whether there is a housing need and how that might best be satisfied. Sometimes, in a strong case, it will be by the provision of a capital sum so that an applicant may purchase a house outright. In other cases, it will be the provision of more income so that rent can be paid or it might be by a trust fund being set up in which the applicant has a life interest.

The payment of debts and the injection of capital into an existing business or the provision of capital to start one up might also be regarded as maintenance.

Although the reasonable needs and resources of an applicant provide a starting point, the inquiry will rarely stop there. The merits of the claim by the particular applicant have to be balanced against claims by other applicants and beneficiaries, particularly those to whom the deceased owed obligations. All this has to be looked at in the context of the size of the net estate which can be crucial in assessing the size of an award. Where the estate is small and the claims on it numerous, the court may well not be able to satisfy even the most basic needs of an applicant by an award. Where the estate is large, the court has more room for manoeuvre but a large estate should not encourage the court to go beyond what is required for the reasonable maintenance of an applicant nor to give more to a claimant whose claim is not particularly meritorious.

In respect of other cases of spouses, civil partners and former spouses and civil partners where death occurs within 12 months of the dissolution of the marriage or civil partnership and where the court exercises its discretion to treat them as spouses and civil partners (s.14 of the Act), the issue is what is a reasonable provision. As set out above, in those cases the court is required to cross-check the provision it is proposing to make against the relief which might have been made on divorce or the dissolution of the civil partnership. It is still important to look at the financial needs and resources of the claimant and the other factors which s.3 requires the court to consider. However, in a large estate, the court will not stop at what is required for the reasonable maintenance of the applicant but will usually be more generous. However, in the case of a modest estate, awarding the spouse or civil partner one half of the joint assets might not provide them with enough to satisfy their reasonable needs and there is no reason in such a case why the court should feel constrained to limit the award in such a way. As the courts have stressed, in a divorce there are two people to provide for, whereas there is only one surviving party to the marriage to provide for on death.

The best approach in each case is to go through the various factors under s.3 of the Act and see which way they point in terms of the award and then come to a conclusion about a range of possible awards which the court might possibly make.

CHAPTER 5

Orders which the court can make

5.1 THE NET ESTATE

Before addressing how the court may order provision to be made for a successful applicant, it is necessary to consider from what assets such provision will be made. Section 2 of the Inheritance (Provision for Family and Dependants) Act 1975 envisages awards being made from the deceased's 'net estate'. 'Net estate' is defined in s.25(1) of the Act as follows:

(a) all property of which the deceased had power to dispose by his will (otherwise than by virtue of a special power of appointment) less the amount of his funeral, testamentary and administration expenses, debts and liabilities, including any capital transfer tax payable out of his estate on his death;

(b) any property in respect of which the deceased held a general power of appointment (not being a power exercisable by will) which has not been exercised;

(c) any sum of money or other property which is treated for the purposes of this Act as part of the net estate of the deceased by virtue of section 8(1) or (2) of this Act;

(d) any property which is treated for the purposes of this Act as part of the net estate of the deceased by virtue of an order made under section 9 of the Act;

(e) any sum of money or other property which is, by reason of a disposition or contract made by the deceased, ordered under section 10 or 11 of this Act to be provided for the purposes of the making of financial provision under this Act.

5.1.1 Generally

This part of the chapter will consider the definition of the 'net estate' generally and will look in particular at nominations and joint property, which are the subject of the definition in s.25(c) and (d), above. Dispositions and contracts under ss.10 and 11 of the Act (s.25(1), definition of 'net estate', subsection (e) above) are dealt with in **Chapter 6**.

The definition of 'net estate' in s.25(a) of the Act will catch the entire estate of most deceased persons. The definition in (a) is of all property which the deceased 'had power to dispose of by his will'. Two points should be noted. The first is that it makes no difference that the deceased may have died wholly or partially intestate: he *had power* to leave his property by will, and (a) encompasses all the property he could have disposed of had he exercised that power. The second point is that an estate may include property payable to a deceased's personal representatives that was not the deceased's property to dispose of in his lifetime. It may be thought such property could not in practice have been disposed of by a will. For example, personal representatives may be paid money under policies of life assurance written on the life of the deceased or they may receive moneys under the terms of the deceased's pension policy. These sums do fall within the definition of 'net estate' in (a). The reason is that this property could be disposed of by the deceased under a gift of residue or even as a specific gift, notwithstanding the property only falls into the deceased's estate on death.

The qualification in s.25(a) 'otherwise than by special power of appointment' is intended to deal with the self-evident proposition that property which may be disposed of by the deceased by will in exercise of a special power of appointment is not property that the deceased owned or could have owned beneficially in his lifetime. In contrast, property in s.25(b) is property that the deceased could have appointed to himself during his lifetime and which otherwise vests in a third party on the death of the deceased in default of the exercise of the general power of appointment. Such property will remain to be treated as part of the deceased's net estate for the purposes of the Act.

The 'net estate' will include:

- foreign property if it passes under an English grant. This will not include foreign immovable property;
- the deceased's share in property held for him and others as tenants in common, including his share in partnership property.

The 'net estate' will not include:

- benefits payable under pension schemes and insurance policies that are not payable to the personal representatives and do not fall within s.8(1) of the Act;
- foreign property that the deceased could not dispose of by will.

The treatment of foreign property, whether as an asset in the 'net estate' or as property passing to the applicant or a beneficiary of the estate, must be investigated by parties to a claim since the ownership and disposition of such assets will be relevant even if they do not fall into the 'net estate' (*Bheekun* v. *Williams* [1999] 2 FLR 229).

In deciding whether to make provision for an applicant and what order to make, the court will consider (amongst other factors listed in s.3 of the Act) 'the size and nature of the net estate'. This consideration will take place at the date of trial and will deal with the property in the net estate in its then current form (s.3(5) and *Dingmar* v. *Dingmar* [2006] EWCA Civ 942, paras 55 and 56). It is important to recognise that s.2(1) of the Act enables the court to make orders specifically related to property in the net estate so that, for example, the court may order the transfer of particular property to the applicant (s.2(1)(c)) rather than simply the periodical or lump sum payment of money (s.2(1)(a) and (b)).

5.1.2 Nominations and property received as *donatio mortis causa*

Section 8(1) of the Act provides that any sum of money or other property nominated by the deceased in someone's favour under 'any enactment' will be treated as part of the net estate 'to the extent of the value thereof at the date of the death of the deceased' after the deduction of any inheritance tax payable in respect of it. It is a requirement that the nomination is in force at the date of death and is made in accordance with the provisions of 'any enactment'. This type of nomination generally encompasses nominations made in respect of sums (whose size is limited by statute) held in accounts subject to the Friendly Societies Act 1974, ss.66 and 67 and the Industrial and Provident Societies Act 1965, ss.23 and 24.

Deceased persons are perhaps more likely to have made a nomination within s.8(1) of the Act under an occupational pension scheme. Section 8(1) will apply if the scheme is founded on an enactment and the employee has a power to nominate. Private sector schemes will generally not have been established by Act of Parliament, so the section will not apply (see *Re Cairnes, sub nom: Howard* v. *Cairnes* (1983) 4 FLR 225). Similarly, any public sector scheme established by statutory instrument rather than Act of Parliament will also fall outside the section. Section 8(1) does not apply where pension benefits are payable automatically under the scheme rules to a specific individual (e.g. a surviving spouse) nor where the trustees of the scheme have a discretion to decide who is to be paid. Benefits payable to the deceased's personal representative are within the s.25 definition of 'net estate' under (a) in any event.

In the rare circumstances where a deceased has made a gift as a *donatio mortis causa* the sum of money or other property the subject of the gift will be treated as an asset in the net estate for the purposes of the Act, subject to the deduction of inheritance tax payable on it, to the extent of the value of the gift at the date of the deceased's death. A gift *donatio mortis causa* will be made where a gift is made by delivery of the subject of the gift, or something representing it, in contemplation of imminent death in terms that make the gift absolute and irrevocable only on death.

Property subject to statutory nomination and *donatio mortis causa* will automatically be treated as part of the net estate without a court order. This is apparent from the s.25 definition and the terms of s.8. The terms of both s.8(1) and (2) refer to the property concerned being treated as part of the net estate 'to the extent of the value thereof at the date of the death of the deceased after deducting therefrom any inheritance tax so payable'. This formula also appears in s.9 (see below for the meaning and effect of this provision in light of the decision in *Dingmar* v. *Dingmar*).

5.1.3   Joint property

Section 9 of the Act contains a provision that is frequently resorted to by applicants in relatively small estates of a deceased person who was a beneficial joint tenant of property that passes by survivorship on his death. Typically this concerns a matrimonial home or property shared by cohabitees. It may also be a business property. Section 9 provides that where a deceased person was a beneficial joint tenant of property that has passed to the survivor or survivors on the death of the deceased, then 'the deceased's severable share of that property, at the value thereof immediately before his death . . . for the purpose of facilitating the making of financial provision for the applicant under this Act' may be 'treated for the purposes of this Act as part of the net estate of the deceased'. Note that (in contrast to s.8 which treats the property concerned as part of the deceased's net estate to the full extent of its value) the deceased's severable share in the joint property is only treated as part of the net estate 'to such extent as appears to the court to be just in all the circumstances of the case'. Thus, an order under s.9 will not be made unless the 'net estate' is otherwise too small for an order for financial provision to be made under the Act.

There is an absolute time limit for applications for orders under s.9. Section 9(1) states that where an application is made for an order under s.2 of the Act within six months of the grant of representation for the estate, then the court shall consider making an order under s.9. In other words, no order can be made under s.9 in any case where the applicant has to apply under s.4 of the Act for an extension of time to make his application. There is no express provision in the Act requiring a s.9 application to be made within the s.4 six-month time limit, only the requirement that a s.2 application must have been made in that period. However, in *Dingmar* v. *Dingmar* Lloyd LJ states at para.23 that a s.9 application must be made within six months of the grant of representation.

Any property can be the subject of a joint tenancy and s.9 expressly refers to 'any property' in its provisions concerning the deceased's severable share. In *Powell* v. *Osborne* [1993] 1 FLR 1001, the court held that the benefit of an endowment policy or a life policy assigned for the benefit of a mortgagee or otherwise intended to discharge a mortgage on joint property on the death of a joint tenant will be taken into account so that any debt secured on the property is set off and the deceased's severable share treated as if free of the burden of the debt.

If the court exercises its power under s.9 it will (under the terms of the section) treat the deceased's severable share in the property 'at the value thereof immediately before his death' as part of the deceased's net estate 'to such extent as appears to the court to be just in all the circumstances'. It had been assumed that by this means there is a cap on the value of the deceased's severable share so that if, for example, his severable share at its probate value represented a half share in the property but at trial it represented only a third of the value of the property, the court would have recourse only to a third of the value of the property in making an order for provision for the applicant under s.2. The Court of Appeal in *Dingmar* v. *Dingmar* reached a different conclusion. The words 'at the value thereof immediately before his death' do not restrict or cap the power of the court to treat property, namely the severable share, as part of the deceased's estate. Under s.9, the court can take the proportionate share of the property that would have belonged to the deceased if there had been severance of joint ownership and treat that proportion of the property as the share of the property which the court is empowered to treat as part of the estate. Thus the property is treated as if there were a deemed severance at the date of the trial.

Dingmar v. *Dingmar* is a surprising decision not only for the construction it puts upon the statute but also because it appears to take no account of the provision in the 1975 Act, s.9(2) and the Inheritance Tax Act 1984, s.146(4) (see **5.5** concerning tax and orders under the Act). Sections 8(1) and (2) and 9(2) of the 1975 Act clearly state that the value of the property concerned as part of the 'net estate' is to be calculated net of inheritance tax payable. The inheritance tax attributable to the deceased's severable share in joint property is payable by the survivor or survivors as the persons in whom the property vests beneficially on the deceased's death (Inheritance Tax Act 1984, s.200(1)(c)). Section 146(4) of the Inheritance Tax Act 1984 provides:

The adjustment in consequence of the provisions of this section or of section 19(1) of the 1975 Act of the tax payable in respect of the transfer of value made by the deceased on his death shall not affect –

(a) the amount of any deduction to be made under section 8 of that Act in respect of tax borne by the person mentioned in subsection (3) of that section, or

(b) the amount of tax to which regard is to be had under section 9(2) of that Act;

and where a person is ordered under that Act to make a payment or transfer property by reason of his holding property treated as part of the deceased's net estate under section 8 or 9 and tax borne by him is taken into account for the purposes of the order, any repayment of that tax shall be made to the personal representatives of the deceased and not to that person.

The effect of s.146(4) is that the donee of the property concerned, whether under s.8 or s.9 of the 1975 Act, will bear the inheritance tax on the deceased's interest in the property as calculated at death but may be ordered to transfer a part or whole of the property that is greater than the value of the deceased's share on death. Further, if there is any repayment of inheritance tax in consequence of the court's order under the 1975 Act (which there may be if, for example, provision is made for an exempt beneficiary) that repayment will be made to the personal representatives who will have no obligation to reimburse the donee who paid the tax in the first place.

5.2 THE COURT'S POWERS: SECTION 2 OF THE INHERITANCE (PROVISION FOR FAMILY AND DEPENDANTS) ACT 1975

5.2.1 Periodical payments

Section 2(1)(a) of the Act provides that the court may make an order for periodical payments to the applicant in a sum and for the period specified in the order. This enables both a start and an end date to be specified in the order. Section 2(2) and (3) make further provision for the mechanics of an order for periodical payments and reflect the likely difficulties inherent in ongoing provision to an applicant by way of periodical payments from an estate. In deciding how to fund an order for periodical payments (and, indeed, whether to make such an order at all) the court will have in mind the size and nature of the net estate. If, for example, the estate includes a share in a family business now vested in beneficiaries, this may be the source of periodical payments but care will be needed to ensure that the payments are secure and that they can be maintained at the requisite level.

Section 2(2)(a)–(c) of the Act provide alternative forms of order for periodical payments and give the court a general power to make such order for periodical payments from the whole or some part or other of the net estate as it thinks fit. Under s.2(3) the court may order the setting aside or appropriation of a part of the net estate (but no larger part than is sufficient at the date of the order) to produce by its income the amount required for the periodical payments. The restriction on the size of the part of the estate that may be set aside or appropriated requires the court to take account of future rates of return on investment. In practice, this means that the court will need to be referred to capitalisation tables or annuity costs in order to gauge the appropriate size of the sum to be set aside or appropriated. (See **5.4** for the provisions in the Act for the variation of periodical payment awards.)

5.2.2   Lump sum payments

Section 2(1)(b) of the Act covers by far the most common type of award that is made under the Act: a lump sum payment. The attraction of such an award is its finality but therein lies one of its shortcomings: there is no provision for a subsequent variation of a lump sum so it is important to factor in contingencies such as inflation and likely alterations in the applicant's circumstances, for example deteriorating health, redundancy, retirement (see *Re Besterman* [1984] Ch 458 at 476).

The court may order a lump sum to be paid by instalments under s.7(1) of the Act. If an order is made for a lump sum to be paid by instalments the payee, the personal representatives or the trustees of the fund from which the lump sum is to be paid may apply under s.7(2) for an order to vary the number of instalments, the date on which the instalments are payable or the amount payable on each instalment. Such an application cannot seek a variation of the quantum of the total lump sum to be paid (in contrast to periodical payments under s.2(1)(a) which may be varied in quantum and terminated altogether under s.6).

5.2.3   Transfer of property in the estate

Under s.2(1)(c) of the Act the court may order the transfer of a particular property in the net estate to an applicant. This may, for example, be the matrimonial home, or a share of it. The transfer of a particular property to an applicant may be made subject to a charge (ordered in exercise of the court's powers under s.2(4)) for the payment of legacies to beneficiaries of the estate. By this means the court has the flexibility to preserve an asset of particular value or utility to the applicant while at the same time making appropriate provision for other applicants or beneficiaries of the estate. It also avoids the trouble and expense that may be involved in settling the same property on trust for the applicant for life under s.2(1)(d) (*Churchill* v. *Roach* [2003] WTLR 779).

5.2.4   Settlement of property

Section 2(1)(d) of the Act allows the court to order the settlement of specific property 'comprised in' the net estate 'for the benefit of the applicant'. That such an order must be for the benefit of the applicant does not mean that it must be for his exclusive benefit and, indeed, it is hard to conceive of a settlement involving limited (rather than absolute) interests in property that would not also be for the benefit of persons other than the applicant. A settlement will be required for a minor child, for example, because such an applicant cannot take a vested interest before the age of 18. The particular requirements of individual applicants need to be considered carefully both in making an order under this subsection and in drafting the terms of any settlement. Do state benefits need to be protected? If so, a discretionary trust may be appropriate, or a limited entitlement to income only with a discretion to advance capital. Is there a risk of bankruptcy or will an award otherwise be for the benefit of the applicant's creditors rather than the applicant himself? If so, property can be settled on a protective trust under the Trustee Act 1925, s.33.

As happened in the following two cases referred to, a court may order a settlement of a house for the occupation of the applicant. The terms of such a trust must make adequate provision for the maintenance and insurance of such property (and any substitute), clearly stating who is liable to pay and the consequences of failing to do so. In *Re Krubert (Deceased)* [1997] Ch 97 at first instance the judge ordered the matrimonial home to be transferred to the applicant absolutely. On appeal the applicant was given an absolute interest in the estate *apart* from the matrimonial home which was settled on trust for her for life. On appeal in *Harrington* v. *Gill* [1983] 4 FLR 265 the applicant (who had lived with the deceased as his wife for six years) was awarded a life interest in the deceased's house in addition to the lump sum and income awarded to her at first instance.

Rather than paying a lump sum to an applicant, a court may order the acquisition of specific property using assets in the estate. The acquired property may then be transferred to the applicant or to trustees to be held on the terms of a settlement (1975 Act, s.2(1)(e)). This is a cumbersome formula that seems of limited value if the acquired property is to be transferred immediately to the applicant absolutely. It is possible that the cost of acquisition may be sufficiently obscure to merit an order in this form rather than a lump sum payment under s.2(1)(b) of the Act. The provision makes more sense in the context of a transfer to trustees to hold for the benefit of the applicant and others which will be necessary where, for example, the applicant is a child or where the court is awarding a limited interest in a dwelling house that needs to be purchased.

5.2.5 Variation of ante-nuptial and post-nuptial settlements and ante- and post-civil partnership settlements

Such settlements are trusts established in anticipation of marriage or civil partnership or during the currency of a marriage or civil partnership for the benefit of parties to that marriage or civil partnership. The settlor of the settlement need not himself be a party to the marriage or civil partnership, he may, for example, be a parent of one of the spouses/civil partners. An express settlement of property made after marriage/civil partnership on the parties to that marriage/civil partnership will be a post-nuptial/civil partnership settlement in all but the rarest of cases. An ante-nuptial/civil partnership settlement is harder to establish because it must be shown that the settlement was made on the parties in contemplation of their marriage/civil partnership and that there was an intention to provide for them in their character as parties to the marriage/civil partnership. This may be plainly obvious from the terms of the settlement but, for example, a settlement for the benefit of a child of the settlor and that child's spouse will not be an ante-nuptial settlement if the spouse in question was not in contemplation at the date of the settlement.

There are other transactions and dispositions that can be classified as ante- post-nuptial/civil partnership settlements apart from express trusts. Life assurance policies that make provision for both parties to a marriage (or civil partnership) may be relevant settlements. It was established in *Brooks* v. *Brooks* [1996] AC 375 that a pension scheme could be varied as a post-nuptial settlement under the Matrimonial Causes Act 1973, s.24(1)(c). That provision has since been amended specifically to exclude pension schemes from the ante-nuptial and post-nuptial variation scheme in the Matrimonial Causes Act 1973, but the treatment of a pension scheme as a relevant settlement under s.2(1)(f) and (g) of the 1975 Act is unaffected if it meets the definition in *Brooks*.

The effect of s.2(1)(f) and (g) of the 1975 Act is to enable the court to vary relevant settlements for the benefit of the surviving spouse/civil partner, a child of the marriage/civil partnership and a person treated as a child of the marriage/civil partnership. The obvious benefit to applicants is that this provision may enable the court to resort to assets outside the definition of the net estate in s.25 of the Act in making orders under s.2.

5.3 INTERIM ORDERS

Under s.5 of the Act the court may make an order for the payment to the applicant out of the net estate a sum or sums by way of interim provision pending the court's final determination of the question whether (or at all) to make an order under s.2 of the Act. The applicant must demonstrate that:

- he is in immediate need of financial assistance;
- it is not yet possible to determine whether a s.2 order should be made; and
- there is property in the net estate that is or can be made available to meet the applicant's needs.

The order will be for a payment of a lump sum or periodical payments of money (rather than, for example, the transfer of property in the estate) and it can be made the subject of restrictions and conditions. A condition for payments on a periodical basis might be that they are to last for as long as the applicant resides at a certain property or is out of employment, or until state benefits are paid (alternatively only for as long as the applicant remains entitled to state benefits). It is normal to make it a condition of any interim award that it is made on account of the provision that may be ordered under s.2 at the final hearing.

In addition to establishing an immediate need for financial assistance, an applicant for an order under s.5 will also need to produce evidence relevant to the factors listed in s.3 of the Act. Section 5(3) states that the court shall have regard to s.3 factors 'so far as the urgency of the case permits'. This proviso absolves the applicant from the necessity to prove his case as if at trial, but not from producing evidence of a good *prima facie* on the merits.

If there is no property from which the provision of 'financial assistance' can be made, the court will not make any order on application under s.5. That is not to say that the court may only make an interim order for provision where there are liquid assets in an estate immediately available for distribution. Section 5(2) provides that s.2(2), (3) and (4) all apply in relation to an order under s.5. This means that the court may make 'consequential and supplemental provisions as the court thinks necessary or expedient for the purpose of giving effect to the order'. Under this provision the court may order the sale of an asset to provide a fund for the making of a lump sum or periodical payments, provided there is property in the estate that 'is or can be made available to meet the needs of the applicant' (s.5(1)(b)).

An application may be included in the claim form, with evidence in the witness statement filed in support. Otherwise an application would be made by interim application under CPR Part 23, with evidence in support. Applications should not be made before a grant of representation has been made in the estate (as to which, and the issue of claims under the Act generally, see **Chapter 8**). Applications may be renewed and interim orders may be varied. There is no express provision within s.5 for the repayment of an interim award in the event that the applicant is ultimately unsuccessful. The terms of s.5(1) expressly recognise the possibility of the court declining to make an order under s.2 at the final hearing.

Personal representatives are protected in paying any sum directed by the court under an order under s.5 from 'any liability by reason of that estate not being sufficient to make the payment' except that the protection is lost if the personal representative has 'reasonable cause to know that the estate is not sufficient'. If he has such reasonable cause and makes the distribution he will be liable to the estate's creditors and beneficiaries, notwithstanding the order of the court. It is obviously important for this reason that personal representatives are active defendants on any application for an interim award, if only on the question of the assets in the net estate and its value.

5.4 CONSEQUENTIAL AND SUPPLEMENTAL ORDERS AND VARIATIONS

Section 2(4) of the Act provides that the court in making an order under that section may make:

such consequential and supplemental provisions as the court thinks necessary or expedient for the purposes of giving effect to the order or for the purposes of securing that the order operates fairly as between one beneficiary of the estate of the deceased and another . . .

It is by this means that the court is able to consider the needs and resources of the beneficiaries of an estate, as it is required to do under s.3(c), and to ensure that the overall disposition of the deceased's net estate, allowing for the order in favour of the applicant, operates fairly and practically. It also enables a court to make orders that are tax efficient.

Section 6 of the Act provides that the court has power to vary or discharge an order made under s.2(1)(a) (periodical payments order) on application by any of the following persons: other eligible applicants for provision under the Act; the deceased's personal representatives; the trustees of any property from which periodical payments are being made; and beneficiaries of the deceased's estate. Note that other eligible applicants may apply even though they did not make an application within time in the first instance. A 'beneficiary' as defined in s.25 includes the donee of property subject to s.8 of the Act but not the surviving joint tenant of property subject to s.9 of the Act. An application under s.6 may be made more than once by the same (or different) applicants. The discharge of an order for periodical payments will be final but the court does have power to 'suspend' the operation of an order so that it may be reactivated on later application. If an order was made under s.2(1)(a) in favour of an applicant, then on application to vary that original order the court may make a 'new' order for periodical payments in favour of a different s.1 applicant.

Section 6 orders can only be made in respect of the property referred to in s.6(6), defined as 'relevant property', which is the property from which periodical payments are being or have been made. In the latter case, where periodical payments have ceased on the occurrence of a specific event (unless the specified event was remarriage or the formation of a new civil partnership) or a limited period has expired, s.6(3) requires the application to be made within six months of the date the payments ceased.

Under s.6 of the Act, the court may order discharge or suspension, variation of the amount up or down, a lump sum payment to the applicant or a transfer of the property from which the periodical payments are being made. It cannot make any of the orders that it had power to make under s.2(1)(d), (e) and (f) nor ss.9, 10 and 11 of the Act (see s.6(9)). In practice, there will be little flexibility to make meaningful variations other than those that seek to discharge the order and dispose of the capital from which the periodical payments are made. In making an order the court will have regard to all the circumstances of the case, including any change concerning matters it had regard to when the original order was made.

5.5 TAX

Section 19(1) of the Act provides:

> Where an order is made under section 2 of this Act then for all purposes, including the purposes of the enactments relating to inheritance tax, the will or the law relating to intestacy, or both the will and the law relating to intestacy, as the case may be, shall have effect and be deemed to have had effect as from the deceased's death subject to the provisions of the order.

The provisions made in the order are therefore treated as if they had appeared in the will or on intestacy. This may have an impact on the inheritance tax position and will affect the income and capital gains tax position.

Section 19 is reflected in the Inheritance Tax Act 1984, s.146(1) which provides specifically for any order made under the 1975 Act to have retrospective effect for inheritance tax. There is no corresponding provision for capital gains or income tax but s.19 itself makes clear that the order is retrospective for all purposes. This is on the basis that the court makes an order under the Act. Where the claim is compromised the matter is not so straightforward and **Chapter 9** on compromise and the tax implications of that should be consulted.

Section 146(6) of the Inheritance Tax Act 1984 provides that anything which is done in compliance with an order under the 1975 Act or occurs on the coming into force of such an order, and which would constitute an occasion on which tax is chargeable under any provision of the Act (apart from the 10–yearly charge applicable to trusts containing relevant property), should not be treated as such an event and where an order under the 1975 Act provides for property to be settled or for the variation of a settlement, and (apart from this subsection) tax would be charged under s.52(1) of the Act (which imposes a charge to tax when an interest in possession comes to an end) on the coming into force of the order, s.52(1) shall not apply. Therefore, insofar as the order requires something to be done (such as property to be settled or an interest in possession to be terminated) which cannot be read back into the will or intestacy, there are no tax implications.

CHAPTER 6

Anti-avoidance provisions

6.1   INTRODUCTION

Sections 10 to 13 of the Inheritance (Provision for Family and Dependants) Act 1975 contain provisions which enable the court to set aside or inhibit transactions entered into by the deceased with a view to defeating a claim for provision out of his estate under the Act.

The sections can only apply to transactions entered into by the deceased after the commencement of the Act (1 April 1976).

6.2   DISPOSITIONS INTENDED TO DEFEAT APPLICATIONS FOR FINANCIAL PROVISION

Section 10 of the Act provides as follows:

(1)   Where an application is made to the court for an order under section 2 of this Act, the applicant may, in the proceedings on that application, apply to the court for an order under subsection (2) below.

(2)   Where on an application under subsection (1) above the court is satisfied –

    (a)   that, less than six years before the date of the death of the deceased, the deceased with the intention of defeating an application for financial provision under this Act made a disposition, and

    (b)   that full valuable consideration for that disposition was not given by the person to whom or for the benefit of whom the disposition was made (in this section referred to as 'the donee') or by any other person, and

    (b)   that the exercise of the powers conferred by this section would facilitate the making of financial provision for the applicant under this Act,

then, subject to the provisions of this section and sections 12 and 13 of this Act, the court may order the donee (whether or not at the date of the order he holds any interest in the property disposed of to him or for his benefit by the deceased) to provide, for the purpose of the making of that financial provision, such sum of money or other property as may be specified in the order.

6.3 PRELIMINARY POINTS ON SECTION 10

An application under s.10 of the Act can only be made in circumstances where the claimant has made an application for an order making financial provision under s.2 of the Act. However, provided an application for an order under s.2 has been made within the time limit specified in s.4 (or outside that time limit with the permission of the court), a s.10 application can be made at any time before the application for an order under s.2 has been finally determined.

The court can only make an order under s.10 if such an order will 'facilitate the making of financial provision' for the claimant under s.2. Section 2(1)(a)–(e) list various forms of order which the court can make in relation to the deceased's 'net estate' so as to make provision for the claimant. Section 25(1) of the Act includes in the definition of the 'net estate' any sum of money or other property which is ordered to be provided under s.10. Thus, if the deceased left no property in his estate by reason of having made a disposition within the ambit of s.10, it would still be open to the claimant to apply for an order under s.2 together with an order under s.10 of the Act.

An order made under s.10 is made against the 'donee' whether or not he still retains any interest in the property which was disposed of to him or for his benefit by the deceased. However, the donee's potential liability is limited to the value of the money paid to him by the deceased (after any inheritance tax paid by him is deducted) or, in the case of a recipient of property, the value which that property had at the date of death of the deceased (again, after deduction of the relevant inheritance tax). If the donee has transferred the property to a third party, the donee's liability will be limited to the value of that property at the date of that disposal.

The section does not give rise to a proprietary remedy; the claimant cannot trace the property disposed of by the deceased into the hands of the ultimate owner. Thus, any liability which the donee owes pursuant to an order made under s.10 would not take priority over other liabilities in his bankruptcy. Section 10(5) does, however, enable both a donee who has been made subject to an application under s.10 and the claimant to seek a similar order against any person to whom the donee disposed of the property in question for less than full valuable consideration.

Section 12(3) of the Act enables the court, when making an order under s.10 (or s.11), to make such consequential directions as it thinks fit for giving effect to that order or securing a 'fair adjustment for the rights of the persons affected thereby'. Section 12(4) provides that the court's power to make orders under ss.10 (and 11) against a donee are exercisable in like manner against the personal representative of the donee. However, the subsection provides protection for a personal representative of a donee who distributes without notice of a s.10 (or s.11) claim.

6.4 THE DISPOSITION

For the court's s.10 powers to come into play, there must have been a disposition within the ambit of the section. Any dispositions made by will, *donatio mortis causa*, nomination within s.8 of the Act or any exercise of a special power of appointment are expressly excluded from its ambit. Otherwise, s.10(7) defines disposition widely so as to include within the ambit of the section 'any payment of money (including the payment of a premium under a policy of life assurance) and any conveyance, assurance, appointment or gift of property of any description, whether made by an instrument or otherwise'.

There is a more rigid time limit on the scope of transactions within s.10 than there is in relation to s.11. For a disposition to fall within s.10, it must have been made within six years of the date of death of the deceased.

The disposition must have been made for less than 'full valuable consideration'. Section 25(2) of the Act makes clear that 'valuable consideration' does not include marriage or a promise of marriage. It is assumed that 'full' consideration means consideration of a value equal to the market value of the asset disposed of. However, it is unclear whether 'full' consideration should mean something in addition to market value in the case of a special purchaser.

6.5 THE INTENTION

For an application under s.10 to succeed, the claimant must show that, on the balance of probabilities, the deceased made the disposition with the intention, though not necessarily the sole intention, of preventing an order for financial provision being made under the Act, or reducing the amount of provision which may have been granted (see s.12(1) of the Act).

There is no statutory presumption to assist the claimant with this task (*cf.* s.37(5) of the Matrimonial Causes Act 1973 and s.12(2) of the Act) and, without doubt, establishing the requisite intention on the part of the deceased will be the most difficult hurdle which the claimant will face when seeking to make an application under s.10.

Perhaps this evidential difficulty explains why there are few reported decisions concerning applications under s.10 of the Act. Some guidance as to the likely approach of the court can be gathered from authorities on other similar statutory provisions, such as s.37 of the Matrimonial Causes Act 1973 (court's power to set aside dispositions made with the intention of defeating claims for financial relief under that Act) or s.423 of the Insolvency Act 1986 (court's power to set aside transactions at an undervalue made for the purpose of defeating creditors).

In *Kemmis* v. *Kemmis* [1988] 2 FLR 223 at 230, 241, the Court of Appeal held, in the context of an appeal concerning s.37 of the Matrimonial Causes

Act 1973, that, in circumstances where the statutory presumption in s.37(5) did not apply, the applicant must establish intention in a subjective sense; that is, by reference to the state of mind of the deceased rather than the natural consequences of his acts alone. The approach of the court considering a s.10 claim (where no presumption arises) will be similar. The claimant is not, however, required to show that the intention in question was the dominant intention of the party making the disposition, only that the intention concerned played a substantial part in his intentions as a whole (see *Kemmis* at 246).

It appears that the claimant need not show that the deceased had in mind the act itself: a general desire to protect his asset from the claimant after his death will suffice (see e.g. *Dawkins* v. *Judd* [1986] 2 FLR 360; *Re Kennedy (Deceased), sub nom: Kennedy* v. *the Official Solicitor* (unreported, 22 May 1980, Shoreditch CC).

Moreover, as was pointed out in *Kemmis* (at 241), in any case where the court is asked to determine whether a person had a particular intention, the court will usually be thrown back on inference and, when drawing inferences in the context of an application under s.10, it will be proper for the court to take into account the natural consequences of the deceased's act; although those consequences should not, of themselves, be sufficient to establish the necessary intention.

In some cases the deceased's contemporaneous declarations will (provided they are disclosed – on this subject please refer to the discussion on privilege in **Chapter 8**) make the claimant's task of establishing the requisite intention relatively straightforward (as was the case in *Dawkins* v. *Judd* (above) and in *Hanbury* v. *Hanbury* [1999] 2 FLR 255). However, in the vast majority of cases there will be very little material, beyond the natural consequences of the act in question, available to the claimant and establishing the requisite intention will be highly problematical, if not impossible.

6.6   FACTORS THE COURT WILL TAKE INTO ACCOUNT

In contrast to the court's powers under s.37 of the Matrimonial Causes Act 1973, s.10 of the Act enables the court to make an order against the donee even if the donee provided valuable consideration (provided that the consideration which he or any other party provided was not 'full'), acted in good faith and received the property in question with no notice of the deceased's intention to defeat a claim under the Act.

However, the court's powers under s.10 are discretionary and s.10(6) directs the court to take into account the circumstances in which the disposition was made and any valuable consideration given for it as well as the relationship of the donee to the deceased, the conduct and financial resources of the donee and all the other circumstances of the case when determining whether and in what manner to exercise its powers under s.10. It is considered most unlikely that the court would choose to exercise its powers under s.10 so as to make an order against a person who provided consideration which was close to the full value of the property concerned and who acted in good faith.

6.7   CONTRACTS TO LEAVE PROPERTY BY WILL

Section 11 of the Act provides:

(1)   Where an application is made to a court for an order under section 2 of this Act, the applicant may, in the proceedings on that application, apply to the court for an order under this section.

(2)   Where on an application under subsection (1) above the court is satisfied –

(a)   the deceased made a contract by which he agreed to leave by his will a sum of money or other property to any person or by which he agreed that a sum of money or other property would be paid or transferred to any person out of his estate, and

(b)   that the deceased made that contract with the intention of defeating an application for financial provision under this Act, and

(c)   that when the contract was made full valuable consideration for that contract was not given or promised by the person with whom or for the benefit of whom the contract was made (in this section referred to as 'the donee') or by any other person, and

(d)   that the exercise of the powers under this section would facilitate the making of financial provision for an applicant under this Act, then, subject to the provisions of this section and sections 12 and 13 of this Act, the court may make any one or more of the following orders . . .

6.8   PRELIMINARY POINTS ON SECTION 11

The preliminary points made in relation to s.10 above also apply to s.11 of the Act. An application for an order under s.11 can only be made if it is coupled with an application for an order under s.2; it can be made at any time within existing proceedings for an order under s.2; the court may only exercise its s.11 powers to facilitate making provision under s.2 and, if the s.11 powers are exercised, they do not give rise to a tracing remedy. In addition to making an order that the donee or his personal representative repay any money or property paid or transferred to him pursuant to a contract within the ambit of the section, the court can, under s.11(2)(ii) make an order preventing the deceased's personal representatives from giving effect to the contract in question.

Section 11(3) limits the scope of the s.11 powers so that they may only be exercised to the extent that the property transferred or money paid pursuant to the relevant contract exceeds the value of the consideration given.

6.9 CONTRACTS WITHIN THE AMBIT OF THE SECTION

In order for an agreement by the deceased to leave money or property by will or to dispose of money or property in his estate to fall within the ambit of the section, that agreement must be a 'contract' made by the deceased.

The agreement will not amount to a contract unless the essential characteristics of a contract, including offer and acceptance, are present (see e.g. *Irani* v. *Irani and Others* [2006] EWHC 1811). Moreover, the agreement will only amount to a binding contract if it was either made under seal or supported by consideration, i.e. something of value in the eye of the law (see *Thomas* v. *Thomas* (1842) 2 QB 851) passing from the other contracting party to the deceased (see *Schaeffer* v. *Schuhmann* [1972] AC 572; *Maddison* v. *Alderson* (1882–3) LR 8 App Cas 467). Gratuitous promises or assurances made by the deceased, even those which induce detrimental reliance on the part of the promisee which may be enforceable in equity under the doctrine of proprietary estoppel, will not fall within the ambit of s.11. (Although, somewhat incongruously, the other contracting party is referred to in s.11 as 'the donee'.) Moreover, the agreement must comply with any relevant formality requirements (see e.g. *Irani* v. *Irani* above).

Any contract of the nature specified in s.11(2)(a) may fall within the ambit of s.11 provided that it was made after the commencement of the Act itself.

6.10 THE REQUISITE INTENTION

To be within the ambit of the section, the contract must have been made with the intention of defeating an application for financial provision under the Act. The approach of the court on this issue is likely to be similar to s.10 save in one respect. Section 12(2) of the Act provides that:

> Where an application is made under section 11 of this Act with respect to any contract made by the deceased and no valuable consideration was given or promised by any person for that contract then ... it shall be presumed, unless the contrary is shown, that the deceased made that contract with the intention of defeating an application for financial provision under this Act.

In the vast majority of cases where the deceased agreed to leave property by will or to dispose of his estate in a particular way for no valuable consideration, the agreement will have been gratuitous and, accordingly, will not amount to a contract at all and will be outside the ambit of s.11 altogether. However, there may be rare cases where the deceased made an agreement under seal or an agreement for nominal consideration or an agreement for inadequate consideration, all of which could amount to contracts within the ambit of s.11, but where the presumption in s.12(2) would apply.

6.11 FACTORS THE COURT WILL TAKE INTO ACCOUNT

Just as is the case with its power under s.10 of the Act, the court's power
under s.11 is discretionary. Section 11(4) directs the court to take into
account the circumstances in which the contract was made, the relationship,
if any, of the donee to the deceased, the conduct and financial resources of
the donee and all the other circumstances of the case when determining
whether, and to what extent, to exercise its powers.

6.12 TRUSTEES

Section 13 of the Act contains special provisions which apply in the case of
any application made under either s.10 or s.11 in respect of a disposition or
contract made between the deceased and a trustee, or the donee and a trustee.
In such a case, the order made by the court against the donee must be limited
to the aggregate value of the money or property transferred (or property
representing that property) in the hands of the trustee at the time the order is
made. Moreover, a trustee is not to be made liable to account on the basis
that he has distributed without taking account of the possibility of a claim
under s.10 or s.11 (see s.13(2) of the Act).

The fact that the claimant's remedy under ss.10 and 11 against a trustee is
limited to the value of the property in the hands of the trustee at the time the
order is made means that the claimant could be severely prejudiced by distributions made by the trustee before his s.10 or s.11 claim is determined.
Presumably, if an application has been made under s.10 or s.11 against a trustee
and that trustee is put on notice of the application but refuses to provide an
undertaking not to make any distributions of the relevant property pending
determination of the claim, it would be possible for the claimant to seek
injunctive relief so as to restrain the trustee from making such distributions.

CHAPTER 7

Variation of matrimonial, dissolution and separation orders

7.1 INTRODUCTION

Sections 14 to 18 of the Inheritance (Provision for Family and Dependants) Act 1975 are specific to the break up of marriage and civil partnership. They contain powers:

(a) to prohibit a prospective claim brought under the Act in the order finalising separation;
(b) where one party dies within 12 months of the order finalising the separation, to assess the surviving party's claim as if the relationship had ended by death;
(c) to vary secured periodical payment orders;
(d) to vary maintenance agreements; and
(e) to extend anti-avoidance provisions to post-death variations.

Because the specific nature of these powers is limited, relevant procedural issues are addressed at the end of this chapter rather than in **Chapter 6**.

7.2 RESTRICTION PROHIBITING APPLICATION

7.2.1 Court's power

On or after granting a decree absolute of divorce or nullity, or decree of judicial separation (spouses), or a dissolution, nullity, separation or presumption of death order (civil partners), the court may order that the survivor shall not be entitled to apply for provision under the Act on the death of the other (ss.15 and 15ZA of the Act).

In *Cameron* v. *Treasury Solicitor* [1996] 2 FLR 716, Thorpe LJ suggested that the omission of such provision in any clean-break order would be 'so irregular as to suggest fundamental error in drafting'.

The court has power, under s.17 of the Matrimonial and Family Proceedings Act 1984 and Sched.7, Part 1, para. 9 to the Civil Partnership Act 2004, to make orders for property adjustment and financial provision following an overseas divorce or dissolution. Sections 15A and 15B of the 1984 Act mirror ss.15 and 15ZA of the 1975 Act and empower the court, when exercising those powers, to include an order that the surviving party shall not be entitled on the death of the other to apply for provision under the 1975 Act.

7.2.2   Taking instructions on a claim

When taking instructions on a potential claim brought under the 1975 Act from a former spouse or civil partner, practitioners must ensure that the client has the standing to bring a claim, i.e. that they have not subsequently remarried or formed a new civil partnership (eliminating their entitlement to apply under s.1(1)(b)). It is also crucial to check the terms of any decree or financial order which finalised the separation to ensure that the client has the right to bring a claim.

7.2.3   Alternative claims?

Where a claim brought under the Act is precluded, there may be scope for provision by way of variation of orders for secured periodical payments or variation and revocation of maintenance agreements, as to which see below. Otherwise, the claimant may have to explore alternative claims, as to which see **Chapter 11**.

See **Chapter 4** for an analysis of the treatment of former spouses and civil partners where there is no restriction on the bringing of a claim under the Act.

The standard s.15 order wording would appear to exclude a claim brought under the Act in any capacity. In extraordinarily meritorious circumstances, for instance where the parties recommenced cohabitation or some form of dependency and the surviving party had nursed the deceased, a court may strive to achieve a just result – perhaps by determining that a s.15 order only precludes applications brought under s.1(1)(b). Alternatively, where the s.15 order was by consent, it may allow the claim to proceed on the basis that, because a s.15 order lies within the court's discretion and requires proper consideration by the court, by rubber stamping a consent order the court did not properly exercise its discretion

7.2.4   Death as a *Barder* event?

In exceptional circumstances, where an order for ancillary relief has been made (following divorce, judicial separation, nullity or civil partnership proceedings) and one of the parties dies following the making of the order, an application may be made for leave to appeal the order out of time.

In *Barder* v. *Barder (Caluori intervening)* [1988] AC 20, the House of Lords set out the conditions that must be met for such an application to be made:

1. A new event must have occurred since the making of the order which invalidates the basis, or a fundamental assumption, upon which the order was made, so that, if leave to appeal out of time is granted, the appeal would be certain, or very likely, to succeed.
2. The new event should have occurred within a relatively short time of the order having been made.
3. The application for permission should be made reasonably promptly in the circumstances of the case.
4. Third parties who have acquired an interest in property which is the subject-matter of the relevant order in good faith and for valuable consideration should not be prejudiced.

A further requirement has been added: that the event(s) must not only invalidate the order, but must also not have been reasonably foreseeable when the order was made.

The 'new event' can be the death of one of the parties. In *Reid* v. *Reid* [2004] 1 FLR 736, the wife died two months after a consent order which stated that the husband would receive 60 per cent of the net proceeds of sale of the former matrimonial home. The husband applied within three months of his wife's death. Permission to appeal was granted and, on appeal, he was granted 75 per cent of the net proceeds. The court rejected an argument that, at the age of 74, early death should have been recognised as reasonably foreseeable: it was legitimate to refer to life expectancy tables indicating average life expectancy of 13 years.

In *Barber* v. *Barber* [1993] 1 FCR 65, death three months after the order of a woman with severe liver disease where medical evidence had indicated a reasonable hope of living for five years justified altering the provisions of the order.

Death does not always constitute a new event which justifies setting an order aside. The court must ascertain whether, when the order was made, there was any reason to consider the death of one of the parties as more than a theoretical possibility. If a party's continued good health was not the basis upon which the assets were divided, then the order will not be set aside (*Amey* v. *Amey* [1992] 1 FCR 289).

The reasonably unforeseeable event in itself is insufficient – there must be a basis for arguing that the order itself is invalidated. That will be the case where provision has been needs based, as in *Smith* v. *Smith (Smith intervening)* [1992] Fam 69, where the wife had committed suicide within six months of an order for which her housing needs had been a predominant consideration.

Similarly, in *Benson* v. *Benson (Deceased)* [1996] 1 FLR 692 where, although a long marriage, capitalised maintenance according to Duxbury principles had formed part of the basis on which the consent order was made (the application failed, however, because it was not made reasonably promptly).

7.3   DEATH OCCURRING WITHIN 12 MONTHS OF SEPARATION

7.3.1   Circumstances where higher standard of provision potentially available

Specific provision applies where a former or judicially separated spouse or civil partner dies within 12 months of a decree absolute of divorce or nullity, or decree of judicial separation (spouses), or a dissolution, nullity, separation or presumption of death order (civil partners), but where no final order for ancillary relief has been made (ss.14 and 14A of the 1975 Act). In such instances, where the surviving party brings an application for provision, the court may treat the survivor as if the relationship was terminated by death rather than separation. In other words, the court may assess the application for financial provision on the more generous test of what is reasonable provision for a surviving spouse or civil partner without reference to maintenance requirements.

In the case of judicial separation or separation order, the order must have been in force and the separation continuing at the date of death.

Where a presumption of death order has been made under s.55 of the Civil Partnership Act 2004, then s.14A of the 1975 Act also extends the court's discretion to treat an application, brought within 12 months by a surviving former civil partner, as if the relationship had terminated on death.

7.3.2   Discretionary nature of power

The court's power to determine whether to treat the application as if the relationship had terminated on death is discretionary. Section 14 of the Act states that the power is to be applied 'if it thinks just to do so'. The section appears to be rarely considered, the Court of Appeal's unreported decision in *Eeles* v. *Evans* (1989) where the power was exercised, being an isolated example.

In practice, the court is unlikely to refuse to exercise the power. Even where the parties had reached final agreement on the terms of financial separation and lodged agreed terms with the court, it is highly likely that the court will exercise its power for the simple reason that on divorce or dissolution there are two parties to the relationship to provide for whereas following death only one remains.

7.4 VARIATION OF ORDERS FOR SECURED PERIODICAL PAYMENTS

7.4.1 Secured periodical payments

Secured periodical payments require one spouse or civil partner to make regular payments, usually monthly, to the other on dissolution of the marriage or partnership. Either capital or property is secured to protect the receiving party against eventualities such as the bankruptcy of the paying party. Unlike unsecured periodical payments, secured periodical payments survive the death of the paying party. Orders are made under the Matrimonial Causes Act 1973, s.23 or the Civil Partnership Act 2004, Sched.5.

7.4.2 Power to vary post-death

There is provision under the Matrimonial Causes Act 1973, s.31(6) and the Civil Partnership Act 2004, Sched.5, para.60 for the variation or discharge of orders for secured periodical payments following the death of the paying party. The application may be brought either by the claimant or by the deceased's personal representative.

The Matrimonial Causes Act 1973 and Civil Partnership Act 2004, as under the 1975 Act, provide the court with discretion to allow applications made outside the six-month deadline from a grant of representation.

Sections 18 and 18A of the 1975 Act extend its anti-avoidance provisions (see **Chapter 6**) to applications brought under the Matrimonial Causes Act 1973, s.31(6) and the Civil Partnership Act 2004, Sched.5, para.60.

Section 16 of the Act also provides that the court has power to vary or discharge any secured periodical payments order, or alternatively to revive the operation of any provision on any application under s.2 of the Act.

7.4.3 Potential outcome of application to vary

Unless any application is barred by virtue of a s.15 order (see above), the wider scope of orders under s.2 may make applications brought under the Act more attractive for claimants.

Section 1(2)(b) of the Act makes clear that the object of the legislation is to ensure such financial provision for the applicant as is reasonable in all the circumstances. Thus, there is no certainty that periodical payments will continue at the same level following death. The receiving party may seek continued or even enhanced payments. Given judicial preference for clean-break arrangements where achievable, capital provision out of the secured sum is a more likely outcome. However, the secured fund will form part of an estate that may be chargeable to inheritance tax and subject to competing claims from other family or dependants.

7.4.4 Position of personal representatives

The deceased's personal representatives are entitled to seek the variation or discharge of any secured periodical payments order on the bringing of any application by the recipient under s.2 of the Act.

Evidently, personal representatives do not want to be in a position where they are unable to distribute the estate because of secured periodical payments. However, they need to be conscious that they should adopt a neutral role on any application.

7.5 VARIATION AND REVOCATION OF MAINTENANCE AGREEMENTS

7.5.1 Meaning of maintenance agreement

A maintenance agreement, defined in the Matrimonial Causes Act 1973, s.34(2) (and in the Civil Partnership Act 2004, Sched.5, para.67), for the purposes of the 1975 Act is a written agreement between the deceased and any spouse or civil partner whereby the deceased assumed obligations towards the other.

7.5.2 Power to vary post-death

Where the agreement provided for payments to continue following death, there is provision under the Matrimonial Causes Act 1973, s.36(1) and the Civil Partnership Act 2004, Sched.5, Part 13, para.73 for the variation or revocation of maintenance agreements following the death of the paying party.

Sections 18 and 18A extend the anti-avoidance provisions of the Act (see **Chapter 6**) to applications brought under the Matrimonial Causes Act 1973, s.36(1) and the Civil Partnership Act 2004, Sched.5, Part 13, para.73.

As with s.16 of the 1975 Act, in relation to secured periodical payments (see above), s.17 of the Act provides that the court has power to vary or revoke such agreements under the Act. Again, the court has discretion to allow applications out of time under all three statutes.

7.5.3 In practice

Separation agreements often constitute maintenance agreements and the court's power to vary pursuant to s.17 of the Act is relevant if they incorporate obligations that survive death. In practice, practitioners are unlikely to grapple with the section and there are no reported cases.

7.6   PROCEDURE

7.6.1   1975 Act, section 14

No procedural requirements are stipulated for the provisions of ss.14 and 14A of the Act. The authors suggest that an application should be issued by the applicant under s.1(1)(b) of the Act, for an order under s.2 (and any other relevant section), reciting the date of the marriage or civil partnership, date of divorce or dissolution, etc. and date of death.

7.6.2   1975 Act, sections 16 and 17

If relief is sought under ss.16 and 17 of the Act, reference should be made on the face of the Part 8 claim form that an order is sought.

CHAPTER 8

Procedure

8.1 PRE-ACTION STEPS

There is no CPR pre-action protocol for claims under the Inheritance (Provision for Family and Dependants) Act 1975. The Association of Contentious Trust and Probate Specialists (ACTAPS) has produced Practice Guidance for the Resolution of Probate and Trust Disputes ('the ACTAPS Code') including claims under the Act. The ACTAPS Code can be found at **Appendix C2**. A draft Letter of Claim can be found at **Appendix B1**.

The early commencement of a dialogue between the parties to a claim will often lead to settlement without the necessity to issue proceedings. This depends, however, not only upon the claimant making appropriate overtures at an early stage but also upon the relevant defendants – i.e. the beneficiaries of the estate concerned – being involved from the beginning. A common problem encountered in claims under the Act is the misplaced zeal of personal representatives who adopt the role of guardians of the status quo, whether there is a will or on an intestacy, and seek to 'protect' the estate from the claimant's claim. This in turn leads to the exclusion of the beneficiaries from negotiations, when they are the persons whose consent is essential to any compromise or settlement. See **8.2.5** and **8.7.3** for information about the role of personal representatives in proceedings brought under the Act.

Any pre-action approach by a claimant should ensure that the defendants are made aware of the basis for the claim. This means that the claimant must address the relevant sections of the Act and state: his or her status as an eligible applicant under s.1; that the disposition of the deceased's estate fails to make reasonable financial provision; and what the claimant seeks by way of financial provision. In stating that the claimant has not received 'reasonable financial provision', it is essential that a letter of claim addresses the s.3 factors under the Act, at least so far as this is possible at that stage of the proceedings. In particular, it is important that the claimant states his or her present and future financial needs and resources, and provides documents to corroborate the statement where possible.

A claim under the Act may be an alternative remedy to be pursued in the event a primary claim fails. For example, a claim may be made against the validity of a will, or for a remedy based upon proprietary estoppel. The claim under the Act will be made in the event the primary claim fails. It is tempting in such circumstances to put off the consideration of the details of the claim under the Act, pending the resolution of the principal claim. This is a short-sighted approach to litigation, particularly if the aim is to settle the case, as it should be. Claimants should be encouraged to work on the merits of the claim for financial provision since this may well concentrate the minds of defendants who are otherwise minded to resist a primary claim that could deprive them of any benefit at all from an estate.

There is often some confusion when a possible claimant first seeks advice about his remedies under the Act, whether it is necessary to issue a caveat to prevent the sealing of a grant of representation for the deceased's estate under the Non-Contentious Probate Rules 1987, rule 44. While anyone may issue a caveat (whether or not they have any claim against or interest in an estate of a deceased), the purpose of a caveat is to prevent the issue of a grant on a temporary basis so that, if appropriate, a substantive case can be made against a grant, for example in respect of a disputed will. The whole point about a claim under the Act is that it is predicated on an undisputed distribution of an estate save that the claimant seeks the court's intervention to make 'reasonable financial provision' for him because the will or intestacy distribution otherwise fails to do so. An unnecessary caveat issued by a claimant under the Act will often cause irritation to defendants that is ultimately counter-productive to swift settlement of the claim. A caveat is not necessary where the only relief sought is provision under the Act.

A claimant may need to issue a standing search under the Non-Contentious Probate Rules 1987, rule 43 so that he has notice of a grant once it is made. Notice will be given of any grant made up to 12 months before and six months after the date of application. Application is made to the probate manager at the Principal Registry or to any district or sub-registry on payment of a fee, and must be renewed every six months. Some personal representatives and beneficiaries are reluctant to divulge details of a deceased's estate, including whether or not a grant has been obtained and by whom. This is unnecessary and obstructive unless it is plain beyond doubt that the claim has no merit.

8.2   DISCLOSURE OF WILL FILE

Claimants frequently anticipate that the will file contains information that may be pertinent to their claim. Notes or correspondence may reveal the testator's reasoning (the testator is, of course, no longer able to cast light on that process).

How should firms holding will files respond to requests to inspect the original will file and/or for copies of previous wills? Similarly, what stance should personal representatives adopt?

8.2.1 Relevance of privilege

Legal professional privilege provides that solicitor–client communications for the purpose of obtaining legal advice are protected from disclosure.

It appears that the relevance of privilege and will files has not been addressed by the court in any reported claim under the Act. That may well be because (other than for applications under s.10 of the Act) the deceased's reasons are, strictly speaking, not relevant to the objective assessment of whether or not reasonable financial provision has been made, and because as a matter of practice, personal representatives agree to disclose.

8.2.2 Where does privilege lie?

Privilege survives the death of the testator and vests in the testator's personal representatives and successors in title.

Halsbury's Laws of England (4th edn Reissue, Vol. 17(2) at para.291, LexisNexis) states that 'privilege belongs equally to all who derive title under the testator, whether personal representatives [or] beneficiaries'.

8.2.3 ACTAPS Code and analogy with *Larke* v *Nugus*

The ACTAPS Code makes clear that copies of all wills, drafts, written instructions and so forth should be disclosed (see **Appendix C2**). The ACTAPS Code is specifically intended to apply to claims under the Act. This is clearly predicated on the basis that a claim under the Act is analogous to a contentious probate action and the reasoning in the Court of Appeal decision in *Larke* v. *Nugus* [2000] WTLR 1033 applies to claims under the Act. In *Larke* v. *Nugus* the solicitor draftsman was heavily criticised for failing to provide information about the drafting of a contested will.

Tyler's Family Provision (R. D. Oughton, 3rd edn at p.363, Tottel Publishing) suggests that failure to allow professional privilege to be claimed on a claim under the Act might lead to capricious results, for example, if a former spouse were allowed to see otherwise privileged communications passing between the deceased and his lawyers in matrimonial proceedings. However, there is no suggestion in *Larke* v. *Nugus* that the waiver of privilege extends to any documents other than those relating to the preparation of wills.

8.2.4   Position of will drafting firm

The significant difference between a contentious probate action (where *Larke* v. *Nugus* undoubtedly does apply to solicitor draftsmen) and a claim under the Act is that in a contentious probate action the identity of the personal representative is yet to be established whereas with a claim under the Act a grant is already in place.

As any privilege belongs to the personal representatives, firms holding the original will file must seek the permission of the personal representatives before disclosing any documents covered by privilege. (In New Zealand it has been held that earlier wills of the testator are not privileged (*Re Moore* [1965] NZLR 895 – see *Tyler's Family Provision*, 3rd edn at p.363).)

8.2.5   Position of personal representatives

Personal representatives are defendants to any claim under the Act. The Practice Direction to CPR Part 57 states that the written evidence filed by a personal representative must state any facts which might affect the exercise of the court's powers under the Act.

That provision does not mention privileged information. Statutory provisions have to state expressly that they are overriding legal professional privilege if they are to have that effect. It is therefore the personal representatives' choice whether or not they waive privilege in respect of the will file.

In a probate claim, where the considerations are somewhat different, the personal representatives' duty is to those who benefit from the estate and they should bear in mind the words of Lord Rodger in *Three Rivers D.C.* v. *Bank of England* [2005] 1 AC 610 at 656, when rejecting the Court of Appeal's assertion that there was no good reason for privilege to attach to the presentation of a will: 'Divulging the provisions during the testator's lifetime or disclosing the reasons for them after the testator's death could often cause incalculable harm and misery.'

A waiver of privilege must be exercised carefully in order to avoid unintended collateral waiver, which occurs where waiver of privilege in respect of one document is held to extend to all documents relating to the same transaction. Waiver should be for documents relating to the preparation of the will and only those documents.

It appears that personal representatives face alternatives. The first is to confirm whether or not they hold any will file for the deceased and to seek agreement to disclosure from those with a beneficial interest who are defending the claim brought under the Act. If that agreement is withheld they can put the onus for an application for pre-action disclosure onto the claimant, making clear that they will be neutral and that those objecting must bear the cost risks of opposing disclosure.

The second – and in the authors' view preferable
personal representatives should disclose to all parties.
brought under the Act is not a claim against the estate
to benefit from the estate. Asserting privilege over test
inconsistent with the personal representatives' neut
riding objective of the CPR, and with the Practice Di
To protect themselves from criticism, a personal representative m
be satisfied that there is some merit to any purported claim and may for that
purpose require to see a draft witness statement.

8.2.6 Position of claimants

Claimants may draw comfort in any event from cases such as *Westendorp* v.
Warwick [2006] EWHC 915 (non-disclosure of medical evidence in a will
validity action) which suggest that courts may well draw adverse inferences
from any refusal by defendants to waive privilege.

8.3 WHERE TO ISSUE PROCEEDINGS

The High Court and the county court both have jurisdiction to hear claims
under the Act, regardless of the size of the deceased's estate or the size and
nature of the claimant's claim. The county court's unlimited jurisdiction is
conferred by the County Courts Act 1984, s.25 as amended by the High
Court and County Courts Jurisdiction Order 1991, SI 1991/724. Article 7(3)
and (4) of the Order suggest that claims with a value of less than £25,000
should be tried in the county court, while those worth more than £50,000
should be tried in the High Court. In practice, it is common to see claims
under the Act with values of in excess of £100,000 being tried in the county
court.

In the High Court, proceedings under the Act may be commenced in or
transferred to either the Chancery or the Family Division (CPR rule 57.15).
There is no simple answer to the question which is more appropriate; this will
depend upon a number of factors. On the one hand, a spouse claim that relies
heavily on the 'deemed divorce' provision in s.3(2) of the 1975 Act may fare
better in the Family than in the Chancery Division. On the other hand, the
Chancery Division will be the appropriate venue if there are difficulties in
dealing with or holding assets pending the disposal of the claim, or if consideration of the tax implications of an award is likely to be of importance.
There may also be other claims in the proceedings (e.g. construction of the
will; proprietary estoppel; beneficial interest claims) that will dictate the
choice of the Chancery Division.

WHEN TO ISSUE PROCEEDINGS

The simple rule is that a claim under the Act must be issued within six months of the grant of representation. Section 4 of the Act provides as follows:

> An application for an order under section 2 of the Act shall not, except with permission of the court, be made after the end of the period of six months from the date on which representation with respect to the estate of the deceased is first taken out.

Time does not include the day the grant of representation is issued so that if a grant is taken out on 27 April, proceedings must be issued at the latest on 27 October. This is implicit in the remarks of Brooke LJ at para.6 in *Hannigan* v. *Hannigan* [2000] 2 FCR 650, CA. It is also supported by *Trow* v. *Ind Coope (West Midlands)* [1967] 2 QB 899, a case concerning the computation of a period of time by reference to a date 'beginning with . . .'. The contrary view, that the six months includes the day on which the grant of representation is granted, has been expressed and caution indicates that a claim is best not left to be issued at the last minute.

A claimant may be faced with the difficulty that no grant of representation has been obtained by those entitled to one. Can a claim be issued in such circumstances? The short answer is no. In *Re McBroom (Deceased)* [1992] 2 FLR 49 the court held that an application issued prior to a grant of representation was premature. Earlier authority (*Re Searle* [1949] Ch 73) found to the contrary but it has not been followed since.

8.4.1 What type of grant?

A limited grant of representation may be issued in a particular case, for example a grant *ad colligenda bona*, which does not permit distribution of the estate to beneficiaries and may leave unresolved any doubt there may be about the disposition of the estate by will or on intestacy. Is such a grant one that will start time running under s.4 of the Act? The section itself refers to the date upon which representation is 'first taken out'. This would certainly appear to include any type of grant, apart from those listed in s.23 of the Act which specifically excludes grants limited to settled land and trust property from the computation of time running under s.4. The existence of s.23 and the general terms of s.4 both suggest that any other type of grant will start time running. This is surprising given that a limited grant may be issued in the course of a probate action, the outcome of which may determine whether or not a claim under the Act will be made at all. The procedural rules governing the conduct of these claims appear to envisage a full grant rather than a limited one. For example, a claimant is required to exhibit to his or her witness statement filed in support of the claim 'every testamentary document in respect of which probate or letters of administration were granted' (CPR rule 57.16(3)). The personal representatives must file evidence of the persons beneficially interested in the estate, and the values of their interests (para.16 of the Practice Direction to CPR Part 57). The premise of any claim is that the disposition of the deceased's estate fails to make reasonable provision for the claimant. It is hard to see how such a proposition can be established on the evidence in the face of doubt as to the disposition of the estate, notwithstanding a grant has been issued.

Common sense suggests that a limited grant should not start time running and there is authority to the effect that a grant *ad litem* (pending the outcome of litigation brought by the deceased's estate) will not start time running (*Re Johnson (Deceased)* [1987] CLY 3882). However, it is known that a claimant has persuaded a High Court master to issue a limited grant solely for the purpose of enabling a claimant to issue a claim under the Act, notwithstanding a contentious probate action in relation to the deceased's will. This question is not beyond doubt and it is suggested that a claimant may be well advised to issue a claim in the event that a limited grant is obtained, advise the personal representatives that a claim form has been issued, delay service of the claim form for the available period (generally four months from issue) and seek a stay on the proceedings.

8.4.2 Late claims

Section 4 of the Act permits late claims to be brought with the permission of the court. The Act contains no guidance about the court's exercise of its discretion in permitting a late application. Assistance can be obtained from *Re Salmon (Deceased)* [1981] Ch 167 which lists the following as (non-exhaustive) guidelines to be applied by the court in deciding whether to permit a late application:

1. The court's discretion is unfettered and must be exercised judicially, in accordance with what is right and proper.
2. The onus is on the claimant to show sufficient grounds for not applying the time bar. The claimant must make out a substantive case for it being just and proper for the court to exercise its statutory discretion to extend the time limit.
3. It is material to consider whether the claimant has acted promptly and the circumstances in which he applied for an extension of time after the expiry of the time limit.
4. It is material whether or not negotiations were begun within the time limit.
5. It is material whether the estate has been distributed before the claim was notified to the defendants.

6.   It is material whether dismissal would leave the claimant without recourse to anyone.

Since *Re Salmon (Deceased)*, courts have tended also to consider the substantive merits of the claimant's claim as a factor to be taken into account. In *McNulty* v. *McNulty* [2002] WTLR 737 the strong merits of the claim were a decisive reason for granting the application where there had been no distribution of the estate and in the absence of any prejudice to the beneficiaries, despite a substantial and unexplained delay even after the claimant had been made aware of her remedy under the Act and the expiry of the time limit.

It may be difficult to justify a late claim against an estate where the claimant has an obvious remedy against professional advisers. It should be borne in mind that damages for 'loss of a chance' to bring a claim under the Act may be discounted to reflect the 'litigation risk' inherent in such a professional negligence claim. Moreover, a remedy in damages will not give the claimant the variety of orders available to him as an applicant for an order under s.2 of the Act. Further, a claimant entitled to public funding from the Legal Services Commission to make a claim under the Act is likely to find that the same public funding is not available to support a claim against a negligent professional adviser.

Claimants seeking permission to make a claim after the expiry of the six-month limit must ensure their applications are supported by evidence that will address:

(a)   the chronology of the delay and, in particular, the date upon which the claimant became aware of the availability of a remedy under the Act and all the steps taken since that date including consultation with solicitors and counsel, notice of the claim to the defendants and any negotiations;

(b)   the merits of the claim. If (as is most likely) the application for permission under s.4 of the Act is included in the claim form with the claim for provision under s.2 of the Act, the evidence served with the claim form should include all the evidence in support of the substantive claim. Any temptation to foreshorten the evidence for the substantive claim in anticipation of an opportunity to serve further evidence once permission has been granted should be resisted;

(c)   why a remedy in a professional negligence claim will either be inadequate and inappropriate, or otherwise unavailable.

8.5   STARTING A CLAIM

The procedure to adopt in making a claim under the Act is governed by CPR rules 57.14–57.16 and the Practice Direction to CPR Part 57. Rule 57.16

states: 'A claim under section 1 of the Act must be made by issuing a claim form in accordance with Part 8.' There is no scope for the issue of a Part 7 claim form and particulars of claim, nor any legitimate reason for a defendant to object to the use of the Part 8 procedure. If an additional claim is brought by the claimant this can be included in the Part 8 claim form and addressed in the claimant's evidence. Directions can be sought subsequently for points of claim and defence to be served. The only exception to this is if there is an alternative claim in contentious probate which requires the use of the Part 7 procedure (see CPR rule 57.3). In such a case the claims should be issued separately and directions for a single trial can be made subsequently.

Rule 8.2 of the CPR and para.2.2 of the accompanying Practice Direction requires all Part 8 claim forms to be in Practice Form N208 and to include:

(a)   a statement that CPR Part 8 applies to the claim;
(b)   a reference to any enactment under which the claim is being bought. Thus, a claim form issued for provision under the Act should include a statement 'This claim is bought under the Inheritance (Provision for Family and Dependants) Act 1975' and the heading should include the words 'In the matter of the Inheritance (Provision for Family and Dependants) Act 1975';
(c)   a statement of the remedy sought and the legal basis for that remedy;
(d)   if either the claimant or any of the defendants sue or are being sued in a representative capacity, a description of that representative capacity. In a claim under the Act the only obvious application of this requirement is in the description of the deceased's personal representatives as such.

The Part 8 procedure is modified in the following respects for claims under the Act by CPR rule 57.16(3)–(5):

1.   The claimant is required to exhibit to the witness statement filed in support of the claim:

   (a)   a copy of the grant of representation of the deceased's estate (whether of probate or of letters of administration); and
   (b)   any testamentary document in respect of which the grant of representation was made.

2.   A defendant has 21 days after service of the claim form to file and serve an acknowledgement of service and the written evidence upon which he intends to rely. There are further modifications for responses to a claim form served out of the jurisdiction (CPR rule 57.16(4A)).

3.   A defendant who is a personal representative must file and serve in evidence the information required by para.16 of the Practice Direction to CPR Part 57, as set out in **8.8**.

4.   A defendant who is a personal representative may file an acknowledgement of service stating that he will not take any part in the proceedings

but will abide and be bound by the outcome of the proceedings (para.15 of the Practice Direction to CPR Part 57).

5. A claimant may serve further evidence in reply within 14 days of the defendant's evidence (see CPR rule 8.5(5)).

8.6 WHAT TO INCLUDE IN THE CLAIM FORM

8.6.1 Details of claim

The claim form need do no more than:

(a) identify the deceased by name and date of death, stating the date that a grant of representation was taken out and identifying a will or intestacy as appropriate;

(b) identify the claimant and state that he applies under s.1 of the Act (placing the claimant within the relevant subsection);

(c) state the grounds for the application being that the disposition of the deceased's estate fails to make reasonable financial provision for the claimant;

(d) state the claimant seeks provision from the deceased's estate under s.2 of the Act (there is no necessity to say precisely what provision is sought);

(e) identify the defendants and state whether they are the deceased's personal representatives or the beneficiaries of the deceased's estate (or both) and/or defendants for the purpose of an application under ss.8, 9, 10 and 11 of the Act (see further below);

(f) make applications under other sections of the Act:

    (i) s.4, for permission to apply out of time;

    (ii) s.5, for interim relief;

    (iii) s.8, to treat nominated property and property the subject of a *donatio mortis causa* as property available to satisfy a claim for provision from the deceased's estate;

    (iv) s.9, to treat the deceased's jointly owned property passing by survivorship as property available to satisfy a claim for provision from the deceased's estate;

    (v) ss.10 and 11, to treat property the subject of a transaction intended to defeat the Act as property available to satisfy a claim for provision from the deceased's estate;

(g) state the claimant's costs to be paid out of the estate.

8.6.2 Relief under ss.4, 5, 8, 9, 10 and 11

An order under s.9 of the Act cannot be made in a claim that is issued after the expiry of the six-month time limit in s.4, even where the court gives permission for the late application to be made (see s.9(1)). This does not necessarily mean that in any case it is essential that the s.9 application is included in the claim form for a claim made within the six-month limit. It may be that a claimant only realises the necessity to use s.9 when evidence concerning the assets in the estate is filed by the personal representative. There is nothing in the Act to prevent a claim for an order under s.9 being made later, even at trial, in a claim that was issued within the time limit in s.4. However, prudence and the recent decision in *Dingmar* v. *Dingmar* [2006] EWCA Civ 942 (see 5.1.3) suggest that an application under s.9 must be issued within six months of the grant of representation. Furthermore, if the defendant to a s.9 claim is otherwise not a party to the claim, being neither a personal representative nor a beneficiary, he may well succeed in opposing an application to amend and add him as the surviving joint tenant as a party.

An application for interim relief under s.5 need not be made on issue of the claim form, but again there is no reason not to include it if the evidence is available and the necessity is apparent. In an appropriate case, an interim application will tend to concentrate the minds of the defendants and make them realise both the seriousness of the claim and the practical consequences of having to satisfy it.

8.7 PARTIES AND CONFLICTS OF INTEREST

8.7.1 Claimants

The general rule is that claimants suing together must have identical interests, and certainly that they must act through one solicitor. In claims under the Act the general rule still applies, but with some modification. Paragraph 17(1) of the Practice Direction to CPR Part 57 provides that, where it appears there is a conflict of interest between two or more claimants who are making a claim jointly, any claimant may choose to be represented by separate solicitors or counsel, or may appear in person. If the claimants, or one or more of them, fail to take appropriate action in the face of a conflict of interest, the court may do so. Para.17(2) of the Practice Direction to CPR Part 57 provides that where the court considers such a conflict has arisen it may adjourn the application until the conflicted parties have separate representation.

This question will arise most frequently where a widow or widower sues jointly with her or his children. There is obvious sense in such parties taking joint advice, particularly where the children are minors. There is also a real difficulty for such litigants to accept that they may be in conflict. However, they frequently will be. While a mother may profess herself unwilling to take anything from her children, in practice the decision about how her claim (and theirs) is to be satisfied is ultimately one for the court to decide.

8.7.2   Defendants

There is no rule specifying who should be made defendants to a claim under the Act. The deceased's personal representatives are necessary parties and must be joined. However, the beneficiaries of the estate are equally necessary parties since it is their interests in the deceased's estate that will be affected by any order the court decides to make. The residuary beneficiaries should certainly be joined save that a large class of residuary beneficiaries could be represented by just one of their number. If a claimant decided not to join all residuary beneficiaries, it would be necessary to seek a representation order under CPR rule 19.7(2)(d) and also to give notice of the proceedings to those affected under CPR rule 19.8A(2). The claimant may not be best placed to decide who out of the residuary beneficiaries should defend the claim on behalf of the rest. The orders under CPR Part 19 are matters to be dealt with at the first directions hearing (see below).

Other beneficiaries may be joined but some thought should be given to whether their interests are likely to be affected and whether notice of the claim will be sufficient. For example, beneficiaries of small pecuniary legacies, particularly in a large estate, are unlikely to want to defend a claim and may well find that their legacies are left untouched in any event. A claimant may state that he will not claim against particular bequests and legacies. While this would not prevent the court from considering how to satisfy a claim, nor stop other defendant beneficiaries seeking to persuade the court to ring fence their interests and look elsewhere in the estate for funds to pay the claimant, nevertheless in practice this can be a useful means to limit the number of defendants and keep costs down.

Other defendants who may be neither beneficiaries nor personal representatives are those affected by applications under ss.8, 9 10 and 11 of the Act. They must be joined.

8.7.3   Personal representatives

It has already been stated that personal representatives must be joined as defendants, but what if the claimant is also a personal representative? There is no reason why a claimant personal representative cannot make a claim and continue to act as a personal representative. Accordingly, there is no need to renounce the right to a grant. To do so would only increase costs and cause delay while an eligible alternative was appointed. A claimant or defendant beneficiary who is also a personal representative must comply with the requirements of CPR rule 57.16 concerning evidence but then go on to include any evidence that he considers relevant to his claim (or defence).

Personal representatives should not take a partisan approach to claims under the Act. Their duty is to collect in, administer and preserve the estate for the benefit of those entitled to it. A claim under the Act should not be treated as a claim 'hostile' to the estate: it does not seek to diminish the assets available for distribution but only to establish the claim of someone who seeks to be treated as a beneficiary.

8.7.4 Children and patients

Just as joint claimants must consider whether there may be a conflict between them, so too must defendants where questions arise concerning who should act as the litigation friend of a child or patient under CPR Part 21. It is often seen that a parent of a minor child is appointed litigation friend for his offspring when there is a serious risk that the child and parent may have reasons to protect their interest in the estate at the expense of that of the other. The same may apply to a litigation friend for a party who, by reason of mental disorder within the meaning of the Mental Health Act 1983, is incapable of managing and administering his property and affairs and is a patient within CPR rule 21.1(2)(b).

CPR rule 21.4(3) requires that a person who is to act as a litigation friend can fairly and competently conduct proceedings on behalf of the child or patient and has no interest adverse to that of the child or patient. The court has power under CPR rule 21.7 to terminate the appointment of a litigation friend if that person does not satisfy the requirements of CPR rule 21.4(3).

8.8 EVIDENCE

The Practice Direction to CPR Part 57 at para.16 covers evidence to be filed by parties – and they could be defendants or claimants – who are personal representatives. This evidence must include (to the best of the person's ability) full details of:

(a) the deceased's net estate, as defined in s.25(1) of the Act (see **Chapter 5**);
(b) the persons or classes of persons beneficially interested in the estate and

    (i)   the names and (unless they are parties to the claim) the addresses of all living beneficiaries; and
    (ii) the value of their interests, as far as known;
    (iii) whether any living beneficiary (naming him) is a child or patient within CPR rule 21.1(2);
    (iv) any fact which might affect the exercise of the court's powers under the Act.

Personal representatives who are not beneficiaries or claimants and who are otherwise unaffected by the relief sought by the claim are best advised to confine evidence of 'any fact that might affect the exercise of the court's powers' to matters known to them as personal representatives. They should avoid comment on the merits of the case or other contentious but arguably irrelevant issues like, for example, the deceased's reasons for making a will in the terms he did.

A claimant should address the following issues in the witness statement served with the claim form:

1. The deceased's death and the disposition of the estate, by will or intestacy, describing the claimant's benefit under either, if any; the identity of the personal representatives; and the date of the grant of representation to the personal representatives. A copy of the death certificate, the will (if there is one) and the grant of representation should be exhibited.

2. The status of the claimant as an applicant under s.1(1) of the Act. The formal relationship (if any) between the deceased and the claimant should be described and the relevant documentary evidence exhibited: birth certificate for a child claimant; marriage or civil partnership certificate for a spouse/civil partner; evidence of divorce or judicial separation. The informal relationship (if any) between claimant and the deceased should be described: for example, how they lived together as if married or how the claimant was treated as a child of the family or how the claimant was maintained by the deceased. This part of the evidence is important and should address issues of responsibility and obligation (s.3(1)(d) of the Act) and any other relevant matter (s.3(1)(g)) as well as the age of the claimant and the duration of the marriage/civil partnership, and the claimant's contribution to the deceased's family's welfare, including looking after the home and caring for the family.

3. The claimant's present net income and expenditure, identifying the source of any income and the claimant's prospects including, for example, promotion, redundancy or retirement. Expenditure should be presented in an easily understood form and by reference to corresponding income periods so that it is possible to tell at a glance whether the claimant is living within his income, or not. It is important to be comprehensive in the survey of expenditure and not to ignore apparently inessential and non-recurrent items (e.g. building repairs, car maintenance, gifts and holidays).

4. The claimant's future income and expenditure. Depending upon the age of a claimant, it is important to look ahead to any likely alteration in a claimant's circumstances.

5. The claimant's present and future capital resources including savings, house (net of any mortgage), investments, car, pension rights, other valuable capital assets. Again, the evidence should address any likely depletion (or increase) expected to affect these assets.

The claimant's and the defendants' evidence should avoid irrelevant observations on the deceased's conduct. Relevant evidence will generally be confined to s.3 matters and while this does permit evidence of conduct it should be borne in mind always that the rationale behind the Act is to provide financial provision to applicants who satisfy the statutory requirement that the disposition of the deceased's estate fails to make reasonable financial provision for them. The Act's purpose is not to make a 'fair' distribution of the deceased's estate, nor to make reparation for any perceived wrongful conduct on the part of the deceased. The inclusion of irrelevant evidence by claimants and defendants tends to make it difficult for the parties to focus on the real merits of a claim and reach a negotiated settlement.

There are no rules governing evidence from defendants who are not personal representatives. They may wish to adduce evidence of their own present and future financial needs and resources, this being a relevant consideration for the court under s.3(1)(c), but they are not obliged to do so. In the absence of any evidence concerning a beneficiary's financial position the court will discount this as a matter to be taken into account.

8.9 DIRECTIONS

Part 8 claims are allocated to the multi-track and case management directions are covered by CPR Part 29. It is normal for the court to fix a case management hearing at which the following will be considered:

(a) disclosure and inspection;
(b) expert evidence;
(c) further evidence of fact;
(d) stay for alternative dispute resolution;
(e) directions for trial;
(f) further case management;
(g) other matters, including joinder of parties, representation of interested parties, other claims.

While many if not most of the documents upon which parties intend to rely will (or should) have been exhibited to the evidence served with the claim form and in response, it may be necessary to obtain an order for standard disclosure and inspection. This is particularly likely to relate to evidence concerning financial needs and resources and may also deal with assets in the estate.

Expert evidence is most likely to concern valuation. Valuation ought to be an area where a single joint expert can be appointed.

The evidence that the court will consider is the evidence of the parties' circumstances at trial (as opposed to at the date of death or the date of issue of the claim) (1975 Act, s.3(5)). For this reason it is appropriate for the parties to be directed to file further evidence shortly before trial.

It is common for a stay of proceedings to be ordered to enable parties to seek a settlement or compromise by alternative dispute resolution. Mediation is a preferred option for many parties involved in claims brought under the

Act. Mediation tends to take place once all parties have served evidence and given disclosure.

The court will consider whether to order the trial of a preliminary issue (e.g. whether the claimant qualifies as a cohabitant under s.1(1)(ba)). It will also give directions as to place, length and date of trial, the filing and exchange of skeleton arguments and the trial timetable. Further case management may be ordered in an appropriate case.

The first case management conference should consider whether all necessary parties have been joined and whether any representation order is needed for unborn or unascertained persons (CPR rule 19.7) or for members of a class of beneficiaries (CPR rule 19.6) and whether notice of the proceedings should be served on any non-party under CPR rule 19.8A.

8.10 HEARINGS

Trials are generally in public but there is provision for a claim brought under the Act to be heard in private if it involves confidential information, including information concerning personal finances (CPR rule 39.2(1), (3) and para 1.5 of the Practice Direction to CPR Part 39). The Practice Direction also provides that transcripts of hearings in private will not be provided to non-parties unless permitted by the court.

High Court masters and district judges in the county court both have jurisdiction to try claims under the Act (see CPR rule 2.4 and Practice Direction B to CPR Part 2). Note that there are limits to a master's and district judge's jurisdiction to approve compromises of claims under the Act (para.5.1(a)of Practice Direction B to CPR Part 2).

As with other contentious litigation, evidence from witnesses is given orally although the general rule is that their witness statement will stand as their evidence-in-chief. Witnesses may amplify the evidence in their witness statement and give evidence concerning things that have arisen since statements were filed and served. Witnesses may be subject to cross-examination on their evidence (see, generally, CPR rules 32.5 and 32.11).

8.11 APPEALS

Appeals from the decision of a district judge or master will be to the circuit judge or High Court judge as appropriate. Appeals from the circuit judge are to the High Court judge and from the High Court judge are to the Court of Appeal (para.2A.1 of the Practice Direction to CPR Part 52).

There is no right of appeal from a decision in an application under the Act. A would-be appellant requires permission from the tribunal that heard the case at first instance (the lower court) or from the appeal court on application by notice (CPR rule 52.3(1)). A litigant is well advised to seek permission from the lower court, by oral application at the conclusion of the proceedings. This involves no additional cost to either party and leaves a further opportunity to apply for permission if the application is refused. Also, it does not commit the litigant to continuing with the appeal process if he decides not to. The lower court is best placed in the first instance to consider the merits of the application.

If it is necessary to apply by notice for permission to appeal, the application must be made within the notice of appeal (or respondent's notice) (CPR rules 52.4(2) and 52.5(3)). The notice must be filed within 14 days after the decision that the litigant wishes to appeal (or on the expiry of such period as set by the lower court). CPR rule 52.5(4) deals with the date for service of a respondent's notice.

An appeal will succeed only where the decision of the lower court was wrong or unjust because of a serious procedural or other irregularity in the proceedings of the lower court (CPR rule 52.11(3)). 'Wrong' means that a judge has:

> ... not merely preferred an imperfect solution which is different from an alternative imperfect solution which the Court of Appeal might or would have adopted, but has exceeded the generous ambit within which a reasonable disagreement is possible (*per* Lord Fraser in *G* v. *G (Minors: Custody Appeal)* [1985] 1 WLR 647 at 652 cited by Brooke LJ at para.32 of *Tanfern Ltd* v. *Cameron-MacDonald* [2000] 1 WLR 1311).

An appeal is a review of a decision and not a re-hearing. Except in exceptional circumstances, no oral evidence or new evidence will be admitted.

8.12 COSTS

The general principle under the CPR is that costs follow the event. It should not be assumed that the parties' costs of litigation will be awarded from the estate. An unsuccessful applicant may well not have their costs met from the estate, especially where the estate is small, and even apart from the cases where improper or unreasonable conduct merits an adverse costs order, there is a good argument that litigation under the Act should be treated no differently from any other contentious matter.

A personal representative will expect to recover his costs from the estate on an indemnity basis to the extent they are not recovered from any other party (see CPR rule 48.4(2)). If a personal representative has acted inappropriately in the proceedings (e.g. by actively opposing the claimant's claim) he may be denied the usual indemnity.

An unsuccessful respondent whose award under the Act was reduced on appeal was effectively still protected on costs in that her costs of appeal were taken into account in the capital sum awarded to her (see *Cunliffe* v. *Fielden* [2006] Ch 361).

A successful claimant who refuses to pursue any alternative dispute resolution (ADR) may be penalised in costs. The court will consider the following in deciding whether the refusal was unreasonable:

(a)   the nature of the dispute: not all disputes are amenable to ADR;
(b)   the merits of the case: a claimant with a clear-cut strong case on the merits is not unreasonable in refusing ADR;
(c)   whether other settlement methods have been attempted: this may make it plain that ADR would not have succeeded;
(d)   whether the costs of mediation would be disproportionately high;
(e)   delay: if ADR is suggested too late, it is not unreasonable to refuse;
(f)   whether the mediation had a reasonable prospect of success.

(See *Halsey* v. *Milton Keynes General NHS Trust* [2004] 1 WLR 3002.)

CHAPTER 9

Compromise

9.1 INTRODUCTION

The vast majority of claims under the Inheritance (Provision for Family and Dependants) Act 1975 are compromised. The focus in civil litigation since the introduction of the Civil Procedure Rules 1998 has been on alternative dispute resolution and mediation has become widespread. Alternative dispute resolution is particularly appropriate for claims of this kind where often the only issue between the parties is the amount of an award which can be negotiated.

Some courts have adopted the 'neutral evaluation' hearing approach to these claims which is used frequently in family cases. This involves a district judge looking at the file, hearing brief submissions from both sides as to the merits of their claim and then providing his view of the likely outcome of the case. The whole procedure takes about an hour-and-a-half and frequently prompts a settlement, particularly in cases where one party has an unrealistic view of the merits of his case.

There are undoubted advantages in compromising rather than fighting a case. The first is that a bitterly fought contested claim often between members of the family will go nowhere towards healing family rifts. It also means that the settlement can be structured in a tax efficient manner which can make a compromise extremely attractive if, for example, it is possible to fund provision for a widow partially out of saved inheritance tax. Furthermore, this jurisdiction can be notoriously unpredictable and therefore the certainty of a negotiated settlement can be preferable to leaving the matter in the hands of the judge.

There are various ways in which a claim can be compromised. Sometimes it is possible to settle the claim before proceedings are issued by use of a Deed of Variation. If that is entered into within two years of the date of death it may have certain tax advantages as set out below. That is not always the most tax efficient way of proceeding and sometimes cases have to be settled by way of a court order. The circumstances in which this is the case and the form of that order are dealt with below.

Particular problems can arise where there are parties to the claim or bene-ficiaries who are patients or children. The particular problems which can arise in such cases are dealt with below.

There may also be cases where the estate is held wholly or partly on discre-tionary trusts and it is the trustees of those trusts who, far from being able to take the neutral stance which executors can take, have to defend an action and decide on what basis to compromise it. There has been doubt expressed as to whether personal representatives have power under the Trustee Act 1925, s.15 (which provides that trustees can compromise any claim made in respect of the estate) to compromise claims under the 1975 Act. Certainly, as a matter of good practice, in normal circumstances personal representatives would not compromise a claim without consulting with and obtaining the consent of all adult beneficiaries who have capacity. The position is different for trustees of a discretionary trust and it is clear that they have power under the Trustee Act 1925, s.15 to compromise the claim. However, like all trustees, they can seek the directions of the court under the *Beddoes* jurisdiction (in accordance with the procedure set out in CPR Part 64) to sanction a compro-mise into which they wish to enter which will then afford them protection against any complaint by the beneficiaries. Such an application should be brought by a separate CPR Part 8 claim outside the proceedings of the 1975 Act with representatives of the beneficiaries joined.

9.2   COMPROMISE WITHOUT PROCEEDINGS

Leaving aside cases which involve children and patients, in theory a claim under the Act can be settled at any time out of court. However, in reality the decision as to whether there needs to be a court order or not will usually be driven by tax considerations.

The effect of the Inheritance Tax Act 1984, s.146 (as set out below) is to read the terms of any order back to the disposition on death so any award will be treated for inheritance tax purposes as if it devolved under the terms of the will or intestacy. That reading back *includes* terms contained in a schedule to any Tomlin order. Therefore, if a claim is brought in an estate where the benefici-aries are exempt, i.e. spouses, civil partners or charities, there is a real incentive for parties to negotiate a compromise before proceedings are issued so that the benefit of the inheritance tax exemption is not forfeited and the terms are not retrospective. Comfort can be taken, if negotiations are still in process but the six-month deadline imminent, from cases such as *Re Salmon (Deceased)* [1981] Ch 167 (see **Chapter 8**) which indicate strongly that the court will not deny permission for leave to issue out of time if negotiations are in progress. Nevertheless, it would be sensible for exempt defendants to confirm well in advance of the six-month deadline expiring that they will not object to an application to issue out of time to allow discussions to proceed.

If, however, it is wished to ensure that the effect of any agreed terms are retrospective for tax, a deed of variation which alters the dispositions made by the will or on the intestacy of the deceased has certain favourable tax consequences if made within two years of the date of death. For the purposes of inheritance tax, the variation is treated as if the deceased had made a will in those terms (Inheritance Tax Act 1984, s.142(1)) and the estate will be charged to tax accordingly. Therefore, for parties giving up interests in the estate in order to make the provision, they will not be treated as making any sort of transfer of value for inheritance tax. It is important if advantage is to be taken of this section that the deed of variation states that s.142 is intended to apply to it.

There is a similar provision in respect of capital gains tax contained in the Taxation of Chargeable Gains Act 1992, s.62(6) which provides that a variation does not constitute a disposal for the purposes of capital gains tax. That is important, of course, because frequently a beneficiary will be giving up rights in the estate or to property in order to satisfy a claim. Secondly, the variation is treated for the purposes of s.62 (which specifies the capital gains tax treatment on death) as if the variation had been made by the deceased. There are subtle but nevertheless important differences between this and the provision in the Inheritance Tax Act 1984, s.142. Section 142 makes the deed of variation effective for *all* inheritance tax purposes whereas the Taxation of Chargeable Gains Act 1992, s.62 makes it retrospective only for the provisions relating to death.

This may be of importance if, for example, the deed of variation sets up a trust. For inheritance tax purposes the settlor will be the deceased. However, for capital gains tax purposes, it will be the person who is giving up assets to create that trust who will be regarded as the settlor (see *Marshall (Inspector of Taxes)* v. *Kerr* [1994] STC 638).

What is more, the fiction that the deed is retrospective does not extend to anything other than inheritance and capital gains tax. The provisions of the deed are not as a matter of general law retrospective. Neither are they retrospective for income tax purposes. So if a settlement is created the person providing the funds for that settlement will be the settlor, and if there is income payable to a beneficiary prior to the deed being entered into that beneficiary will be entitled to the income (subject to the deed providing to the contrary) and will be liable to income tax on it.

Sometimes concern is expressed that the compromise of the proceedings amounts to external consideration for the variation which disqualifies the deed from falling within s.142, by reason of s.142(3). HMRC does not take the point in respect of the compromise of proceedings under the 1975 Act and, as a matter of practice, numerous claims are dealt with in this way without the need for proceedings being brought.

There are certain procedural requirements which have to be complied with as far as the deed of variation is concerned. There is, in fact, no requirement that the variation be effected by deed (although that is how it is usually done) and all that is needed is an instrument in writing. The personal representatives need only be parties, strictly speaking, if the variation results in more tax being paid but it is usual to join them and since they are necessary parties to any claim under the 1975 Act, it would be unusual not to do so. The other parties should inlcude any beneficiary whose entitlement is affected and, of course, the claimant if not a beneficiary. Since August 2002 every instrument must contain a statement of intent to the following effect:

> The parties to this variation intend that the provisions of section 142(1) Inheritance Tax Act 1984 and section 62(6) Taxation of Chargeable Gains Act 1992 shall apply.

It is important to get the deed of variation right first time round. There can be no second variation purporting to re-direct the same property (*Russell* v. *Inland Revenue Commissioners* [1988] STC 195) although if evidence is available the court will rectify the deed (*Lake* v. *Lake* [1989] STC 865).

Compromise of a claim in this way is only possible if the claimant and all the affected beneficiaries are of full age and capacity. If there are beneficiaries under the age of 18 or patients whose entitlement under the will is affected then there has to be an application to the court for approval in the ways suggested below, or the court can approve the deed of variation on behalf of the children or patients under its jurisdiction under the Variation of Trusts Act 1958. This is dealt with in more detail below.

A deed under s.142 may be unnecessary in cases where the potential claimant is a beneficiary under a discretionary trust set up by the will. Section 144 of the Inheritance Tax Act 1984 provides that an appointment out of a discretionary trust within two years of the date of death is treated as if the will had provided for the property to be held as specified in the appointment. What is more, it is not treated as a chargeable event for inheritance tax purposes.

9.3   ORDERS OF THE COURT

If proceedings are already underway the obvious way forward is to seek an order of the court. In other cases, the two-year period may have expired and so the retrospective tax effects of a deed of variation may no longer be available and an order under the Act might be the answer.

Section 19 of the Act provides:

> Where an order is made under section 2 of this Act then for all purposes, including the purposes of the enactments relating to inheritance tax, the will or the law relating to intestacy, or both the will and the law relating to intestacy, as the case

may be, shall have effect and be deemed to have had effect as from the deceased's death subject to the provisions of the order.

The provisions made in the order are therefore treated as if they had appeared in the will or on intestacy. This may have an impact on the inheritance tax position and will affect the income and capital gains tax position.

That is the case in respect of orders made under the Act. However, the most usual way of settling cases of this kind is by way of a Tomlin order – that is, an order which stays the proceedings save for the purpose of carrying the agreed terms into effect. Those terms are contained in a schedule to the order and are in effect a contract between the parties. Except where the order has to be approved on behalf of children or patients, the court is unconcerned as to the nature of those terms. A Tomlin order has the distinct advantage that the parties can include in the scheduled terms a compromise of any matters which might be between them and not just those relating to the proceedings under the Act. However, such an order is, arguably, not an order made under s.2 of the Act as required by s.19.

There is no problem with an order of this kind as far as inheritance tax is concerned because the Inheritance Tax Act 1984, s.146(8) provides that where an order is made staying or dismissing proceedings under the 1975 Act on terms set out in or scheduled to the order, the section (which makes orders retrospective for inheritance tax purposes) shall have effect as if any of those terms which could have been included in an order under s.2 or s.10 of the 1975 Act were provisions of such an order. Therefore, insofar as the terms in the schedule to the Tomlin order relate to provision for the applicant, they will be effective for inheritance tax purposes as if they were dispositions made by the deceased by his will or on his intestacy.

Unfortunately, the position is not so straightforward as far as capital gains tax is concerned. This can be important because some beneficiaries may be giving up interests under the estate to satisfy a claim and these would constitute a disposal for capital gains tax purposes if not read back into the dispositions on death. If the terms are scheduled to a Tomlin order and the court is not required to approve them on behalf of a child or patient (as to which see below), then the order will not be regarded as retrospective for capital gains tax. If it is made within two years and there is a statement of intention to the effect that the Taxation of Chargeable Gains Act 1992, s.62(6) applies, then the retrospective effect will be available. However, if the order is made more than two years after death and there could be a capital gains tax disposal by a beneficiary, a Tomlin order should not be used. There is always a particular concern that a beneficiary might be regarded not as disposing of any particular asset but of his interest in the unadministered estate and the base cost for that would be nil, although in practice HMRC appears not to take the point.

In practice, the answer is for the parties to ask the court to make an order under s.2 of the Act rather than to have a Tomlin order. This will mean that there will usually have to be a short hearing to persuade the court that the compromise which has been reached is such that the court could make an order to that effect under s.2 of the Act.

9.4 PATIENTS AND CHILDREN

As set out above, it is not possible to settle a claim under the Act out of court where there is a patient or child involved. CPR rule 21.1(2) defines a child as a person under 18 and a patient as a person who by reason of mental disorder within the meaning of the Mental Health Act 1983 is incapable of managing and administering his property and affairs. It is important to appreciate who is a patient within this definition. It is not simply someone for whom a receiver has been appointed by the Court of Protection. What is more, the capacity to deal with property and affairs is issue specific (see *Masterman-Lister* v. *Brutton & Co* [2003] 1 WLR 1511) and therefore the question is whether the person is capable of understanding (with legal assistance) the proceedings and the settlement which is being proposed.

There are a number of ways in which a claim under the Act can be settled where there are children and patients involved:

1. Deed of variation approved on behalf of the child or patient by the court or the Court of Protection as being for their benefit.
2. Application to the court using the procedure under CPR rule 21.10(2) for the approval of the compromise on behalf of the child or patient.
3. Order made in proceedings under the Act and approved by the court.

9.4.1 Deed of variation

In the case of a deed of variation to which all parties who have capacity have consented, and where one of the parties is a patient, application should be made to the Court of Protection for its approval under the Mental Health Act 1983 which is a cheaper and easier procedure than a full-blown application under the Variation of Trusts Act 1958. If there is a patient and someone else on whose behalf the approval of the court is sought, then the Court of Protection should be asked to give its approval on behalf of the patient first and then an application can be made as set out below to the Chancery Division of the High Court.

In a case where a child is involved, the application is to the Chancery Division of the High Court and the procedure can be found in the CPR Part 64 and the Practice Directions to those rules. That practice can be summarised as follows:

1. A Part 8 claim is brought supported by written evidence which exhibits the proposed deed of variation (referred to in this jurisdiction as the arrangement).
2. Minor children need separate representation and the litigation friend appointed on their behalf needs to file evidence exhibiting the opinion of the lawyer representing the children that it is for their benefit.
3. When the application is ready to be heard, a certificate signed by all lawyers involved needs to be filed as the application goes straight to the judge. An eye needs to kept on the two-year time limit when listing the case. Generally, the court will entertain applications at short notice if necessary.

As set out above, if there are children and patients, then the Court of Protection rules whether it is for the benefit of the patient prior to an application being made to the court for approval on behalf of the children. In all cases the court will only approve the arrangement if it is satisfied that the application is for the benefit of the child or patient concerned. In doing that the court will, of course, take into account the fact that a claim under the Act is being compromised. As set out above, the practice requires an opinion from counsel or other suitably qualified lawyer on behalf of the child or patient which sets out why the proposed variation is for their benefit.

9.4.2 Application under CPR rule 21.10(2)

This procedure enables an application to be made to the court before proceedings are issued solely for the purpose of the court approving the compromise on behalf of the child or patient. The application is made by way of a Part 8 claim supported by a statement of the litigation friend appointed specifically for the purpose of this application which sets out the following information: the age and occupation (if any) of the child or patient; the litigation friend's approval of the settlement or compromise; and which exhibits an opinion of counsel or solicitor for the child or patient and, if not clear from that opinion, the instructions which gave rise to it which set out the benefit of the compromise to the child or patient. The latter requirement is stated by the rules not to apply to clear cases but it is unlikely that a claim under the Act would ever fall within that category. Such applications are usually heard by a master or district judge unless there is something particularly complex about the matter.

9.4.3 Order in the proceedings

In cases where there are proceedings underway, the obvious course will be to have a consent order in the proceedings themselves. In other cases there may be good reason for starting proceedings in order to settle them and have the court approve the settlement within the proceedings. That is often the course taken where more than two years have passed since the date of death of the deceased and it is not possible to take advantage of the provisions of s.142 of the Inheritance Tax Act 1984 and s.62(6) of the Taxation of Chargeable Gains Act 1992. This is because, as explained above, orders under the 1975 Act have retrospective effect for all purposes (see s.19 of the Act). However, the position is not so straightforward where a Tomlin-type order is used and that is discussed further below. In such a case the court needs to approve the order on behalf of the child or patient and will almost always require an opinion from counsel or the solicitor acting to the effect that the terms proposed are for the benefit of the child or patient.

As set out above, a Tomlin order will be regarded as retrospective for inheritance tax purposes. However, for capital gains tax purposes, it will generally not be regarded as such. The position is different where the court has to approve the Tomlin order on behalf of a child or patient. In those circumstances, provided that the court directs the personal representatives to carry the terms of the compromise into effect, rather than simply gives them liberty to enter into the compromise, HMRC regards the Tomlin order as retrospective for capital gains tax purposes.

If the child is the claimant then thought needs to be given as to whether the sum agreed by way of provision should be paid into court or held on private trusts. It is probably right to say that if the award is substantial a private trust is more flexible as applications do not have to be made to court whenever the child needs money. On the other hand, if the award is modest the court may not be keen on the fund having to bear the expense of trust administration. Having said that, if members of the family are prepared to act free of charge, it can still be worth considering.

Sometimes the child will be a defendant – perhaps entitled on intestacy to a fund on attaining 18. When compromising a claim the parties often wish to take the opportunity to postpone the date on which the children will obtain capital from 18 to, say, 21 or 25. It is at best doubtful whether the court has jurisdiction to do this as part of an order made under the Act, bearing in mind that in general the court does not have power to settle the property of a child. In any event, as a matter of practice, capital which is to vest in defendant children at 18 is frequently postponed to a later date. The Finance Act 2006 introduced changes to the way in which trusts for children, usually framed as accumulation and maintenance trusts within s.71 of the Inheritance Tax Act 1984, are taxed and this is a further consideration to bear in mind if asking a court to approve an order which involves the postponement of capital.

The Finance Act 2006 abolished the special treatment which accumulation and maintenance trusts received. Instead, the treatment was initially limited to trusts for bereaved minors as set out in the new s.71A of the Inheritance Tax Act 1984. These are trusts established by will by a parent of the child in question where the child obtains capital at 18. These trusts will apply to wills which are varied either by a Deed of Variation under s.142 of the Inheritance Tax Act 1984 which has been approved by the court as set out above, or a consent order under the 1975 Act which has retrospective effect for tax purposes in respect of deaths after 22 March 2000. At a very late stage the government introduced s.71D of the 1984 Act which provides that trusts will obtain special tax treatment if set up by the will of a deceased parent where capital and income vest in the child not later than the age of 25.

The tax implications of such trusts are as follows. While the beneficiary is under the age of 18, there are no anniversary or exit charges. Once the beneficiary attains 18 the special charging regime (laid down in s.71F) applies, namely that inheritance tax becomes payable until the capital vests at a maximum rate of 4.2 per cent on the value of the property. Therefore, while trusts where children do not attain a vested interest in capital until they are 25 are less attractive than they used to be from a tax perspective, the taxation treatment is not disastrous and the sense in keeping capital away from an immature beneficiary at 18 may well outweigh any tax disadvantages.

As far as patients are concerned, it may make a great deal of sense for trusts to be used in respect of any agreed provision for them. Disabled trusts under the Inheritance Tax Act 1984, s.89 have always been regarded as rather inflexible but the definition of those trusts has been widened by the Finance Act 2006 which has introduced s.89B and their use may become more popular. Frequently, the way in which claims on behalf of patients are settled is for a discretionary trust to be established in the patient's favour which will not affect the social security benefits to which they may be entitled and which provide inherent flexibility. The Finance Act 2006 has not made any changes to the way in which those trusts are taxed.

9.5 TAX CONSIDERATIONS: USE OF THE SPOUSE AND CIVIL PARTNERSHIP EXEMPTION

One of the advantages of settling a claim under the Act rather than taking the matter to court, is that the consent order can be structured in such a way as to save inheritance tax where there is a spouse or a civil partner involved. In particular, the use of short-term life interests to obtain the spouse/civil partner exemption where in fact the property will eventually go elsewhere is a very tax efficient way of proceeding. If the court is being asked to approve the order then the comments of the Court of Appeal in *Goodchild* v. *Goodchild* [1997] 1 WLR 1216 at 1231, where artificial arrangements to save tax were being criticised robustly, should be taken into account. However, particularly where provision is being made for a widow/ widower or civil partner the courts are generally sympathetic to orders which are structured to mitigate tax.

95

Thought should therefore be given to conferring on a spouse or civil partner a short-term life interest in a fund which is intended ultimately to go, say, to children. The life interest should last for longer than two years from the date of death. This is because the Inheritance Tax Act 1984, s.142(4) provides that an interest in possession which lasts for less than two years from the date of death is treated as if it had not existed which would mean the spouse/civil partner exemption would be lost. The aim is to attract spouse/civil partner relief for the estate over and above the nil rate band for inheritance tax.

As a matter of practice, HMRC looks at any life interest less than five years with a degree of suspicion but it seems to be generally accepted that this method will work. It is a method which is proposed in *Foster's Inheritance Tax* (Richard Wallington (ed.), looseleaf, LexisNexis) where the editors conclude that the Ramsay doctrine (which applies to tax avoidance schemes) cannot apply in these circumstances. There is a reality about the short-term life interest given to the spouse or civil partner – he or she reaps the benefit of the income from the fund in which he or she has an interest for the short period when it subsists and that can make a great deal of sense when, for example, a widow has actually been living in a property which it is agreed she will have to vacate. Moreover, when the short-term life interest comes to an end, there will be a potentially exempt transfer on the part of the spouse/civil partner which could result in inheritance tax having to be paid if they do not survive for seven years. It is usual to insure against this eventuality.

Drastic changes to the way in which trusts are subjected to inheritance tax were introduced in the Finance Act 2006. In essence, an interest in possession trust where the beneficiary had hitherto been treated as absolutely beneficially entitled to the trust property is to be taxed in the same way as discretionary trusts with charges on each 10-year anniversary and charges to inheritance tax when property leaves the trust. The changes as initially drafted had a considerable impact on life interests for surviving spouses/civil partners and the way in which claims under the Act could be settled tax efficiently. The changes do not affect interests in possession in existence on 22 March 2006 when the changes were announced in the Budget.

However, the government withdrew some of the more controversial aspects of its proposed reforms which would have restricted considerably the ability to leave a life interest for a spouse/civil partner. The Finance Act 2006 introduces as an exception to the way in which trusts will now be taxed the concept of an immediate post-death interest in possession. Such a trust will be taxed in the same way as an interest in possession trust established prior to the changes (see s.49(1A)(iii) of the Inheritance Tax Act 1984). Such a trust can only be established by a will or by a Deed of Variation or order under the 1975 Act which varies that will. The existence of powers of appointment or advancement will not prevent an interest in possession qualifying as an immediate post-death interest in possession. It does not have to

be in favour of a spouse or civil partner but the exception is crucially important in this context to the compromise of claims where interest in possession
trusts in favour of a surviving spouse or civil partner are established in order
to take advantage of the spouse/civil partner exemption.

Considerable care does have to be taken when the immediate post-death
interest in possession is terminated. Unlike under the old rules where that
would be a potentially exempt transfer and therefore only taxable if the
surviving spouse/civil partner failed to survive for seven years, the termination of the immediate post-death interest in possession during the lifetime of
the surviving spouse/civil partner will only be a potentially exempt transfer
if the trust comes to an end (subject to a few limited exceptions). If the
surviving spouse's/civil partner's interest is followed, say, by a life interest in
favour of another beneficiary, that will be taxed as if it were a discretionary
trust under the new regime and the termination of the immediate post-death
interest in possession will be immediately chargeable.

The other point to note is that any termination of a surviving spouse's/civil
partner's interest after 22 March 2006 will be treated as a gift for the purposes
of the gift with reservation rules (see Finance Act 1986, s.102ZA introduced
by the Finance Act 2006). It is therefore important that the immediate post-
death interest in possession is not followed, say, by a discretionary trust under
which the surviving spouse/civil partner is a beneficiary. Otherwise, on the
death of the surviving spouse/civil partner the property in the trust will be
treated as part of his estate for inheritance tax purposes.

9.6 CHARITIES

Some care has to be taken where charities are beneficiaries of the estate and
a claim for provision is being claimed. For inheritance tax purposes, a gift to
charity is exempt and therefore the retrospective effect of any deed of variation or order compromising a claim might result in more inheritance tax
being payable rather than less. Clearly, if the claim is made by another exempt
beneficiary, such as a spouse or civil partner, then no difficulty arises.
Similarly, the nil rate band for inheritance tax might be available and any
claim settled within that band.

The important trap to watch for is that an instrument which falls within
the Inheritance Tax Act 1984, s.142 and any order compromising proceedings
(and thus falling within the 1984 Act, s.146(1)) will be read back into the will
or the intestacy. Therefore, the charity exemption can be lost if the compromise is settled in this way and the payment to the claimant will be treated as
chargeable and tax paid on it accordingly if the nil rate band is exceeded.

One solution to the problem (if it is possible) is to settle the claim without
proceedings being issued. This may involve the charity in agreeing not to take
a point on the six-month time limit (although there is some risk to the

claimant in such a course as the court could, in theory, refuse to extend time although that would be most unlikely to happen in practice). Care still needs to be taken. Section 29A of the Inheritance Tax Act 1984 provides that if, in settlement of a claim against the deceased's estate, a charity effects a disposition of property not derived from the transfer (that is, from the estate), then the result would be much the same as if s.146 had applied.

There is a further argument under the Inheritance Tax Act 1984, s.23(5) that property passing to the claimant in settlement of the claim is not property of charities or held on trust for charitable purposes only. One argument against this is that if s.23(5) is used in this way to restrict the charity tax relief then this would render s.29A meaningless. The argument might also be avoided if the personal representatives make a transfer to the charity from the estate and those funds are then used to settle the claim.

A charity may wish to involve the Charity Commissioners in any compromise. The Charity Commission's consent is not required to any compromise of a claim under the 1975 Act, but if the charity is in doubt about the propriety of settling or compromising the claim, the Commission can be asked to sanction it under s.26 of the Charities Act 1993 on the basis that it is expedient in the interests of the charity.

CHAPTER 10

Will drafting and the interrelation between the Inheritance (Provision for Family and Dependants) Act 1975 and other claims

10.1 LIABILITY OF THE WILL DRAFTSMAN IN RESPECT OF CLAIMS UNDER THE 1975 ACT

When a will draftsman prepares a will the last thing on his mind might be the possibility of the provision he is carefully inserting being set aside after a claim under the Inheritance (Provision for Family and Dependants) Act 1975. However, it is something to which he should have regard.

It is certainly good practice for the will draftsman to consider the possibility that the disposition of a testator's estate might result in a claim under the Act. However, it is not clear that he is under a positive duty to consider and advise on the matter.

There has been no judicial decision where a will draftsman has been held liable for failure to consider the possibility of a claim under the Act. Two possible lines of attack can be seen:

1. A claim on behalf of beneficiaries disappointed in their entitlement under the will because a claimant under the Act has succeeded in having the provisions of the will varied.
2. A claim on behalf of the estate for the costs incurred in defending proceedings under the Act.

The first sort of claim would be doomed to fail on the question of causation: it is the order made under the Act which has caused loss to beneficiaries deprived of their entitlement under the will, and not the negligence of the solicitor. The second possibility cannot be dismissed so lightly. At present the possibility of such a claim has to be regarded as an open question. Bearing in mind how many family provision claims are made every year, it is perhaps remarkable that blame for the costs has not been laid at the door of the will draftsman.

In *Grattan* v. *McNaughton* [2001] WTLR 1305 the wife of the deceased unsuccessfully sued the solicitor who had drawn up their wills on the basis he had failed to carry out their instructions, and then successfully sought provision out of the estate of her late husband. There was no claim by the estate against the solicitors. It was in many ways a clear case where each spouse was cutting the other out of their will, but there was no suggestion that the solicitor had been negligent in failing to advise that this might give rise to a claim under the Act.

There are obvious difficulties in expecting a solicitor who is an experienced draftsman and not a litigator to understand all the ramifications in any given case of the particular manner in which the testator wishes to dispose of his estate. What is more, the situation at the death of the deceased may be very different from the situation at the date the will is made. While the will at the date it is made may open the estate to a possible claim under the Act, that claim might well not lie by the date of death. Take, for example, someone who is dependent on the deceased at the time when he makes the will but by the time he dies is no longer being maintained by the deceased. The answer probably is that in a clear case good practice dictates that the draftsman ought to mention the possibility of a claim to the testator.

All this, however, is good practice but whether a failure to deal with these matters could be characterised as negligence on the part of the solicitor is another matter altogether. There would seem to be no reason why such a claim by the estate to recover the costs of a successful family provision claim could not lie in a clear case, particularly if the testator was at the time of making the will close to death and his circumstances were unlikely to change.

10.2   STATEMENT OF REASONS FOR EXCLUDING A BENEFICIARY

The court can take into account the reasons of the testator for leaving someone out of his will, and a written statement is admissible under s.21 of the Act. This may assist the court and if the testator is determined to go ahead and leave someone out of their will who could have a good claim, then a statement either in the body of the will itself or in a letter accompanying it which explains why a potential claimant has been excluded might have some limited effect.

It should, however, not be forgotten that although the court can take such a statement into account, the jurisdiction is an objective one and the subjective view of the testator that he has made reasonable provision for a potential claimant may not objectively be a good reason for the lack of provision. Caution needs to be exercised. In *Singer* v. *Isaac* [2001] WTLR 1045, memoranda were described as 'manifestly prepared with the benefit of legal advice' and 'self-serving documents, being self-justificatory of the deceased's conduct'. The existence of such documents can be seen by a jaundiced court as recognition that, subject to the explanation or reasons put forward, reasonable financial provision has not been made.

A testator, determined to thwart potential claims, is well advised to ensure that reasons given in a side letter are sustainable, and to keep reviewing on a regular basis any side letter. *Singer* v. *Isaac* suggests that home-made letters may possibly be regarded as more convincing. That leads onto questions of whether solicitors should retain file notes of discussions with a testator recording reasons given for excluding beneficiaries or whether those files notes are best destroyed.

10.3   AGREEMENTS TO EXCLUDE THE ACT

There are few ways out of the Act. Ante-nuptial agreements are not, in fact, enforceable in England and Wales and so a provision agreeing that there will be no claim made under the Act by a spouse would not be enforceable.

In Australia it was decided in *Lieberman* v. *Morris* (1944) ALR 150 that a contract not to make a claim under the Act as part of an ante-nuptial agreement is void for public policy reasons.

10.4   NON-DISPUTATION CLAUSES

Some testators try to avoid any dispute over their will by using a non-disputation clause. For example, if B disputes or contests the will he will lose his interest under it. Although such clauses are generally valid as a matter of law (see *Cooke* v. *Turner* (1846) 15 M & W 727) there has been some question as to whether they would be void for public policy reasons if they prevented an application under the Act. Two Commonwealth cases held that clauses which prevent an application under similar family provision legislation would be void for public policy reasons (see *Re Gaynor* [1960] VLR 640; *Re Kent* (1982) 139 DLR (3d) 318).

The English courts have taken a different line, and in *Nathan* v. *Leonard* [2003] 1 WLR 827 the court held that such a clause of very wide ambit in a home-made codicil which in effect provided that all beneficiaries would lose their interests if any challenge was made to the will would (had it not been void for uncertainty) have been valid to prevent a claim being made under the Act. The judge was influenced by the fact that such a condition does not prevent an application being made and if the claimant has a meritorious case the fact that the condition operates to deprive him of any benefit under the will counts in favour of the claim and not against it. On the other hand, if the claim is more questionable, the condition may have the effect of deterring the applicant from bringing the claim. This opens the doors to the possibility of using a non-disputation clause in a will to try to discourage a claim. However, in a case where there was a clear failure to make proper provision for someone, it would always be open to them to decide to make a claim under the Act and lose their provision under the will.

10.5 ADVICE CONCERNING ANTI-AVOIDANCE

Once advice has been given to a testator concerning the potential impact of the Act, he may wish to try to avoid its impact by perhaps disposing of property during his lifetime. Such tactics may not work. As set out in **Chapter 6**, the court has power under s.10 of the Act to set aside dispositions made for less than full valuable consideration less than six years before the death with the intention of defeating an application under the Act. Such applications are rare because of the difficulty of establishing the requisite intention, but a solicitor's attendance note has sometimes provided the necessary proof.

A contract made by the deceased to leave property by will to a third party with the intention of defeating an application under the Act can also be set aside under s.11 of the Act. These provisions are dealt with in more detail in **Chapter 6** but the draftsman should alert any testator to these anti-avoidance provisions in appropriate cases.

10.6 INTERACTION WITH OTHER CLAIMS

Quite often an attack will be launched against a will in a number of ways with a claim under the Act being just a part of that. *Grattan* v. *McNaughton* [2001] WTLR 1305 referred to above was a striking example.

In that case, the claimant took the unorthodox approach of suing the solicitor for negligence, failing and then claiming rectification of the will. When all else failed she brought a claim as a widow under the Act which finally succeeded. It is the timing of such claims and the appropriate case management which needs to be considered.

10.6.1 Rectification of wills

The jurisdiction of the court to rectify a will is contained in the Administration of Justice Act 1982, s.20 and it only applies where the testator died after 31 December 1982. That section provides:

> If a court is satisfied that a will is so expressed that it fails to carry out the testator's intentions, in consequence – (a) of a clerical error; or (b) of a failure to understand his instructions, it may order that the will shall be rectified so as to carry out his intentions.

The section was considered in *Re Segelman* [1996] Ch 171 where it was made clear that strong evidence was required to establish that the will did not carry out the intentions of the deceased. A claim to rectify a will has imposed on it the same six-month time limit as a claim under the Act. There may be cases where, if a will were rectified, that would provide adequate provision for a potential claimant or would affect their resources and hence the claim. Therefore, how should a case where both possibilities arise be dealt with? A further problem is that family provision proceedings really do need to be brought separately from the other proceedings as they are governed by a specific procedure, which is unique to them (as to which, see **Chapter 8**). A claim for rectification of a will should in general be brought by a Part 7 claim. There are two possible ways forward. The fist possibility is to bring the claim to rectify the will as part of the family provision proceedings which is probably procedurally inaccurate but has the virtue of simplicity. The second possibility is to issue two sets of separate claims and to try to make sure that the case management conference for them comes on at the same time. That has the added disadvantage that there are two sets of issue fees. There will need to be an order staying the family provision proceedings until the rectification claim has been heard because the entitlement of the claimant under the will is a crucial piece of information which the judge hearing the family provision claim will need to know.

10.6.2 Solicitors' negligence claim

It was accepted in *Grattan* v. *McNaughton* [2001] WTLR 1305 and *Walker* v. *Geo. Medlicott & Son* [1999] 1 All ER 685 that before a disappointed beneficiary sues a solicitor for negligence for the way in which a will is drafted, the possibility of a rectification claim should be exhausted first. However, if there is a claim against a solicitor which can be brought without a rectification claim being brought, care needs to be taken to consider whether a claim under the Act is also apposite. In such a case problems can arise in respect of timing. There is, in general terms, a six-year limitation period in respect of claims against negligent solicitors although whether that is six years from the date of the will or the date of death is something of a moot point. However, the point is that proceedings under the Act have to be brought within the six-month time limit or there is a risk that the court will not extend time. Therefore, any claim should be brought and stayed pending the outcome of the negligence claim on the basis that any damages derived from that will have an impact on the merits of the claim under the Act and may render it unnecessary.

10.6.3   Proprietary estoppel

There may be a claim against the estate based on proprietary estoppel and a claim under the Act which was the case in *Ottey v Grundy* [2003] WTLR 1253 where the claim in proprietary estoppel succeeded. The principles of proprietary estoppel were set out in *Gillett* v. *Holt* [2001] Ch 210 and essentially require encouragement or representations by someone, detrimental reliance by the other party which leads the court to conclude that it would be unconscionable for the first party to rely on strict legal rights. Once these factors have been established, it is a question of looking at the extent of the equity which has been established, and then satisfying that equity (see *Jennings* v. *Rice* [2003] 1 P&CR 8). Again, any claim against the estate based on the principles of proprietary estoppel needs to be dealt with by the court before it can consider the claim under the Act. In *Ottey* v. *Grundy* the two claims were heard together and that is certainly one way of proceeding. The other way is to have the claim under the Act stayed to await the outcome of the proprietary estoppel claim.

10.6.4   Mutual wills

In order to succeed in a claim that mutual wills were executed, it must be established by clear evidence that there was a contract enforceable in law between the two parties making the wills and that the survivor would not revoke them under any circumstances. If the survivor does then revoke the will, the beneficiaries can claim that the estate is held on constructive trust for them on the terms of the first will (see *Re Cleaver (Deceased)* [1981] 1 WLR 939 and *Goodchild* v. *Goodchild* [1997] 1 WLR 1216). There is no time limit for making such a claim and so it can be seen that there could well be a case where a party has a claim under the Act but only if their mutual wills claim fails, or which would be affected by the outcome of their mutual wills claim. Again, proceedings under the Act should be issued within the six-month time limit and then be stayed pending the outcome of the mutual wills claim. It is important not to fight out the claim under the Act first as that could involve the implicit acceptance that the terms of the last will of the deceased (and not the mutual wills) govern the disposition of the estate.

10.6.5   Contentious probate claim

If there is a challenge to the very validity of the will, that can pose problems for an applicant under the Act. Until there is a grant (and grants such as those pending the outcome of the action which are limited and do not permit distribution are left out of account for these purposes (see *Re Johnson (Deceased)* [1987] CLY 3882, no application can be brought under the Act (see *Re McBroom (Deceased)* [1992] 2 FLR 49 and **Chapter 8** above).

Therefore, any claim will have to await the result of the contentious probate proceedings.

10.6.6   Forfeiture Act 1982

The impact of the rule of public policy known as the forfeiture rule is such that a person who unlawfully kills another cannot benefit from that person's estate. It seems clear that the rule applies in all cases where there is a conviction for manslaughter and has been held to apply to a case of aiding and abetting a suicide (see *Dunbar* v. *Plant* [1997] 4 All ER 289). Under the Forfeiture Act 1982, s.2(1) the court has power to modify the effect of the rule in cases apart from murder. However, there is a strict time limit imposed by s.2(3) that an application must be made within three months of the date of the conviction. Until the enactment of the 1982 Act, it was considered that public policy prevented a person who had unlawfully killed another from applying under the 1975 Act (see *Re Royse (Deceased)* [1985] Ch 22). However, s.3(1) of the 1982 Act provides that: 'The forfeiture rule shall not be taken to preclude any person from making any application under . . . any provision of the Inheritance (Provision for Family and Dependants) Act 1975.' In *Re Royse (Deceased)* the Court of Appeal indicated (albeit that it was not part of its decision) that a person who, in fact, benefited under the will or intestacy of the deceased but lost those benefits because of the forfeiture rule could not apply because they could not get over the hurdle of establishing that the will or intestacy did not make reasonable financial provision for them. In the recent case of *Land* v. *Land* [2006] WTLR 1447 a decision of HHJ Norris QC sitting as a deputy of the Chancery Division in Birmingham, the court refused to follow the *dicta* of the Court of Appeal and held that full effect had to be given to the Forfeiture Act 1982, s.3 in accordance with the Human Rights Act 1998. He also held that it could not be right that s.3 would allow those who did not benefit under the will or intestacy to apply if they unlawfully killed the deceased when it prevented those who did benefit. It therefore seems that someone who loses their right to benefit from the estate of the deceased because of the forfeiture rule and who fails to make an application under the Forfeiture Act 1982 in time or successfully, will still be able to apply under the 1975 Act.

APPENDICES

A. Statutory Extracts

Administration of Estates Act 1925, Part IV, ss.45–52

PART IV DISTRIBUTION OF RESIDUARY ESTATE

45 Abolition of descent to heir, curtesy, dower and escheat

(1) With regard to the real estate and personal inheritance of every person dying after the commencement of this Act, there shall be abolished –

    (a) All existing modes rules and canons of descent, and of devolution by special occupancy or otherwise, of real estate, or of a personal inheritance, whether operating by the general law or by the custom of gavelkind or borough english or by any other custom of any county, locality, or manor, or otherwise howsoever; and

    (b) Tenancy by the curtesy and every other estate and interest of a husband in real estate as to which his wife dies intestate, whether arising under the general law or by custom or otherwise; and

    (c) Dower and freebench and every other estate and interest of a wife in real estate as to which her husband dies intestate, whether arising under the general law or by custom or otherwise: Provided that where a right (if any) to freebench or other like right has attached before the commencement of this Act which cannot be barred by a testamentary or other disposition made by the husband, such right shall, unless released, remain in force as an equitable interest; and

    (d) Escheat to the Crown or the Duchy of Lancaster or the Duke of Cornwall or to a mesne lord for want of heirs.

(2) Nothing in this section affects the descent or devolution of an entailed interest.

46 Succession to real and personal estate on intestacy

(1) The residuary estate of an intestate shall be distributed in the manner or be held on the trusts mentioned in this section, namely:

    (i) If the intestate leaves a spouse or civil partner, then in accordance with the following Table:

TABLE

If the intestate –

(1)	leaves –
	   (a) no issue, and
	   (b) no parent, or brother or sister of the whole blood, or issue of a brother or sister of the whole blood
		the residuary estate shall be held in trust for the surviving spouse or civil partner absolutely.

(2)	leaves issue (whether or not persons mentioned in sub-paragraph (b) above also survive)	the surviving spouse or civil partner shall take the personal chattels absolutely and, in addition, the residuary estate of the intestate (other than the personal chattels) shall stand charged with the payment of a fixed net sum, free of death duties and costs, to the surviving spouse or civil partner with interest thereon from the date of the death . . . at such rate as the Lord Chancellor may specify by order until paid or appropriated, and, subject to providing for that sum and the interest thereon, the residuary estate (other than the personal chattels) shall be held –
		
		   (a) as to one half upon trust for the surviving spouse or civil partner during his or her life, and, subject to such life interest, on the statutory trusts for the issue of the intestate, and
		   (b) as to the other half, on the statutory trusts for the issue of the intestate.

(3)	leaves one or more of the following, that is to say, a parent, a brother or sister of the whole blood, or issue of a brother or sister of the whole blood, but leaves no issue	the surviving spouse or civil partner shall take the personal chattels absolutely and, in addition, the residuary estate of the intestate (other than the personal chattels) shall stand charged with the payment of a fixed net sum, free of death duties and costs, to the surviving spouse or civil partner with interest thereon from the date of the death . . . at such rate as the Lord Chancellor may specify by order until paid or appropriated, and, subject to providing for that sum and the interest thereon, the residuary estate (other than the personal chattels) shall be held –
		
		   (a) as to one half in trust for the surviving spouse or civil partner absolutely, and
		   (b) as to the other half –

(i) where the intestate leaves one parent or both parents (whether or not brothers or sisters of the intestate or their issue also survive) in trust for the parent absolutely or, as the case may be, for the two parents in equal shares absolutely

(ii) where the intestate leaves no parent, on the statutory trusts for the brothers and sisters of the whole blood of the intestate.

The fixed net sums referred to in paragraphs (2) and (3) of this Table shall be of the amounts provided by or under section 1 of the Family Provision Act 1966

(ii) If the intestate leaves issue but no spouse or civil partner, the residuary estate of the intestate shall be held on the statutory trusts for the issue of the intestate;

(iii) If the intestate leaves no spouse or civil partner and no issue but both parents, then ... the residuary estate of the intestate shall be held in trust for the father and mother in equal shares absolutely;

(iv) If the intestate leaves no spouse or civil partner and no issue but one parent, then ... the residuary estate of the intestate shall be held in trust for the surviving father or mother absolutely;

(v) If the intestate leaves no spouse or civil partner and no issue and no parent, then ... the residuary estate of the intestate shall be held in trust for the following persons living at the death of the intestate, and in the following order and manner, namely:

First, on the statutory trusts for the brothers and sisters of the whole blood of the intestate; but if no person takes an absolutely vested interest under such trusts; then

Secondly, on the statutory trusts for the brothers and sisters of the half blood of the intestate; but if no person takes an absolutely vested interest under such trusts; then

Thirdly, for the grandparents of the intestate and, if more than one survive the intestate, in equal shares; but if there is no member of this class; then

Fourthly, on the statutory trusts for the uncles and aunts of the intestate (being brothers or sisters of the whole blood of a parent of the intestate); but if no person takes an absolutely vested interest under such trusts; then

Fifthly, on the statutory trusts for the uncles and aunts of the intestate (being brothers or sisters of the half blood of a parent of the intestate)
...

(vi) In default of any person taking an absolute interest under the foregoing provisions, the residuary estate of the intestate shall belong to the Crown or to the Duchy of Lancaster or to the Duke of Cornwall for the time being, as the case may be, as bona vacantia, and in lieu of any right to escheat.

The Crown or the said Duchy or the said Duke may (without preju dice to the powers reserved by section nine of the Civil List Act 1910, or any other powers), out of the whole or any part of the property devolving on them respectively, provide, in accordance with the existing practice, for dependents, whether kindred or not, of the intestate, and other persons for whom the intestate might reasonably have been expected to make provision.

(1A) The power to make orders under subsection (1) above shall be exercisable by statutory instrument subject to annulment in pursuance of a resolution of either House of Parliament; and any such order may be varied or revoked by a subsequent order made under the power.

(2) A husband and wife shall for all purposes of distribution or division under the foregoing provisions of this section be treated as two persons.

(2A) Where the intestate's spouse or civil partner survived the intestate but died before the end of the period of 28 days beginning with the day on which the intestate died, this section shall have effect as respects the intestate as if the spouse or civil partner had not survived the intestate.

(3) Where the intestate and the intestate's spouse or civil partner have died in circumstances rendering it uncertain which of them survived the other and the intestate's spouse or civil partner is by virtue of section one hundred and eighty-four of the Law of Property Act 1925, deemed to have survived the intestate, this section shall, nevertheless, have effect as respects the intestate as if the spouse or civil partner had not survived the intestate.

(4) The interest payable on the fixed net sum payable to a surviving spouse or civil partner shall be primarily payable out of income.

47 Statutory trusts in favour of issue and other classes of relatives of intestate

(1) Where under this Part of this Act the residuary estate of an intestate, or any part thereof, is directed to be held on the statutory trusts for the issue of the intestate, the same shall be held upon the following trusts, namely:

(i) In trust, in equal shares if more than one, for all or any the children or child of the intestate, living at the death of the intestate, who attain the age of eighteen years or marry under that age or form a civil partnership under that age, and for all or any of the issue living at the death of the intestate who attain the age of eighteen years or marry, or form a civil partnership, under that age of any child of the intestate who predeceases the intestate, such issue to take through all degrees, according to their stocks, in equal shares if more than one, the share which their parent would have taken if living at the death of the intestate, and so that no issue shall take whose parent is living at the death of the intestate and so capable of taking;

(ii) The statutory power of advancement, and the statutory provisions which relate to maintenance and accumulation of surplus income, shall apply, but when an infant marries, or forms a civil partnership, such infant shall be entitled to give valid receipts for the income of the infant's share or interest;

(iii) . . .

(iv) The personal representatives may permit any infant contingently interested to have the use and enjoyment of any personal chattels in such manner and subject to such conditions (if any) as the personal representatives may consider reasonable, and without being liable to account for any consequential loss.

(2) If the trusts in favour of the issue of the intestate fail by reason of no child or other issue attaining an absolutely vested interest –

(a) the residuary estate of the intestate and the income thereof and all statutory accumulations, if any, of the income thereof, or so much thereof as may not have been paid or applied under any power affecting the same, shall go, devolve and be held under the provisions of this Part of this Act as if the intestate had died without leaving issue living at the death of the intestate;

(b) references in this Part of this Act to the intestate 'leaving no issue' shall be construed as 'leaving no issue who attain an absolutely vested interest';

(c) references in this Part of this Act to the intestate 'leaving issue' or 'leaving a child or other issue' shall be construed as 'leaving issue who attain an absolutely vested interest.'

(3) Where under this Part of this Act the residuary estate of an intestate or any part thereof is directed to be held on the statutory trusts for any class of relatives of the intestate, other than issue of the intestate, the same shall be held on trusts corresponding to the statutory trusts for the issue of the intestate (other than the provision for bringing any money or property into account) as if such trusts (other than as aforesaid) were repeated with the substitution of references to the members or member of that class for references to the children or child of the intestate.

(4) References in paragraph (i) of subsection (1) of the last foregoing section to the intestate leaving, or not leaving, a member of the class consisting of brothers or sisters of the whole blood of the intestate and issue of brothers or sisters of the whole blood of the intestate shall be construed as references to the intestate leaving, or not leaving, a member of that class who attains an absolutely vested interest.

(5) . . .

47A Right of surviving spouse to have his own life interest redeemed

(1) Where a surviving spouse or civil partner is entitled to the interest in part of the residuary estate, and so elects, the personal representative shall purchase or redeem the life interest by paying the capital value thereof to the tenant for life, or the persons deriving title under the tenant for life, and the costs of the transaction; and thereupon the residuary estate of the intestate may be dealt with and distributed free from the life interest.

(2) . . .

(3) An election under this section shall only be exercisable if at the time of the election the whole of the said part of the residuary estate consists of property in possession, but, for the purposes of this section, a life interest in property partly in possession and partly not in possession shall be treated as consisting of two separate life interests in those respective parts of the property.

(3A) The capital value shall be reckoned in such manner as the Lord Chancellor may by order direct, and an order under this subsection may include transitional provisions.

(3B) The power to make orders under subsection (3A) above shall be exercisable by statutory instrument subject to annulment in pursuance of a resolution of either House of Parliament; and any such order may be varied or revoked by a subsequent order made under the power.

(4) . . .

(5) An election under this section shall be exercisable only within the period of twelve months from the date on which representation with respect to the estate of the intestate is first taken out:

Provided that if the surviving spouse or civil partner satisfies the court that the limitation to the said period of twelve months will operate unfairly –

   (a) in consequence of the representation first taken out being probate of a will subsequently revoked on the ground that the will was invalid, or

   (b) in consequence of a question whether a person had an interest in the estate, or as to the nature of an interest in the estate, not having been determined at the time when representation was first taken out, or

   (c) in consequence of some other circumstances affecting the administration or distribution of the estate,

the court may extend the said period.

(6) An election under this section shall be exercisable, except where the tenant for life is the sole personal representative, by notifying the personal representative (or, where there are two or more personal representatives of whom one is the tenant for life, all of them except the tenant for life) in writing; and a notification in writing under this subsection shall not be revocable except with the consent of the personal representative.

(7) Where the tenant for life is the sole personal representative an election under this section shall not be effective unless written notice thereof is given to the Senior Registrar of the Family Division of the High Court within the period within which it must be made; and provision may be made by probate rules for keeping a record of such notices and making that record available to the public.

In this subsection the expression 'probate rules' means rules of court made under section 127 of the Supreme Court Act 1981.

(8) An election under this section by a tenant for life who is an infant shall be as valid and binding as it would be if the tenant for life were of age; but the personal representative shall, instead of paying the capital value of the life interest to the tenant for life, deal with it in the same manner as with any other part of the residuary estate to which the tenant for life is absolutely entitled.

(9) In considering for the purposes of the foregoing provisions of this section the question when representation was first taken out, a grant limited to settled land or to trust property shall be left out of account and a grant limited to real estate or to personal estate shall be left out of account unless a grant limited to the remainder of the estate has previously been made or is made at the same time.

48   Powers of personal representative in respect of interests of surviving spouse

(1) ...

(2) The personal representatives may raise –

   (a) the fixed net sum or any part thereof and the interest thereon payable to the surviving spouse or civil partner of the intestate on the security of the whole or any part of the residuary estate of the intestate (other than the personal chattels), so far as that estate may be sufficient for the purpose of the said sum and interest may not have been satisfied by an appropriation under the statutory power available in that behalf; and

   (b) in like manner the capital sum, if any, required for the purchase or redemption of the life interest of the surviving spouse or civil partner of the intestate, or any part thereof not satisfied by the application for that purpose of any part of the residuary estate of the intestate;

and in either case the amount, if any, properly required for the payment of the costs of the transaction.

49   Application to cases of partial intestacy

(1)   Where any person dies leaving a will effectively disposing of part of his property, this Part of this Act shall have effect as respects the part of his property not so disposed of subject to the provisions contained in the will and subject to the following modifications:

   (a)   . . .
   (b)   The personal representative shall, subject to his rights and powers for the purposes of administration, be a trustee for the persons entitled under this Part of this Act in respect of the part of the estate not expressly disposed of unless it appears by the will that the personal representative is intended to take such part beneficially.

(2), (3)   . . .

(4)   The references in subsection (3) of section forty-seven A of this Act to property are references to property comprised in the residuary estate and, accordingly, where a will of the deceased creates a life interest in property in possession, and the remaining interest in that property forms part of the residuary estate, the said references are references to that remaining interest (which, until the life interest determines, is property not in possession).

50   Construction of documents

(1)   References to any Statutes of Distribution in an instrument inter vivos made or in a will coming into operation after the commencement of this Act, shall be construed as references to this Part of this Act; and references in such an instrument or will to statutory next of kin shall be construed, unless the context otherwise requires, as referring to the persons who would take beneficially on an intestacy under the foregoing provisions of this Part of this Act.

(2)   Trusts declared in an instrument inter vivos made, or in a will coming into operation, before the commencement of this Act by reference to the Statutes of Distribution, shall, unless the contrary thereby appears, be construed as referring to the enactments (other than the Intestates' Estates Act 1890) relating to the distribution of effects of intestates which were in force immediately before the commencement of this Act.

(3)   In subsection (1) of this section the reference to this Part of this Act, or the foregoing provisions of this Part of this Act, shall in relation to an instrument inter vivos made, or a will or codicil coming into operation, after the coming into force of section 18 of the Family Law Reform Act 1987 (but not in relation to instruments inter vivos made or wills or codicils coming into operation earlier) be construed as including references to that section.

51   Savings

(1)   Nothing in this Part of this Act affects the right of any person to take beneficially, by purchase, as heir either general or special.

(2)   The foregoing provisions of this Part of this Act do not apply to any beneficial interest in real estate (not including chattels real) to which a person of unsound mind or defective living and of full age at the commencement of this Act, and unable, by reason of his incapacity, to make a will, who thereafter dies intestate in respect of such interest without having recovered his testamentary capacity, was entitled at his death, and any such beneficial interest (not being an interest ceasing on his death) shall, without prejudice to any will of the deceased, devolve

in accordance with the general law in force before the commencement of this Act applicable to freehold land, and that law shall, notwithstanding any repeal, apply to the case.

For the purposes of this subsection, a person of unsound mind or defective who dies intestate as respects any beneficial interest in real estate shall not be deemed to have recovered his testamentary capacity unless his . . . receiver has been discharged.

(3) Where an infant dies after the commencement of this Act without having been married or having formed a civil partnership, and without issue, and independently of this subsection he would, at his death, have been equitably entitled under a trust or settlement (including a will) to a vested estate in fee simple or absolute interest in freehold land, or in any property . . . to devolve therewith or as freehold land, such infant shall be deemed to have had a life interest, and the trust or settlement shall be construed accordingly.

(4) . . .

52   Interpretation of Part IV

In this Part of this Act 'real and personal estate' means every beneficial interest (including rights of entry and reverter) of the intestate in real and personal estate which (otherwise than in right of a power of appointment or of the testamentary power conferred by statute to dispose of entailed interests) he could, if of full age and capacity, have disposed of by his will and references (however expressed) to any relationship between two persons shall be construed in accordance with section 1 of the Family Law Reform Act 1987.

Matrimonial Causes Act 1973, ss.11, 12, 21–25E, 31, 36 and 37

Nullity

11 Grounds on which a marriage is void

A marriage celebrated after 31st July 1971 shall be void on the following grounds only, that is to say –

    (a)   that it is not a valid marriage under the provisions of the Marriage Acts 1949 to 1986 (that is to say where –

        (i)   the parties are within the prohibited degrees of relationship;
        (ii)   either party is under the age of sixteen; or
        (iii)   the parties have intermarried in disregard of certain requirements as to the formation of marriage);

    (b)   that at the time of the marriage either party was already lawfully married or a civil partner;
    (c)   that the parties are not respectively male and female;
    (d)   in the case of a polygamous marriage entered into outside England and Wales, that either party was at the time of the marriage domiciled in England and Wales.

For the purposes of paragraph (d) of this subsection a marriage is not polygamous if at its inception neither party has any spouse additional to the other.

12 Grounds on which a marriage is voidable

A marriage celebrated after 31st July 1971 shall be voidable on the following grounds only, that is to say –

    (a)   that the marriage has not been consummated owing to the incapacity of either party to consummate it;
    (b)   that the marriage has not been consummated owing to the wilful refusal of the respondent to consummate it;
    (c)   that either party to the marriage did not validly consent to it, whether in consequence of duress, mistake, unsoundness of mind or otherwise;
    (d)   that at the time of the marriage either party, though capable of giving a valid consent, was suffering (whether continuously or intermittently) from mental disorder within the meaning of the Mental Health Act 1983 of such a kind or to such an extent as to be unfitted for marriage;
    (e)   that at the time of the marriage the respondent was suffering from venereal disease in a communicable form;

(f) that at the time of the marriage the respondent was pregnant by some person other than the petitioner;

(g) that an interim gender recognition certificate under the Gender Recognition Act 2004 has, after the time of the marriage, been issued to either party to the marriage;

(h) that the respondent is a person whose gender at the time of the marriage had become the acquired gender under the Gender Recognition Act 2004.

PART II FINANCIAL RELIEF FOR PARTIES TO MARRIAGE AND CHILDREN OF FAMILY

Financial provision and property adjustment orders

21 Financial provision and property adjustment orders

(1) The financial provision orders for the purposes of this Act are the orders for periodical or lump sum provision available (subject to the provisions of this Act) under section 23 below for the purpose of adjusting the financial position of the parties to a marriage and any children of the family in connection with proceedings for divorce, nullity of marriage or judicial separation and under section 27(6) below on proof of neglect by one party to a marriage to provide, or to make a proper contribution towards, reasonable maintenance for the other or a child of the family, that is to say –

(a) any order for periodical payments in favour of a party to a marriage under section 23(1)(a) or 27(6)(a) or in favour of a child of the family under section 23(1)(d), (2) or (4) or 27(6)(d);

(b) any order for secured periodical payments in favour of a party to a marriage under section 23(1)(b) or 27(6)(b) or in favour of a child of the family under section 23(1)(e), (2) or (4) or 27(6)(e); and

(c) any order for lump sum provision in favour of a party to a marriage under section 23(1)(c) or 27(6)(c) or in favour of a child of the family under section 23(1)(f), (2) or (4) or 27(6)(f);

and references in this Act (except in paragraphs 17(1) and 23 of Schedule 1 below) to periodical payments orders, secured periodical payments orders, and orders for the payment of a lump sum are references to all or some of the financial provision orders requiring the sort of financial provision in question according as the context of each reference may require.

(2) The property adjustment orders for the purposes of this Act are the orders dealing with property rights available (subject to the provisions of this Act) under section 24 below for the purpose of adjusting the financial position of the parties to a marriage and any children of the family on or after the grant of a decree of divorce, nullity of marriage or judicial separation, that is to say –

(a) any order under subsection (1)(a) of that section for a transfer of property;

(b) any order under subsection (1)(b) of that section for a settlement of property; and

(c) any order under subsection (1)(c) or (d) of that section for a variation of settlement.

21A Pension sharing orders

(1) For the purposes of this Act, a pension sharing order is an order which –

(a) provides that one party's –

    (i)   shareable rights under a specified pension arrangement, or

    (ii)   shareable state scheme rights,

be subject to pension sharing for the benefit of the other party, and

(b) specifies the percentage value to be transferred.

(2) In subsection (1) above –

    (a) the reference to shareable rights under a pension arrangement is to rights in relation to which pension sharing is available under Chapter I of Part IV of the Welfare Reform and Pensions Act 1999, or under corresponding Northern Ireland legislation,

    (b) the reference to shareable state scheme rights is to rights in relation to which pension sharing is available under Chapter II of Part IV of the Welfare Reform and Pensions Act 1999, or under corresponding Northern Ireland legislation, and

    (c) 'party' means a party to a marriage.

Ancillary relief in connection with divorce proceedings, etc.

22   Maintenance pending suit

On a petition for divorce, nullity of marriage or judicial separation, the court may make an order for maintenance pending suit, that is to say, an order requiring either party to the marriage to make to the other such periodical payments for his or her maintenance and for such term, being a term beginning not earlier than the date of the presentation of the petition and ending with the date of the determination of the suit, as the court thinks reasonable.

23   Financial provision orders in connection with divorce proceedings, etc.

(1) On granting a decree of divorce, a decree of nullity of marriage or a decree of judicial separation or at any time thereafter (whether, in the case of a decree of divorce or of nullity of marriage, before or after the decree is made absolute), the court may make any one or more of the following orders, that is to say –

    (a) an order that either party to the marriage shall make to the other such periodical payments, for such term, as may be specified in the order;

    (b) an order that either party to the marriage shall secure to the other to the satisfaction of the court such periodical payments, for such term, as may be so specified;

    (c) an order that either party to the marriage shall pay to the other such lump sum or sums as may be so specified;

    (d) an order that a party to the marriage shall make to such person as may be specified in the order for the benefit of a child of the family, or to such a child, such periodical payments, for such term, as may be so specified;

    (e) an order that a party to the marriage shall secure to such person as may be so specified for the benefit of such a child, or to such a child, to the satisfaction of the court, such periodical payments, for such term, as may be so specified;

    (f) an order that a party to the marriage shall pay to such person as may be so specified for the benefit of such a child, or to such a child, such lump sum as may be so specified;

subject, however, in the case of an order under paragraph (d), (e) or (f) above, to the restrictions imposed by section 29(1) and (3) below on the making of financial provision orders in favour of children who have attained the age of eighteen.

(2)   The court may also, subject to those restrictions, make any one or more of the orders mentioned in subsection (1)(d), (e) and (f) above –

(a)   in any proceedings for divorce, nullity of marriage or judicial separation, before granting a decree; and

(b)   where any such proceedings are dismissed after the beginning of the trial, either forthwith or within a reasonable period after the dismissal.

(3)   Without prejudice to the generality of subsection (1)(c) or (f) above –

(a)   an order under this section that a party to a marriage shall pay a lump sum to the other party may be made for the purpose of enabling that other party to meet any liabilities or expenses reasonably incurred by him or her in maintaining himself or herself or any child of the family before making an application for an order under this section in his or her favour;

(b)   an order under this section for the payment of a lump sum to or for the benefit of a child of the family may be made for the purpose of enabling any liabilities or expenses reasonably incurred by or for the benefit of that child before the making of an application for an order under this section in his favour to be met; and

(c)   an order under this section for the payment of a lump sum may provide for the payment of that sum by instalments of such amount as may be specified in the order and may require the payment of the instalments to be secured to the satisfaction of the court.

(4)   The power of the court under subsection (1) or (2)(a) above to make an order in favour of a child of the family shall be exercisable from time to time; and where the court makes an order in favour of a child under subsection (2)(b) above, it may from time to time, subject to the restrictions mentioned in subsection (1) above, make a further order in his favour of any of the kinds mentioned in subsection (1)(d), (e) or (f) above.

(5)   Without prejudice to the power to give a direction under section 30 below for the settlement of an instrument by conveyancing counsel, where an order is made under subsection (1)(a), (b) or (c) above on or after granting a decree of divorce or nullity of marriage, neither the order nor any settlement made in pursuance of the order shall take effect unless the decree has been made absolute.

(6)   Where the court –

(a)   makes an order under this section for the payment of a lump of sum; and

(b)   directs –

(i)   that payment of that sum or any part of it shall be deferred; or

(ii)   that that sum or any part of it shall be paid by instalments,

the court may order that the amount deferred or the instalments shall carry interest at such rate as may be specified by the order from such date, not earlier than the date of the order, as may be so specified, until the date when payment of it is due.

24 Property adjustment orders in connection with divorce proceedings, etc.

(1) On granting a decree of divorce, a decree of nullity of marriage or a decree of judicial separation or at any time thereafter (whether, in the case of a decree of divorce or of nullity of marriage, before or after the decree is made absolute), the court may make any one or more of the following orders, that is to say –

    (a) an order that a party to the marriage shall transfer to the other party, to any child of the family or to such person as may be specified in the order for the benefit of such a child such property as may be so specified, being property to which the first-mentioned party is entitled, either in possession or reversion;

    (b) an order that a settlement of such property as may be so specified, being property to which a party to the marriage is so entitled, be made to the satisfaction of the court for the benefit of the other party to the marriage and of the children of the family or either or any of them;

    (c) an order varying for the benefit of the parties to the marriage and of the children of the family or either or any of them any ante-nuptial or post-nuptial settlement (including such a settlement made by will or codicil) made on the parties to the marriage, other than one in the form of a pension arrangement (within the meaning of section 25D below);

    (d) an order extinguishing or reducing the interest of either of the parties to the marriage under any such settlement, other than one in the form of a pension arrangement (within the meaning of section 25D below);

subject, however, in the case of an order under paragraph (a) above, to the restrictions imposed by section 29(1) and (3) below on the making of orders for a transfer of property in favour of children who have attained the age of eighteen.

(2) The court may make an order under subsection (1)(c) above notwithstanding that there are no children of the family.

(3) Without prejudice to the power to give a direction under section 30 below for the settlement of an instrument by conveyancing counsel, where an order is made under this section on or after granting a decree of divorce or nullity of marriage, neither the order nor any settlement made in pursuance of the order shall take effect unless the decree has been made absolute.

24A Orders for sale of property

(1) Where the court makes under section 23 or 24 of this Act a secured periodical payments order, an order for the payment of a lump sum or a property adjustment order, then, on making that order or at any time thereafter, the court may make a further order for the sale of such property as may be specified in the order, being property in which or in the proceeds of sale of which either or both of the parties to the marriage has or have a beneficial interest, either in possession or reversion.

(2) Any order made under subsection (1) above may contain such consequential or supplementary provisions as the court thinks fit and, without prejudice to the generality of the foregoing provision, may include –

    (a) provision requiring the making of a payment out of the proceeds of sale of the property to which the order relates, and

    (b) provision requiring any such property to be offered for sale to a person, or class of persons, specified in the order.

(3)   Where an order is made under subsection (1) above on or after the grant of a decree of divorce or nullity of marriage, the order shall not take effect unless the decree has been made absolute.

(4)   Where an order is made under subsection (1) above, the court may direct that the order, or such provision thereof as the court may specify, shall not take effect until the occurrence of an event specified by the court or the expiration of a period so specified.

(5)   Where an order under subsection (1) above contains a provision requiring the proceeds of sale of the property to which the order relates to be used to secure periodical payments to a party to the marriage, the order shall cease to have effect on the death or re-marriage of, or formation of a civil partnership by, that person.

(6)   Where a party to a marriage has a beneficial interest in any property, or in the proceeds of sale thereof, and some other person who is not a party to the marriage also has a beneficial interest in that property or in the proceeds of sale thereof, then, before deciding whether to make an order under this section in relation to that property, it shall be the duty of the court to give that other person an opportunity to make representations with respect to the order; and any representations made by that other person shall be included among the circumstances to which the court is required to have regard under section 25(1) below.

24B Pension sharing orders in connection with divorce proceedings, etc.

(1)   On granting a decree of divorce or a decree of nullity of marriage or at any time thereafter (whether before or after the decree is made absolute), the court may, on an application made under this section, make one or more pension sharing orders in relation to the marriage.

(2)   A pension sharing order under this section is not to take effect unless the decree on or after which it is made has been made absolute.

(3)   A pension sharing order under this section may not be made in relation to a pension arrangement which –

(a)   is the subject of a pension sharing order in relation to the marriage, or
(b)   has been the subject of pension sharing between the parties to the marriage.

(4)   A pension sharing order under this section may not be made in relation to share-able state scheme rights if –

(a)   such rights are the subject of a pension sharing order in relation to the marriage, or
(b)   such rights have been the subject of pension sharing between the parties to the marriage.

(5)   A pension sharing order under this section may not be made in relation to the rights of a person under a pension arrangement if there is in force a requirement imposed by virtue of section 25B or 25C below which relates to benefits or future benefits to which he is entitled under the pension arrangement.

24C Pension sharing orders: duty to stay

(1)   No pension sharing order may be made so as to take effect before the end of such period after the making of the order as may be prescribed by regulations made by the Lord Chancellor.

(2)   The power to make regulations under this section shall be exercisable by statutory instrument which shall be subject to annulment in pursuance of a resolution of either House of Parliament.

24D   Pension sharing orders: apportionment of charges

If a pension sharing order relates to rights under a pension arrangement, the court may include in the order provision about the apportionment between the parties of any charge under section 41 of the Welfare Reform and Pensions Act 1999 (charges in respect of pension sharing costs), or under corresponding Northern Ireland legislation.

25   Matters to which court is to have regard in deciding how to exercise its powers under ss 23, 24 and 24A

(1)   It shall be the duty of the court in deciding whether to exercise its powers under section 23, 24, 24A or 24B above and, if so, in what manner, to have regard to all the circumstances of the case, first consideration being given to the welfare while a minor of any child of the family who has not attained the age of eighteen.

(2)   As regards the exercise of the powers of the court under section 23(1)(a), (b) or (c), 24, 24A or 24B above in relation to a party to the marriage, the court shall in particular have regard to the following matters –

   (a)   the income, earning capacity, property and other financial resources which each of the parties to the marriage has or is likely to have in the foreseeable future, including in the case of earning capacity any increase in that capacity which it would in the opinion of the court be reasonable to expect a party to the marriage to take steps to acquire;
   (b)   the financial needs, obligations and responsibilities which each of the parties to the marriage has or is likely to have in the foreseeable future;
   (c)   the standard of living enjoyed by the family before the breakdown of the marriage;
   (d)   the age of each party to the marriage and the duration of the marriage;
   (e)   any physical or mental disability of either of the parties to the marriage;
   (f)   the contributions which each of the parties has made or is likely in the foreseeable future to make to the welfare of the family, including any contribution by looking after the home or caring for the family;
   (g)   the conduct of each of the parties, if that conduct is such that it would in the opinion of the court be inequitable to disregard it;
   (h)   in the case of proceedings for divorce or nullity of marriage, the value to each of the parties to the marriage of any benefit which, by reason of the dissolution or annulment of the marriage, that party will lose the chance of acquiring.

(3)   As regards the exercise of the powers of the court under section 23(1)(d), (e) or (f), (2) or (4), 24 or 24A above in relation to a child of the family, the court shall in particular have regard to the following matters –

   (a)   the financial needs of the child;
   (b)   the income, earning capacity (if any), property and other financial resources of the child;
   (c)   any physical or mental disability of the child;

(d) the manner in which he was being and in which the parties to the marriage expected him to be educated or trained;

(e) the considerations mentioned in relation to the parties to the marriage in paragraphs (a), (b), (c) and (e) of subsection (2) above.

(4) As regards the exercise of the powers of the court under section 23(1)(d), (e) or (f), (2) or (4), 24 or 24A above against a party to a marriage in favour of a child of the family who is not the child of that party, the court shall also have regard –

(a) to whether that party assumed any responsibility for the child's mainte-nance, and, if so, to the extent to which, and the basis upon which, that party assumed such responsibility and to the length of time for which that party discharged such responsibility;

(b) to whether in assuming and discharging such responsibility that party did so knowing that the child was not his or her own;

(c) to the liability of any other person to maintain the child.

25A Exercise of court's powers in favour of party to marriage on decree of divorce or nullity of marriage

(1) Where on or after the grant of a decree of divorce or nullity of marriage the court decides to exercise its powers under section 23(1)(a), (b) or (c), 24, 24A or 24B above in favour of a party to the marriage, it shall be the duty of the court to consider whether it would be appropriate so to exercise those powers that the financial obligations of each party towards the other will be terminated as soon after the grant of the decree as the court considers just and reasonable.

(2) Where the court decides in such a case to make a periodical payments or secured periodical payments order in favour of a party to the marriage, the court shall in particular consider whether it would be appropriate to require those payments to be made or secured only for such term as would in the opinion of the court be sufficient to enable the party in whose favour the order is made to adjust without undue hardship to the termination of his or her financial dependence on the other party.

(3) Where on or after the grant of a decree of divorce or nullity of marriage an application is made by a party to the marriage for a periodical payments or secured periodical payments order in his or her favour, then, if the court considers that no continuing obligation should be imposed on either party to make or secure periodical payments in favour of the other, the court may dismiss the application with a direction that the applicant shall not be entitled to make any future application in relation to that marriage for an order under section 23(1)(a) or (b) above.

25B Pensions

(1) The matters to which the court is to have regard under section 25(2) above include –

(a) in the case of paragraph (a), any benefits under a pension arrangement which a party to the marriage has or is likely to have, and

(b) in the case of paragraph (h), any benefits under a pension arrangement which, by reason of the dissolution or annulment of the marriage, a party to the marriage will lose the chance of acquiring, and, accordingly, in relation to benefits under a pension arrangement, section 25(2)(a) above shall have effect as if 'in the foreseeable future' were omitted.

(2) ...

(3) The following provisions apply where, having regard to any benefits under a pension arrangement, the court determines to make an order under section 23 above.

(4) To the extent to which the order is made having regard to any benefits under a pension arrangement, the order may require the person responsible for the pension arrangement in question, if at any time any payment in respect of any benefits under the arrangement becomes due to the party with pension rights, to make a payment for the benefit of the other party.

(5) The order must express the amount of any payment required to be made by virtue of subsection (4) above as a percentage of the payment which becomes due to the party with pension rights.

(6) Any such payment by the person responsible for the arrangement –

   (a) shall discharge so much of his liability to the party with pension rights as corresponds to the amount of the payment, and
   (b) shall be treated for all purposes as a payment made by the party with pension rights in or towards the discharge of his liability under the order.

(7) Where the party with pension rights has a right of commutation under the arrangement, the order may require him to exercise it to any extent; and this section applies to any payment due in consequence of commutation in pursuance of the order as it applies to other payments in respect of benefits under the arrangement.

(7A) The power conferred by subsection (7) above may not be exercised for the purpose of commuting a benefit payable to the party with pension rights to a benefit payable to the other party.

(7B) The power conferred by subsection (4) or (7) above may not be exercised in relation to a pension arrangement which –

   (a) is the subject of a pension sharing order in relation to the marriage, or
   (b) has been the subject of pension sharing between the parties to the marriage.

(7C) In subsection (1) above, references to benefits under a pension arrangement include any benefits by way of pension, whether under a pension arrangement or not.

25C Pensions: lump sums

(1) The power of the court under section 23 above to order a party to a marriage to pay a lump sum to the other party includes, where the benefits which the party with pension rights has or is likely to have under a pension arrangement include any lump sum payable in respect of his death, power to make any of the following provision by the order.

(2) The court may –

   (a) if the person responsible for the pension arrangement in question has power to determine the person to whom the sum, or any part of it, is to be paid, require him to pay the whole or part of that sum, when it becomes due, to the other party,

(b)   if the party with pension rights has power to nominate the person to whom the sum, or any part of it, is to be paid, require the party with pension rights to nominate the other party in respect of the whole or part of that sum,

(c)   in any other case, require the person responsible for the pension arrangement in question to pay the whole or part of that sum, when it becomes due, for the benefit of the other party instead of to the person to whom, apart from the order, it would be paid.

(3)   Any payment by the person responsible for the arrangement under an order made under section 23 above by virtue of this section shall discharge so much of his liability in respect of the party with pension rights as corresponds to the amount of the payment.

(4)   The powers conferred by this section may not be exercised in relation to a pension arrangement which –

(a)   is the subject of a pension sharing order in relation to the marriage, or

(b)   has been the subject of pension sharing between the parties to the marriage.

25D Pensions: supplementary

(1)   Where –

(a)   an order made under section 23 above by virtue of section 25B or 25C above imposes any requirement on the person responsible for a pension arrangement ('the first arrangement') and the party with pension rights acquires rights under another pension arrangement ('the new arrangement') which are derived (directly or indirectly) from the whole of his rights under the first arrangement, and

(b)   the person responsible for the new arrangement has been given notice in accordance with regulations made by the Lord Chancellor,

the order shall have effect as if it had been made instead in respect of the person responsible for the new arrangement.

(2)   The Lord Chancellor may by regulations –

(a)   in relation to any provision of sections 25B or 25C above which authorises the court making an order under section 23 above to require the person responsible for a pension arrangement to make a payment for the benefit of the other party, make provision as to the person to whom, and the terms on which, the payment is to be made,

(ab) make, in relation to payment under a mistaken belief as to the continuation in force of a provision included by virtue of section 25B or 25C above in an order under section 23 above, provision about the rights or liabilities of the payer, the payee or the person to whom the payment was due,

(b)   require notices to be given in respect of changes of circumstances relevant to such orders which include provision made by virtue of sections 25B and 25C above,

(ba) make provision for the person responsible for a pension arrangement to be discharged in prescribed circumstances from a requirement imposed by virtue of section 25B or 25C above,

(c)   . . .

(d)   . . .

(e)   make provision about calculation and verification in relation to the valuation of –

     (i)   benefits under a pension arrangement, or

     (ii)   shareable state scheme rights,

for the purposes of the court's functions in connection with the exercise of any of its powers under this Part of this Act.

(2A) Regulations under subsection (2)(e) above may include –

    (a)   provision for calculation or verification in accordance with guidance from time to time prepared by a prescribed person, and

    (b)   provision by reference to regulations under section 30 or 49(4) of the Welfare Reform and Pensions Act 1999.

(2B) Regulations under subsection (2) above may make different provision for different cases.

(2C) Power to make regulations under this section shall be exercisable by statutory instrument which shall be subject to annulment in pursuance of a resolution of either House of Parliament.

(3)   In this section and sections 25B and 25C above –

'occupational pension scheme' has the same meaning as in the Pension Schemes Act 1993;

'the party with pension rights' means the party to the marriage who has or is likely to have benefits under a pension arrangement and 'the other party' means the other party to the marriage;

'pension arrangement' means –

    (a)   an occupational pension scheme,

    (b)   a personal pension scheme,

    (c)   a retirement annuity contract,

    (d)   an annuity or insurance policy purchased, or transferred, for the purpose of giving effect to rights under an occupational pension scheme or a personal pension scheme, and

    (e)   an annuity purchased, or entered into, for the purpose of discharging liability in respect of a pension credit under section 29(1)(b) of the Welfare Reform and Pensions Act 1999 or under corresponding Northern Ireland legislation;

'personal pension scheme' has the same meaning as in the Pension Schemes Act 1993;

'prescribed' means prescribed by regulations;

'retirement annuity contract' means a contract or scheme approved under Chapter III of Part XIV of the Income and Corporation Taxes Act 1988;

'shareable state scheme rights' has the same meaning as in section 21A(1) above; and

'trustees or managers', in relation to an occupational pension scheme or a personal pension scheme, means –

    (a)   in the case of a scheme established under a trust, the trustees of the scheme, and

    (b)   in any other case, the managers of the scheme.

(4)   In this section and sections 25B and 25C above, references to the person responsible for a pension arrangement are –

(a) in the case of an occupational pension scheme or a personal pension scheme, to the trustees or managers of the scheme,

(b) in the case of a retirement annuity contract or an annuity falling within paragraph (d) or (e) of the definition of 'pension arrangement' above, the provider of the annuity, and

(c) in the case of an insurance policy falling within paragraph (d) of the definition of that expression, the insurer.

25E The Pension Protection Fund

(1) The matters to which the court is to have regard under section 25(2) include –

(a) in the case of paragraph (a), any PPF compensation to which a party to the marriage is or is likely to be entitled, and

(b) in the case of paragraph (h), any PPF compensation which, by reason of the dissolution or annulment of the marriage, a party to the marriage will lose the chance of acquiring entitlement to,

and, accordingly, in relation to PPF compensation, section 25(2)(a) shall have effect as if 'in the foreseeable future' were omitted.

(2) Subsection (3) applies in relation to an order under section 23 so far as it includes provision made by virtue of section 25B(4) which –

(a) imposed requirements on the trustees or managers of an occupational pension scheme for which the Board has assumed responsibility in accordance with Chapter 3 of Part 2 of the Pensions Act 2004 (pension protection) or any provision in force in Northern Ireland corresponding to that Chapter, and

(b) was made before the trustees or managers of the scheme received the transfer notice in relation to the scheme.

(3) The order is to have effect from the time when the trustees or managers of the scheme receive the transfer notice –

(a) as if, except in prescribed descriptions of case –

(i) references in the order to the trustees or managers of the scheme were references to the Board, and

(ii) references in the order to any pension or lump sum to which the party with pension rights is or may become entitled under the scheme were references to any PPF compensation to which that person is or may become entitled in respect of the pension or lump sum, and

(b) subject to such other modifications as may be prescribed.

(4) Subsection (5) applies to an order under section 23 if –

(a) it includes provision made by virtue of section 25B(7) which requires the party with pension rights to exercise his right of commutation under an occupational pension scheme to any extent, and

(b) before the requirement is complied with the Board has assumed responsibility for the scheme as mentioned in subsection (2)(a).

(5) From the time the trustees or managers of the scheme receive the transfer notice, the order is to have effect with such modifications as may be prescribed.

(6) Regulations may modify section 25C as it applies in relation to an occupational pension scheme at any time when there is an assessment period in relation to the scheme.

(7) Where the court makes a pension sharing order in respect of a person's shareable rights under an occupational pension scheme, or an order which includes provision made by virtue of section 25B(4) or (7) in relation to such a scheme, the Board subsequently assuming responsibility for the scheme as mentioned in subsection (2)(a) does not affect –

(a) the powers of the court under section 31 to vary or discharge the order or to suspend or revive any provision of it, or

(b) on an appeal, the powers of the appeal court to affirm, reinstate, set aside or vary the order.

(8) Regulations may make such consequential modifications of any provision of, or made by virtue of, this Part as appear to the Lord Chancellor necessary or expedient to give effect to the provisions of this section.

(9) In this section –

'assessment period' means an assessment period within the meaning of Part 2 of the Pensions Act 2004 (pension protection) (see sections 132 and 159 of that Act) or an equivalent period under any provision in force in Northern Ireland corresponding to that Part;

'the Board' means the Board of the Pension Protection Fund;

'occupational pension scheme' has the same meaning as in the Pension Schemes Act 1993;

'prescribed' means prescribed by regulations;

'PPF compensation' means compensation payable under Chapter 3 of Part 2 of the Pensions Act 2004 (pension protection) or any provision in force in Northern Ireland corresponding to that Chapter;

'regulations' means regulations made by the Lord Chancellor;

'shareable rights' are rights in relation to which pension sharing is available under Chapter 1 of Part 4 of the Welfare Reform and Pensions Act 1999 or any provision in force in Northern Ireland corresponding to that Chapter;

'transfer notice' has the same meaning as in section 160 of the Pensions Act 2004 or any corresponding provision in force in Northern Ireland.

(10) Any power to make regulations under this section is exercisable by statutory instrument, which shall be subject to annulment in pursuance of a resolution of either House of Parliament.

Variation, discharge and enforcement of certain orders, etc.

31 Variation, discharge, etc., of certain orders for financial relief

(1) Where the court has made an order to which this section applies, then, subject to the provisions of this section and of section 28(1A) above, the court shall have power to vary or discharge the order or to suspend any provision thereof temporarily and to revive the operation of any provision so suspended.

(2) This section applies to the following orders, that is to say –

(a) any order for maintenance pending suit and any interim order for maintenance;

(b) any periodical payments order;

(c) any secured periodical payments order;

(d) any order made by virtue of section 23(3)(c) or 27(7)(b) above (provision for payment of a lump sum by instalments);

(dd) any deferred order made by virtue of section 23(1)(c) (lump sums) which includes provision made by virtue of –

    (i) section 25B(4), or

    (ii) section 25C (provision in respect of pension rights);

(e) any order for a settlement of property under section 24(1)(b) or for a variation of settlement under section 24(1)(c) or (d) above, being an order made on or after the grant of a decree of judicial separation;

(f) any order made under section 24A(1) above for the sale of property;

(g) a pension sharing order under section 24B above which is made at a time before the decree has been made absolute.

(2A) Where the court has made an order referred to in subsection (2)(a), (b) or (c) above, then, subject to the provisions of this section, the court shall have power to remit the payment of any arrears due under the order or of any part thereof.

(2B) Where the court has made an order referred to in subsection (2)(dd)(ii) above, this section shall cease to apply to the order on the death of either of the parties to the marriage.

(3) The powers exercisable by the court under this section in relation to an order shall be exercisable also in relation to any instrument executed in pursuance of the order.

(4) The court shall not exercise the powers conferred by this section in relation to an order for a settlement under section 24(1)(b) or for a variation of settlement under section 24(1)(c) or (d) above except on an application made in proceedings –

(a) for the rescission of the decree of judicial separation by reference to which the order was made, or

(b) for the dissolution of the marriage in question.

(4A) In relation to an order which falls within paragraph (g) of subsection (2) above ('the subsection (2) order') –

(a) the powers conferred by this section may be exercised –

    (i) only on an application made before the subsection (2) order has or, but for paragraph (b) below, would have taken effect; and

    (ii) only if, at the time when the application is made, the decree has not been made absolute; and

(b) an application made in accordance with paragraph (a) above prevents the subsection (2) order from taking effect before the application has been dealt with.

(4B) No variation of a pension sharing order shall be made so as to take effect before the decree is made absolute.

(4C) The variation of a pension sharing order prevents the order taking effect before the end of such period after the making of the variation as may be prescribed by regulations made by the Lord Chancellor.

(5) Subject to subsections (7A) to (7G) below and without prejudice to any power exercisable by virtue of subsection (2)(d), (dd), (e) or (g) above or otherwise than by virtue of this section, no property adjustment order or pension sharing order shall be made on an application for the variation of a periodical payments or

secured periodical payments order made (whether in favour of a party to a marriage or in favour of a child of the family) under section 23 above, and no order for the payment of a lump sum shall be made on an application for the variation of a periodical payments or secured periodical payments order in favour of a party to a marriage (whether made under section 23 or under section 27 above).

(6) Where the person liable to make payments under a secured periodical payments order has died, an application under this section relating to that order (and to any order made under section 24A(1) above which requires the proceeds of sale of property to be used for securing those payments) may be made by the person entitled to payments under the periodical payments order or by the personal representatives of the deceased person, but no such application shall, except with the permission of the court, be made after the end of the period of six months from the date on which representation in regard to the estate of that person is first taken out.

(7) In exercising the powers conferred by this section the court shall have regard to all the circumstances of the case, first consideration being given to the welfare while a minor of any child of the family who has not attained the age of eighteen, and the circumstances of the case shall include any change in any of the matters to which the court was required to have regard when making the order to which the application relates, and –

   (a) in the case of a periodical payments or secured periodical payments order made on or after the grant of a decree of divorce or nullity of marriage, the court shall consider whether in all the circumstances and after having regard to any such change it would be appropriate to vary the order so that payments under the order are required to be made or secured only for such further period as will in the opinion of the court be sufficient (in the light of any proposed exercise by the court, where the marriage has been dissolved, of its powers under subsection (7B) below) to enable the party in whose favour the order was made to adjust without undue hardship to the termination of those payments;

   (b) in a case where the party against whom the order was made has died, the circumstances of the case shall also include the changed circumstances resulting from his or her death.

(7A) Subsection (7B) below applies where, after the dissolution of a marriage, the court –

   (a) discharges a periodical payments order or secured periodical payments order made in favour of a party to the marriage; or

   (b) varies such an order so that payments under the order are required to be made or secured only for such further period as is determined by the court.

(7B) The court has power, in addition to any power it has apart from this subsection, to make supplemental provision consisting of any of –

   (a) an order for the payment of a lump sum in favour of a party to the marriage;

   (b) one or more property adjustment orders in favour of a party to the marriage;

   (ba) one or more pension sharing orders;

   (c) a direction that the party in whose favour the original order discharged or varied was made is not entitled to make any further application for –

(i)   a periodical payments or secured periodical payments order, or

(ii)   an extension of the period to which the original order is limited by any variation made by the court.

(7C) An order for the payment of a lump sum made under subsection (7B) above may –

(a)   provide for the payment of that sum by instalments of such amount as may be specified in the order; and

(b)   require the payment of the instalments to be secured to the satisfaction of the court.

(7D) Section 23(6) above apply where the court makes an order for the payment of a lump sum under subsection (7B) above as they apply where it makes such an order under section 23 above.

(7E) If under subsection (7B) above the court makes more than one property adjustment order in favour of the same party to the marriage, each of those orders must fall within a different paragraph of section 21(2) above.

(7F) Sections 24A and 30 above apply where the court makes a property adjustment order under subsection (7B) above as they apply where it makes such an order under section 24 above.

(7G) Subsections (3) to (5) of section 24B above apply in relation to a pension sharing order under subsection (7B) above as they apply in relation to a pension sharing order under that section.

(8)   The personal representatives of a deceased person against whom a secured periodical payments order was made shall not be liable for having distributed any part of the estate of the deceased after the expiration of the period of six months referred to in subsection (6) above on the ground that they ought to have taken into account the possibility that the court might permit an application under this section to be made after that period by the person entitled to payments under the order; but this subsection shall not prejudice any power to recover any part of the estate so distributed arising by virtue of the making of an order in pursuance of this section.

(9)   In considering for the purposes of subsection (6) above the question when representation was first taken out, a grant limited to settled land or to trust property shall be left out of account and a grant limited to real estate or to personal estate shall be left out of account unless a grant limited to the remainder of the estate has previously been made or is made at the same time.

(10) Where the court, in exercise of its powers under this section, decides to vary or discharge a periodical payments or secured periodical payments order, then, subject to section 28(1) and (2) above, the court shall have power to direct that the variation or discharge shall not take effect until the expiration of such period as may be specified in the order.

(11) Where –

(a)   a periodical payments or secured periodical payments order in favour of more than one child ('the order') is in force;

(b)   the order requires payments specified in it to be made to or for the benefit of more than one child without apportioning those payments between them;

(c)   a maintenance calculation ('the calculation') is made with respect to one or more, but not all, of the children with respect to whom those payments are to be made; and

(d) an application is made, before the end of the period of 6 months beginning with the date on which the calculation was made, for the variation or discharge of the order,

the court may, in exercise of its powers under this section to vary or discharge the order, direct that the variation or discharge shall take effect from the date on which the calculation took effect or any later date.

(12) Where –

(a) an order ('the child order') of a kind prescribed for the purposes of section 10(1) of the Child Support Act 1991 is affected by a maintenance calculation;

(b) on the date on which the child order became so affected there was in force a periodical payments or secured periodical payments order ('the spousal order') in favour of a party to a marriage having the care of the child in whose favour the child order was made; and

(c) an application is made, before the end of the period of 6 months beginning with the date on which the maintenance calculation was made, for the spousal order to be varied or discharged,

the court may, in exercise of its powers under this section to vary or discharge the spousal order, direct that the variation or discharge shall take effect from the date on which the child order became so affected or any later date.

(13) For the purposes of subsection (12) above, an order is affected if it ceases to have effect or is modified by or under section 10 of the Child Support Act 1991.

(14) Subsections (11) and (12) above are without prejudice to any other power of the court to direct that the variation of discharge of an order under this section shall take effect from a date earlier than that on which the order for variation or discharge was made.

(15) The power to make regulations under subsection (4C) above shall be exercisable by statutory instrument which shall be subject to annulment in pursuance of a resolution of either House of Parliament.

36 Alteration of agreements by court after death of one party

(1) Where a maintenance agreement within the meaning of section 34 above provides for the continuation of payments under the agreement after the death of one of the parties and that party dies domiciled in England and Wales, the surviving party or the personal representatives of the deceased party may, subject to subsections (2) and (3) below, apply to the High Court or a county court for an order under section 35 above.

(2) An application under this section shall not, except with the permission of the High Court or a county court, be made after the end of the period of six months from the date on which representation in regard to the estate of the deceased is first taken out.

(3) A county court shall not entertain an application under this section, or an application for permission to make an application under this section, unless it would have jurisdiction by virtue of section 22 of the Inheritance (Provision for Family and Dependants) Act 1975 (which confers jurisdiction on county courts in proceedings under that Act if the value of the property mentioned in that section does not exceed £ 5,000 or such larger sum as may be fixed by order of the Lord Chancellor) to hear and determine proceedings for an order under section 2 of that Act in relation to the deceased's estate.

(4) If a maintenance agreement is altered by a court on an application made in pursuance of subsection (1) above, the like consequences shall ensue as if the

alteration had been made immediately before the death by agreement between the parties and for valuable consideration.

(5) The provisions of this section shall not render the personal representatives of the deceased liable for having distributed any part of the estate of the deceased after the expiration of the period of six months referred to in subsection (2) above on the ground that they ought to have taken into account the possibility that a court might permit an application by virtue of this section to be made by the surviving party after that period; but this subsection shall not prejudice any power to recover any part of the estate so distributed arising by virtue of the making of an order in pursuance of this section.

(6) Section 31(9) above shall apply for the purposes of subsection (2) above as it applies for the purposes of subsection (6) of section 31.

(7) Subsection (3) of section 22 of the Inheritance (Provision for Family and Dependants) Act 1975 (which enables rules of court to provide for the transfer from a county court to the High Court or from the High court to a county court of proceedings for an order under section 2 of that Act) and paragraphs (a) and (b) of subsection (4) of that section (provisions relating to proceedings commenced in county court before coming into force of order of the Lord Chancellor under that section) shall apply in relation to proceedings consisting of any such application as is referred to in subsection (3) above as they apply in relation to proceedings for an order under section 2 of that Act.

37 Avoidance of transactions intended to prevent or reduce financial relief

(1) For the purposes of this section 'financial relief' means relief under any of the provisions of sections 22, 23, 24, 24B, 27, 31 (except subsection (6)) and 35 above, and any reference in this section to defeating a person's claim for financial relief is a reference to preventing financial relief from being granted to that person, or to that person for the benefit of a child of the family, or reducing the amount of any financial relief which might be so granted, or frustrating or impeding the enforcement of any order which might be or has been made at his instance under any of those provisions.

(2) Where proceedings for financial relief are brought by one person against another, the court may, on the application of the first-mentioned person –

(a) if it is satisfied that the other party to the proceedings is, with the intention of defeating the claim for financial relief, about to make any disposition or to transfer out of the jurisdiction or otherwise deal with any property, make such order as it thinks fit for restraining the other party from so doing or otherwise for protecting the claim;

(b) if it is satisfied that the other party has, with that intention, made a reviewable disposition and that if the disposition were set aside financial relief or different financial relief would be granted to the applicant, make an order setting aside the disposition;

(c) if it is satisfied, in a case where an order has been obtained under any of the provisions mentioned in subsection (1) above by the applicant against the other party, that the other party has, with that intention, made a reviewable disposition, make an order setting aside the disposition;

and an application for the purposes of paragraph (b) above shall be made in the proceedings for the financial relief in question.

(3) Where the court makes an order under subsection (2)(b) or (c) above setting aside a disposition it shall give such consequential directions as it thinks fit for

giving effect to the order (including directions requiring the making of any payments or the disposal of any property).

(4) Any disposition made by the other party to the proceedings for financial relief in question (whether before or after the commencement of those proceedings) is a reviewable disposition for the purposes of subsection (2)(b) and (c) above unless it was made for valuable consideration (other than marriage) to a person who, at the time of the disposition, acted in relation to it in good faith and without notice of any intention on the part of the other party to defeat the applicant's claim for financial relief.

(5) Where an application is made under this section with respect to a disposition which took place less than three years before the date of the application or with respect to a disposition or other dealing with property which is about to take place and the court is satisfied –

(a) in a case falling within subsection (2)(a) or (b) above, that the disposition or other dealing would (apart from this section) have the consequence, or

(b) in a case falling within subsection (2)(c) above, that the disposition has had the consequence,

of defeating the applicant's claim for financial relief, it shall be presumed, unless the contrary is shown, that the person who disposed of or is about to dispose of or deal with the property did so or, as the case may be, is about to do so, with the intention of defeating the applicant's claim for financial relief.

(6) In this section 'disposition' does not include any provision contained in a will or codicil but, with that exception, includes any conveyance, assurance or gift of property of any description, whether made by an instrument or otherwise.

(7) This section does not apply to a disposition made before 1st January 1968.

Inheritance (Provision for Family and Dependants) Act 1975

An Act to make fresh provisions for empowering the court to make orders for the making out of the estate of a deceased person of provision for the spouse, former spouse, child, child of the family or dependant of that person; and for matters connected therewith

[12th November 1975]

BE IT ENACTED by the Queen's most Excellent Majesty, by and with the advice and consent of the Lords Spiritual and Temporal, and Commons, in this present Parliament assembled, and by the authority of the same, as follows:

1   Application for financial provision from deceased's estate

(1)   Where after the commencement of this Act a person dies domiciled in England and Wales and is survived by any of the following persons –

(a)   the spouse or civil partner of the deceased;

(b)   a former spouse or former civil partner of the deceased, but not one who has formed a subsequent marriage or civil partnership;

(ba)   any person (not being a person included in paragraph (a) or (b) above) to whom subsection (1A) or (1B) below applies;

(c)   a child of the deceased;

(d)   any person (not being a child of the deceased) who, in the case of any marriage or civil partnership to which the deceased was at any time a party, was treated by the deceased as a child of the family in relation to that marriage or civil partnership;

(e)   any person (not being a person included in the foregoing paragraphs of this subsection) who immediately before the death of the deceased was being maintained, either wholly or partly, by the deceased;

that person may apply to the court for an order under section 2 of this Act on the ground that the disposition of the deceased's estate effected by his will or the law relating to intestacy, or the combination of his will and that law, is not such as to make reasonable financial provision for the applicant.

(1A) This subsection applies to a person if the deceased died on or after 1st January 1996 and, during the whole of the period of two years ending immediately before the date when the deceased died, the person was living –

(a)   in the same household as the deceased, and

(b)   as the husband or wife of the deceased.

(1B) This subsection applies to a person if for the whole of the period of two years ending immediately before the date when the deceased died the person was living –

    (a)   in the same household as the deceased, and

    (b)   as the civil partner of the deceased.

(2)   In this Act 'reasonable financial provision' –

    (a)   in the case of an application made by virtue of subsection (1)(a) above by the husband or wife of the deceased (except where the marriage with the deceased was the subject of a decree of judicial separation and at the date of death the decree was in force and the separation was continuing), means such financial provision as it would be reasonable in all the circumstances of the case for a husband or wife to receive, whether or not that provision is required for his or her maintenance;

    (aa) in the case of an application made by virtue of subsection (1)(a) above by the civil partner of the deceased (except where, at the date of death, a separation order under Chapter 2 of Part 2 of the Civil Partnership Act 2004 was in force in relation to the civil partnership and the separation was continuing), means such financial provision as it would be reasonable in all the circumstances of the case for a civil partner to receive, whether or not that provision is required for his or her maintenance;

    (b)   in the case of any other application made by virtue of subsection (1) above, means such financial provision as it would be reasonable in all the circumstances of the case for the applicant to receive for his maintenance.

(3)   For the purposes of subsection (1)(e) above, a person shall be treated as being maintained by the deceased, either wholly or partly, as the case may be, if the deceased, otherwise than for full valuable consideration, was making a substantial contribution in money or money's worth towards the reasonable needs of that person.

2   Powers of court to make orders

(1)   Subject to the provisions of this Act, where an application is made for an order under this section, the court may, if it is satisfied that the disposition of the deceased's estate effected by his will or the law relating to intestacy, or the combination of his will and that law, is not such as to make reasonable financial provision for the applicant, make any one or more of the following orders –

    (a)   an order for the making to the applicant out of the net estate of the deceased of such periodical payments and for such term as may be specified in the order;

    (b)   an order for the payment to the applicant out of that estate of a lump sum of such amount as may be so specified;

    (c)   an order for the transfer to the applicant of such property comprised in that estate as may be so specified;

    (d)   an order for the settlement for the benefit of the applicant of such property comprised in that estate as may be so specified;

    (e)   an order for the acquisition out of property comprised in that estate of such property as may be so specified and for the transfer of the property so acquired to the applicant or for the settlement thereof for his benefit;

    (f)   an order varying any ante-nuptial or post-nuptial settlement (including such a settlement made by will) made on the parties to a marriage to which the deceased was one of the parties, the variation being for the benefit of the surviving party to that marriage, or any child of that marriage, or any person who was treated by the deceased as a child of the family in relation to that marriage;

    (g)   an order varying any settlement made –

        (i)   during the subsistence of a civil partnership formed by the deceased, or

        (ii)   in anticipation of the formation of a civil partnership by the deceased,

on the civil partners (including such a settlement made by will), the variation being for the benefit of the surviving civil partner, or any child of both the civil partners, or any person who was treated by the deceased as a child of the family in relation to that civil partnership.

(2)   An order under subsection (1)(a) above providing for the making out of the net estate of the deceased of periodical payments may provide for –

    (a)   payments of such amount as may be specified in the order,

    (b)   payments equal to the whole of the income of the net estate or of such portion thereof as may be so specified,

    (c)   payments equal to the whole of the income of such part of the net estate as the court may direct to be set aside or appropriated for the making out of the income thereof of payments under this section,

or may provide for the amount of the payments or any of them to be determined in any other way the court thinks fit.

(3)   Where an order under subsection (1)(a) above provides for the making of payments of an amount specified in the order, the order may direct that such part of the net estate as may be so specified shall be set aside or appropriated for the making out of the income thereof of those payments; but no larger part of the net estate shall be so set aside or appropriated than is sufficient, at the date of the order, to produce by the income thereof the amount required for the making of those payments.

(4)   An order under this section may contain such consequential and supplemental provisions as the court thinks necessary or expedient for the purpose of giving effect to the order or for the purpose of securing that the order operates fairly as between one beneficiary of the estate of the deceased and another and may, in particular, but without prejudice to the generality of this subsection –

    (a)   order any person who holds any property which forms part of the net estate of the deceased to make such payment or transfer such property as may be specified in the order;

    (b)   varying the disposition of the deceased's estate effected by the will or the law relating to intestacy, or by both the will and the law relating to intestacy, in such manner as the court thinks fair and reasonable having regard to the provisions of the order and all the circumstances of the case;

    (c)   confer on the trustees of any property which is the subject of an order under this section such powers as appear to the court to be necessary or expedient.

3   Matters to which court is to have regard in exercising powers under s.2

(1)   Where an application is made for an order under section 2 of this Act, the court shall, in determining whether the disposition of the deceased's estate effected by his will or the law relating to intestacy, or the combination of his will and that law, is such as to make reasonable financial provision for the applicant and, if the court considers that reasonable financial provision has not been made, in determining whether and in what manner it shall exercise its powers under that section, have regard to the following matters, that is to say –

(a)   the financial resources and financial needs which the applicant has or is likely to have in the foreseeable future;

(b)   the financial resources and financial needs which any other applicant for an order under section 2 of this Act has or is likely to have in the foreseeable future;

(c)   the financial resources and financial needs which any beneficiary of the estate of the deceased has or is likely to have in the foreseeable future;

(d)   any obligations and responsibilities which the deceased had towards any applicant for an order under the said section 2 or towards any beneficiary of the estate of the deceased;

(e)   the size and nature of the net estate of the deceased;

(f)   any physical or mental disability of any applicant for an order under the said section 2 or any beneficiary of the estate of the deceased;

(g)   any other matter, including the conduct of the applicant or any other person, which in the circumstances of the case the court may consider relevant.

(2)   This subsection applies, without prejudice to the generality of paragraph (g) of subsection (1) above, where an application for an order under section 2 of this Act is made by virtue of section 1(1)(a) or (b) of this Act.

The court shall, in addition to the matters specifically mentioned in paragraphs (a) to (f) of that subsection, have regard to –

(a)   the age of the applicant and the duration of the marriage or civil partnership;

(b)   the contribution made by the applicant to the welfare of the family of the deceased, including any contribution made by looking after the home or caring for the family.

In the case of an application by the wife or husband of the deceased, the court shall also, unless at the date of death a decree of judicial separation was in force and the separation was continuing, have regard to the provision which the applicant might reasonably have expected to receive if on the day on which the deceased died the marriage, instead of being terminated by death, had been terminated by a decree of divorce.

In the case of an application by the civil partner of the deceased, the court shall also, unless at the date of the death a separation order under Chapter 2 of Part 2 of the Civil Partnership Act 2004 was in force and the separation was continuing, have regard to the provision which the applicant might reasonably have expected to receive if on the day on which the deceased died the civil partnership, instead of being terminated by death, had been terminated by a dissolution order.

(2A)   Without prejudice to the generality of paragraph (g) of subsection (1) above, where an application for an order under section 2 of this Act is made by virtue of section 1(1)(ba) of this Act, the court shall, in addition to the matters specifically mentioned in paragraphs (a) to (f) of that subsection, have regard to –

(a) the age of the applicant and the length of the period during which the applicant lived as the husband or wife or civil partner of the deceased and in the same household as the deceased;

(b) the contribution made by the applicant to the welfare of the family of the deceased, including any contribution made by looking after the home or caring for the family.

(3) Without prejudice to the generality of paragraph (g) of subsection (1) above, where an application for an order under section 2 of this Act is made by virtue of section 1(1)(c) or 1(1)(d) of this Act, the court shall, in addition to the matters specifically mentioned in paragraphs (a) to (f) of that subsection, have regard to the manner in which the applicant was being or in which he might expect to be educated or trained, and where the application is made by virtue of section 1(1)(d) the court shall also have regard –

(a) to whether the deceased had assumed any responsibility for the applicant's maintenance and, if so, to the extent to which and the basis upon which the deceased assumed that responsibility and to the length of time for which the deceased discharged that responsibility;

(b) to whether in assuming and discharging that responsibility the deceased did so knowing that the applicant was not his own child;

(c) to the liability of any other person to maintain the applicant.

(4) Without prejudice to the generality of paragraph (g) of subsection (1) above, where an application for an order under section 2 of this Act is made by virtue of section 1(1)(e) of this Act, the court shall, in addition to the matters specifically mentioned in paragraphs (a) to (f) of that subsection, have regard to the extent to which and the basis upon which the deceased assumed responsibility for the maintenance of the applicant, and to the length of time for which the deceased discharged that responsibility.

(5) In considering the matters to which the court is required to have regard under this section, the court shall take into account the facts as known to the court at the date of the hearing.

(6) In considering the financial resources of any person for the purposes of this section the court shall take into account his earning capacity and in considering the financial needs of any person for the purposes of this section the court shall take into account his financial obligations and responsibilities.

4   Time-limit for applications

An application for an order under section 2 of this Act shall not, except with the permission of the court, be made after the end of the period of six months from the date on which representation with respect to the estate of the deceased is first taken out.

5   Interim orders

(1) Where an application for an order under section 3 of this Act it appears to the court –

(a) that the applicant is in immediate need of financial assistance, but it is not yet possible to determine what order (if any) should be made under that section; and

(b) that property forming part of the net estate of the deceased is or can be made available to meet the need of the applicant;

the court may order that, subject to such conditions or restrictions, if any, as the court may impose and to any further order of the court, there shall be paid to the applicant out of the net estate of the deceased such sum or sums and (if more than one) at such intervals as the court thinks reasonable; and the court may order that, subject to the provisions of this Act, such payments are to be made until such date as the court may specify, not being later than the date on which the court either makes an order under the said section 2 or decides not to exercise its powers under that section.

(2) Subsections (2), (3) and (4) of section 2 of this Act shall apply in relation to an order under this section as they apply in relation to an order under that section.

(3) In determining what order, if any, should be made under this section the court shall, so far as the urgency of the case admits, have regard to the same matters as those to which the court is required to have regard under section 3 of this Act.

(4) An order made under section 2 of this Act may provide that any sum paid to the applicant by virtue of this section shall be treated to such an extent and in such manner as may be provided by that order as having been paid on account of any payment provided for by that order.

6   Variation, discharge, etc of orders for periodical payments

(1) Subject to the provisions of this Act, where the court has made an order under section 2(1)(a) of this Act (in this section referred to as 'the original order') for the making of periodical payments to any person (in this section referred to as 'the original recipient'), the court, on an application under this section, shall have power by order to vary or discharge the original order or to suspend any provision of it temporarily and to revive the operation of any provision so suspended.

(2) Without prejudice to the generality of subsection (1) above, an order made on an application for the variation of the original order may –

(a) provide for the making out of any relevant property of such periodical payments and for such term as may be specified in the order to any person who has applied, or would but for section 4 of this Act be entitled to apply, for an order under section 2 of this Act (whether or not, in the case of any application, an order was made in favour of the applicant);

(b) provide for the payment out of any relevant property of a lump sum of such amount as may be so specified to the original recipient or to any such person as is mentioned in paragraph (a) above;

(c) provide for the transfer of the relevant property, or such part thereof as may be so specified, to the original recipient or to any such person as is so mentioned.

(3) Where the original order provides that any periodical payments payable thereunder to the original recipient are to cease on the occurrence of an event specified in the order (other than the formation of a subsequent marriage or civil partnership by a former spouse or former civil partner) or on the expiration of a period so specified, then, if, before the end of the period of six months from the date of the occurrence of that event or of the expiration of that period, an application is made for an order under this section, the court shall have power to make any order which it would have had power to make if the application had been made before the date (whether in favour of the original recipient or any

141

such person as is mentioned in subsection (2)(a) above and whether having effect from that date or from such later date as the court may specify).

(4) Any reference in this section to the original order shall include a reference to an order made under this section and any reference in this section to the original recipient shall include a reference to any person to whom periodical payments are required to be made by virtue of an order under this section.

(5) An application under this section may be made by any of the following persons, that is to say –

    (a) any person who by virtue of section 1(1) of this Act has applied, or would but for section 4 of this Act be entitled to apply, for an order under section 2 of this Act,

    (b) the personal representatives of the deceased,

    (c) the trustees of any relevant property, and

    (d) any beneficiary of the estate of the deceased.

(6) An order under this section may only affect –

    (a) property the income of which is at the date of the order applicable wholly or in part for the making of periodical payments to any person who has applied for an order under this Act, or

    (b) in the case of an application under subsection (3) above in respect of payments which have ceased to be payable on the occurrence of an event or the expiration of a period, property the income of which was so applicable immediately before the occurrence of that event or the expiration of that period, as the case may be,

and any such property as is mentioned in paragraph (a) or (b) above is in sub-sections (2) and (5) above referred to as 'relevant property'.

(7) In exercising the powers conferred by this section the court shall have regard to all circumstances of the case, including any change in any of the matters to which the court was required to have regard when making the order to which the application relates.

(8) Where the court makes an order under this section, it may give such consequential directions as it thinks necessary or expedient having regard to the provisions of the order.

(9) No such order as is mentioned in section 2(1)(d), (e) or (f), 9, 10 or 11 of this Act shall be made on an application under this section.

(10) For the avoidance of doubt it is hereby declared that, in relation to an order which provides for the making of periodical payments which are to cease on the occurrence of an event specified in the order (other than the formation of a subsequent marriage or civil partnership by a former spouse or former civil partner) or on the expiration of a period so specified, the power to vary an order includes power to provide for the making of periodical payments after the expiration of that period or the occurrence of that event.

7   Payment of lump sums by instalments

(1) An order under section 2(1)(b) or 6(2)(b) of this Act for the payment of a lump sum may provide for the payment of that sum by instalments of such amount as may be specified in the order.

(2) Where an order is made by virtue of subsection (1) above, the court shall have power, on an application made by the person to whom the lump sum is payable, by the personal representatives of the deceased or by the trustees of the property

out of which the lump sum is payable, to vary that order by varying the number of instalments payable, the amount of any instalment and the date on which any instalment becomes payable.

8   Property treated as part of 'net estate'

(1)   Where a deceased person has in accordance with the provisions of any enactment nominated any person to receive any sum of money or other property on his death and that nomination is in force at the time of his death, that sum of money, after deducting therefrom any inheritance tax payable in respect thereof, or that other property, to the extent of the value thereof at the date of the death of the deceased after deducting therefrom any inheritance tax so payable, shall be treated for the purposes of this Act as part of the net estate of the deceased; but this subsection shall not render any person liable for having paid that sum or transferred that other property to the person named in the nomination in accordance with the directions given in the nomination.

(2)   Where any sum of money or other property is received by any person as a *donatio mortis causa* made by a deceased person, that sum of money, after deducting therefrom any inheritance tax payable thereon, or that other property, to the extent of the value thereof at the date of the death of the deceased after deducting therefrom any inheritance tax so payable, shall be treated for the purposes of this Act as part of the net estate of the deceased; but this subsection shall not render any person liable for having paid that sum or transferred that other property in order to give effect to that *donatio mortis causa*.

(3)   The amount of inheritance tax to be deducted for the purposes of this section shall not exceed the amount of that tax which has been borne by the person nominated by the deceased or, as the case may be, the person who has received a sum of money or other property as a *donatio mortis causa*.

9   Property held on a joint tenancy

(1)   Where a deceased person was immediately before his death beneficially entitled to a joint tenancy of any property, then, if, before the end of the period of six months from the date on which representation with respect to the estate of the deceased was first taken out, an application is made for an order under section 2 of this Act, the court for the purpose of facilitating the making of financial provision for the applicant under this Act may order that the deceased's severable share of that property, at the value thereof immediately before his death, shall, to such extent as appears to the court to be just in all the circumstances of the case, be treated for the purposes of this Act as part of the net estate of the deceased.

(2)   In determining the extent to which any severable share is to be treated as part of the net estate of the deceased by virtue of an order under subsection (1) above, the court shall have regard to any inheritance tax payable in respect of that severable share.

(3)   Where an order is made under subsection (1) above, the provisions of this section shall not render any person liable for anything done by him before the order was made.

(4)   For the avoidance of doubt it is hereby declared that for the purposes of this section there may be a joint tenancy of a chose in action.

Powers of court in relation to transactions intended to defeat applications for financial provision

10   Dispositions intended to defeat applications for financial provision

(1)   Where an application is made to the court for an order under section 2 of this Act, the applicant may, in the proceedings on that application, apply to the court for an order under subsection (2) below.

(2)   Where on an application under subsection (1) above the court is satisfied –

(a)   that, less than six years before the date of the death of the deceased, the deceased with the intention of defeating an application for financial provision under this Act made a disposition, and

(b)   that full valuable consideration for that disposition was not given by the person to whom or for the benefit of whom the disposition was made (in this section referred to as 'the donee') or by any other person, and

(c)   that the exercise of the powers conferred by this section would facilitate the making of financial provision for the applicant under this Act,

then, subject to the provisions of this section and of sections 12 and 13 of this Act, the court may order the donee (whether or not at the date of the order he holds any interest in the property disposed of to him or for his benefit by the deceased) to provide, for the purpose of the making of that financial provision, such sum of money or other property as may be specified in the order.

(3)   Where an order is made under subsection (2) above as respects any disposition made by the deceased which consisted of the payment of money to or for the benefit of the donee, the amount of any sum of money or the value of any property ordered to be provided under that subsection shall not exceed the amount of the payment made by the deceased after deducting therefrom any inheritance tax borne by the donee in respect of that payment.

(4)   Where an order is made under subsection (2) above as respects any disposition made by the deceased which consisted of the transfer of property (other than a sum of money) to or for the benefit of the donee, the amount of any sum of money or the value of any property ordered to be provided under that subsection shall not exceed the value at the date of the death of the deceased of the property disposed of by him to or for the benefit of the donee (or if that property has been disposed of by the person to whom it was transferred by the deceased, the value at the date of that disposal thereof) after deducting therefrom any inheritance tax borne by the donee in respect of the transfer of that property by the deceased.

(5)   Where an application (in this subsection referred to as 'the original application') is made for an order under subsection (2) above in relation to any disposition, then, if on an application under this subsection by the donee or by any applicant for an order under section 2 of this Act the court is satisfied –

(a)   that, less than six years before the date of the death of the deceased, the deceased with the intention of defeating an application for financial provision under this Act made a disposition other than the disposition which is the subject of the original application, and

(b)   that full valuable consideration for that other disposition was not given by the person to whom or for the benefit of whom that other disposition was made or by any other person,

the court may exercise in relation to the person to whom or for the benefit of whom that other disposition was made the powers which the court would have had under subsection (2) above if the original application had been made in respect of that other disposition and the court had been satisfied as to the matters set out in paragraphs (a), (b) and (c) of that subsection; and where any application is made under this subsection, any reference in this section (except in subsection (2)(b)) to the donee shall include a reference to the person to whom or for the benefit of whom that other disposition was made.

(6) In determining whether and in what manner to exercise its powers under this section, the court shall have regard to the circumstances in which any disposition was made and any valuable consideration which was given therefor, the relationship, if any, of the donee to the deceased, the conduct and financial resources of the donee and all the other circumstances of the case.

(7) In this section 'disposition' does not include –

(a) any provision in a will, any such nomination as is mentioned in section 8(1) of this Act or any *donatio mortis causa*, or

(b) any appointment of property made, otherwise than by will, in the exercise of a special power of appointment,

but, subject to these exceptions, includes any payment of money (including the payment of a premium under a policy of assurance) and any conveyance, assurance, appointment or gift of property of any description, whether made by an instrument or otherwise.

(8) The provisions of this section do not apply to any disposition made before the commencement of this Act.

11 Contracts to leave property by will

(1) Where an application is made to a court for an order under section 2 of this Act, the applicant may, in the proceedings on that application, apply to the court for an order under this section.

(2) Where on an application under subsection (1) above the court is satisfied –

(a) that the deceased made a contract by which he agreed to leave by his will a sum of money or other property to any person or by which he agreed that a sum of money or other property would be paid or transferred to any person out of his estate, and

(b) that the deceased made that contract with the intention of defeating an application for financial provision under this Act, and

(c) that when the contract was made full valuable consideration for that contract was not given or promised by the person with whom or for the benefit of whom the contract was made (in this section referred to as 'the donee') or by any other person, and

(d) that the exercise of the powers conferred by this section would facilitate the making of financial provision for the applicant under this Act, then, subject to the provisions of this section and of sections 12 and 13 of this Act, the court may make any one or more of the following orders, that is to say –

(i) if any money has been paid or any other property has been transferred to or for the benefit of the donee in accordance with the contract, an order directing the donee to provide, for the purpose of the making of that financial provision, such sum of money or other property as may be specified in the order;

      (ii)   if the money or all the money has not been paid or the property or all the property has not been transferred in accordance with the contract, an order directing the personal representatives not to make any payment or transfer any property, or not to make any further payment or transfer any further property, as the case may be, in accordance therewith or directing the personal representatives only to make such payment or transfer such property as may be specified in the order.

(3)   Notwithstanding anything in subsection (2) above, the court may exercise its powers thereunder in relation to any contract made by the deceased only to the extent that the court considers that the amount of any sum of money paid or to be paid or the value of any property transferred or to be transferred in accordance with the contract exceeds the value of any valuable consideration given or to be given for that contract, and for this purpose the court shall have regard to the value of property at the date of the hearing.

(4)   In determining whether and in what manner to exercise its powers under this section, the court shall have regard to the circumstances in which the contract was made, the relationship, if any, of the donee to the deceased, the conduct and financial resources of the donee and all the other circumstances of the case.

(5)   Where an order has been made under subsection (2) above in relation to any contract the rights of any person to enforce that contract or to recover damages or to obtain other relief for the breach thereof shall be subject to any adjustment made by the court under section 12(3) of this Act and shall survive to such extent only as is consistent with giving effect to the terms of that order.

(6)   The provisions of this section do not apply to a contract made before the commencement of this Act.

12   Provisions supplementary to ss.10 and 11

(1)   Where the exercise of any of the powers conferred by section 10 or 11 of this Act is conditional on the court being satisfied that a disposition or contract was made by a deceased person with the intention of defeating an application for financial provision under this Act, that condition shall be fulfilled if the court is of the opinion that, on a balance of probabilities, the intention of the deceased (though not necessarily his sole intention) in making the disposition or contract was to prevent an order for financial provision being made under this Act or to reduce the amount of the provision which might otherwise be granted by an order thereunder.

(2)   Where an application is made under section 11 of this Act with respect to any contract made by the deceased and no valuable consideration was given or promised by any person for that contract then, notwithstanding anything in subsection (1) above, it shall be presumed, unless the contrary is shown, that the deceased made that contract with the intention of defeating an application for financial provision under this Act.

(3)   Where the court makes an order under section 10 or 11 of this Act it may give such consequential directions as it thinks fit (including directions requiring the making of any payment or the transfer of any property) for giving effect to the order or for securing a fair adjustment of the rights of the persons affected thereby.

(4)   Any power conferred on the court by the said section 10 or 11 to order the donee, in relation to any disposition or contract, to provide any sum of money or other

property shall be exercisable in like manner in relation to the personal representative of the donee, and –

(a) any reference in section 10(4) to the disposal of property by the donee shall include a reference to disposal by the personal representative of the donee, and

(b) any reference in section 10(5) to an application by the donee under that subsection shall include a reference to an application by the personal representative of the donee;

but the court shall not have power under the said section 10 or 11 to make an order in respect of any property forming part of the estate of the donee which has been distributed by the personal representative; and the personal representative shall not be liable for having distributed any such property before he has notice of the making of an application under the said section 10 or 11 on the ground that he ought to have taken into account the possibility that such an application would be made.

13   Provisions as to trustees in relation to ss.10 and 11

(1) Where an application is made for –

(a) an order under section 10 of this Act in respect of a disposition made by the deceased to any person as a trustee, or

(b) an order under section 11 of this Act in respect of any payment made or property transferred, in accordance with a contract made by the deceased, to any person as a trustee,

the powers of the court under the said section 10 or 11 to order that trustee to provide a sum of money or other property shall be subject to the following limitation (in addition, in a case of an application under section 10, to any provision regarding the deduction of inheritance tax) namely, that the amount of any sum of money or the value of any property ordered to be provided –

(i) in the case of an application in respect of a disposition which consisted of the payment of money or an application in respect of the payment of money in accordance with a contract, shall not exceed the aggregate of so much of that money as is at the date of the order in the hands of the trustee and the value at that date of any property which represents that money or is derived therefrom and is at that date in the hands of the trustee;

(ii) in the case of an application in respect of a disposition which consisted of the transfer of property (other than a sum of money) or an application in respect of the transfer of property (other than a sum of money) in accordance with a contract, shall not exceed the aggregate of the value at the date of the order of so much of that property as is at that date in the hands of the trustee and the value at that date of any property which represents the first mentioned property or is derived therefrom and is at that date in the hands of the trustee.

(2) Where any such application is made in respect of a disposition made to any person as a trustee or in respect of any payment made or property transferred in pursuance of a contract to any person as a trustee, the trustee shall not be liable for having distributed any money or other property on the ground that he ought

to have taken into account the possibility that such an application would be made.

(3)   Where any such application is made in respect of a disposition made to any person as a trustee or in respect of any payment made or property transferred in accordance with a contract to any person as a trustee, any reference in the said section 10 or 11 to the donee shall be construed as including a reference to the trustee or trustees for the time being of the trust in question and any reference in subsection (1) or (2) above to a trustee shall be construed in the same way.

Special provisions relating to cases of divorce, separation, etc

14   Provision as to cases where no financial relief was granted in divorce proceedings, etc

(1)   Where, within twelve months from the date on which a decree of divorce or nullity of marriage has been made absolute or a decree of judicial separation has been granted, a party to the marriage dies and –

(a)   an application for a financial provision order under section 23 of the Matrimonial Causes Act 1973 or a property adjustment order under section 24 of that Act has not been made by the other party to that marriage, or

(b)   such an application has been made but the proceedings thereon have not been determined at the time of the death of the deceased,

then, if an application for an order under section 2 of this Act is made by that other party, the court shall, notwithstanding anything in section 1 or section 3 of this Act, have power, if it thinks it just to do so, to treat that party for the purposes of that application as if the decree of divorce or nullity of marriage had not been made absolute or the decree of judicial separation had not been granted, as the case may be.

(2)   This section shall not apply in relation to a decree of judicial separation unless at the date of the death of the deceased the decree was in force and the separation was continuing.

14A Provision as to cases where no financial relief was granted in proceedings for the dissolution etc of a civil partnership

(1)   Subsection (2) below applies where –

(a)   a dissolution order, nullity order, separation order or presumption of death order has been made under Chapter 2 of Part 2 of the Civil Partnership Act 2004 in relation to a civil partnership,

(b)   one of the civil partners dies within twelve months from the date on which the order is made, and

(c)   either –

(i)   an application for a financial provision order under Part 1 of Schedule 5 to that Act or a property adjustment order under Part 2 of that Schedule has not been made by the other civil partner, or

(ii)   such an application has been made but the proceedings on the application have not been determined at the time of the death of the deceased.

(2)   If an application for an order under section 2 of this Act is made by the surviving civil partner, the court shall, notwithstanding anything in section 1 or section 3 of this Act, have power, if it thinks it just to do so, to treat the surviving civil partner as if the order mentioned in subsection (1)(a) above had not been made.

(3)   This section shall not apply in relation to a separation order unless at the date of the death of the deceased the separation order was in force and the separation was continuing.

15   Restriction imposed in divorce proceedings, etc on application under this Act

(1)   On the grant of a decree of divorce, a decree of nullity of marriage or a decree of judicial separation or at any time thereafter the court, if it considers it just to do so, may, on the application of either party to the marriage, order that the other party to the marriage shall not on the death of the applicant be entitled to apply for an order under section 2 of this Act.
In this subsection 'the court' means the High Court or, where a county court has jurisdiction by virtue of Part V of the Matrimonial and Family Proceedings Act 1984, a county court.

(2)   In the case of a decree of divorce or nullity of marriage an order may be made under subsection (1) above before or after the decree is made absolute, but if it is made before the decree is made absolute it shall not take effect unless the decree is made absolute.

(3)   Where an order made under subsection (1) above on the grant of a decree of divorce or nullity of marriage has come into force with respect to a party to a marriage, then, on the death of the other party to that marriage, the court shall not entertain any application for an order under section 2 of this Act made by the first-mentioned party.

(4)   Where an order made under subsection (1) above on the grant of a decree of judicial separation has come into force with respect to any party to a marriage, then, if the other party to that marriage dies while the decree is in force and the separation is continuing, the court shall not entertain any application for an order under section 2 of this Act made by the first-mentioned party.

15A   Restriction imposed in proceedings under Matrimonial and Family Proceedings Act 1984 on application under this Act

(1)   On making an order under section 17 of the Matrimonial and Family Proceedings Act 1984 (orders for financial provision and property adjustment following overseas divorces, etc) the court, if it considers it just to do so, may, on the application of either party to the marriage, order that the other party to the marriage shall not on the death of the applicant be entitled to apply for an order under section 2 of this Act.
In this subsection 'the court' means the High Court or, where a county court has jurisdiction by virtue of Part V of the Matrimonial and Family Proceedings Act 1984, a county court.

(2)   Where an order under subsection (1) above has been made with respect to a party to a marriage which has been dissolved or annulled, then, on the death of the other party to that marriage, the court shall not entertain an application under section 2 of this Act made by the first-mentioned party.

(3)   Where an order under subsection (1) above has been made with respect to a party to a marriage the parties to which have been legally separated, then, if the

other party to the marriage dies while the legal separation is in force, the court shall not entertain an application under section 2 of this Act made by the first-mentioned party.

15B Restriction imposed in proceedings under Schedule 7 to the Civil Partnership Act 2004 on application under this Act

(1) On making an order under paragraph 9 of Schedule 7 to the Civil Partnership Act 2004 (orders for financial provision, property adjustment and pension-sharing following overseas dissolution etc of civil partnership) the court, if it considers it just to do so, may, on the application of either of the civil partners, order that the other civil partner shall not on the death of the applicant be entitled to apply for an order under section 2 of this Act.

(2) In subsection (1) above 'the court' means the High Court or, where a county court has jurisdiction by virtue of Part 5 of the Matrimonial and Family Proceedings Act 1984, a county court.

(3) Where an order under subsection (1) above has been made with respect to one of the civil partners in a case where a civil partnership has been dissolved or annulled, then, on the death of the other civil partner, the court shall not entertain an application under section 2 of this Act made by the surviving civil partner.

(4) Where an order under subsection (1) above has been made with respect to one of the civil partners in a case where civil partners have been legally separated, then, if the other civil partner dies while the legal separation is in force, the court shall not entertain an application under section 2 of this Act made by the surviving civil partner.

15ZA Restriction imposed in proceedings for the dissolution etc of a civil partnership on application under this Act

(1) On making a dissolution order, nullity order, separation order or presumption of death order under Chapter 2 of Part 2 of the Civil Partnership Act 2004, or at any time after making such an order, the court, if it considers it just to do so, may, on the application of either of the civil partners, order that the other civil partner shall not on the death of the applicant be entitled to apply for an order under section 2 of this Act.

(2) In subsection (1) above 'the court' means the High Court or, where a county court has jurisdiction by virtue of Part 5 of the Matrimonial and Family Proceedings Act 1984, a county court.

(3) In the case of a dissolution order, nullity order or presumption of death order ('the main order') an order may be made under subsection (1) above before (as well as after) the main order is made final, but if made before the main order is made final it shall not take effect unless the main order is made final.

(4) Where an order under subsection (1) above made in connection with a dissolution order, nullity order or presumption of death order has come into force with respect to a civil partner, then, on the death of the other civil partner, the court shall not entertain any application for an order under section 2 of this Act made by the surviving civil partner.

(5) Where an order under subsection (1) above made in connection with a separation order has come into force with respect to a civil partner, then, if the other civil partner dies while the separation order is in force and the separation is continuing, the court shall not entertain any application for an order under section 2 of this Act made by the surviving civil partner.

16 Variation and discharge of secured periodical payments orders made under Matrimonial Causes Act 1973

(1) Where an application for an order under section 2 of this Act is made to the court by any person who was at the time of the death of the deceased entitled to payments from the deceased under a secured periodical payments order made under the Matrimonial Causes Act 1973 or Schedule 5 to the Civil Partnership Act 2004, then, in the proceedings on that application, the court shall have power, if an application is made under this section by that person or by the personal representative of the deceased, to vary or discharge that periodical payments order or to revive the operation of any provision thereof which has been suspended under section 31 of that Act of 1973 or Part 11 of that Schedule.

(2) In exercising the powers conferred by this section the court shall have regard to all the circumstances of the case, including any order which the court proposes to make under section 2 or section 5 of this Act and any change (whether resulting from the death of the deceased or otherwise) in any of the matters to which the court was required to have regard when making the secured periodical payments order.

(3) The powers exercisable by the court under this section in relation to an order shall be exercisable also in relation to any instrument executed in pursuance of the order.

17 Variation and revocation of maintenance agreements

(1) Where an application for an order under section 2 of this Act is made to the court by any person who was at the time of the death of the deceased entitled to payments from the deceased under a maintenance agreement which provided for the continuation of payments under the agreement after the death of the deceased, then, in the proceedings on that application, the court shall have power, if an application is made under this section by that person or by the personal representative of the deceased, to vary or revoke that agreement.

(2) In exercising the powers conferred by this section the court shall have regard to all the circumstances of the case, including any order which the court proposes to make under section 2 or section 5 of this Act and any change (whether resulting from the death of the deceased or otherwise) in any of the circumstances in the light of which the agreement was made.

(3) If a maintenance agreement is varied by the court under this section the like consequences shall ensue as if the variation had been made immediately before the death of the deceased by agreement between the parties and for valuable consideration.

(4) In this section 'maintenance agreement', in relation to a deceased person, means any agreement made, whether in writing or not and whether before or after the commencement of this Act, by the deceased with any person with whom he formed a marriage or civil partnership, being an agreement which contained provisions governing the rights and liabilities towards one another when living separately of the parties to that marriage or of the civil partners (whether or not the marriage or civil partnership has been dissolved or annulled) in respect of the making or securing of payments or the disposition or use of any property, including such rights and liabilities with respect to the maintenance or education of any child, whether or not a child of the deceased or a person who was treated by the deceased as a child of the family in relation to that marriage or civil partnership.

18 Availability of court's powers under this Act in applications under ss.31 and 36 of the Matrimonial Causes Act 1973

(1) Where –

    (a) a person against whom a secured periodical payments order was made under the Matrimonial Causes Act 1973 has died and an application is made under section 31(6) of that Act for the variation or discharge of that order or for the revival of the operation of any provision thereof which has been suspended, or

    (b) a party to a maintenance agreement within the meaning of section 34 of that Act has died, the agreement being one which provides for the continuation of payments thereunder after the death of one of the parties, and an application is made under section 36(1) of that Act for the alteration of the agreement under section 35 thereof,

the court shall have power to direct that the application made under the said section 31(6) or 36(1) shall be deemed to have been accompanied by an application for an order under section 2 of this Act.

(2) Where the court gives a direction under subsection (1) above it shall have power, in the proceedings on the application under the said section 31(6) or 36(1), to make any order which the court would have had power to make under the provisions of this Act if the application under the said section 31(6) or 36(1), as the case may be, had been made jointly with an application for an order under the said section 2; and the court shall have power to give such consequential directions as may be necessary for enabling the court to exercise any of the powers available to the court under this Act in the case of an application for an order under section 2.

(3) Where an order made under section 15(1) of this Act is in force with respect to a party to a marriage, the court shall not give a direction under subsection (1) above with respect to any application made under the said section 31(6) or 36(1) by that party on the death of the other party.

18A Availability of court's powers under this Act in applications under paragraphs 60 and 73 of Schedule 5 to the Civil Partnership Act 2004

(1) Where –

    (a) a person against whom a secured periodical payments order was made under Schedule 5 to the Civil Partnership Act 2004 has died and an application is made under paragraph 60 of that Schedule for the variation or discharge of that order or for the revival of the operation of any suspended provision of the order, or

    (b) a party to a maintenance agreement within the meaning of Part 13 of that Schedule has died, the agreement being one which provides for the continuation of payments under the agreement after the death of one of the parties, and an application is made under paragraph 73 of that Schedule for the alteration of the agreement under paragraph 69 of that Schedule,

the court shall have power to direct that the application made under paragraph 60 or 73 of that Schedule shall be deemed to have been accompanied by an application for an order under section 2 of this Act.

(2) Where the court gives a direction under subsection (1) above it shall have power, in the proceedings on the application under paragraph 60 or 73 of that Schedule, to make any order which the court would have had power to make under the

provisions of this Act if the application under that paragraph had been made jointly with an application for an order under section 2 of this Act; and the court shall have power to give such consequential directions as may be necessary for enabling the court to exercise any of the powers available to the court under this Act in the case of an application for an order under section 2.

(3)   Where an order made under section 15ZA(1) of this Act is in force with respect to a civil partner, the court shall not give a direction under subsection (1) above with respect to any application made under paragraph 60 or 73 of that Schedule by that civil partner on the death of the other civil partner.

Miscellaneous and supplementary provisions

19   Effect, duration and form of orders

(1)   Where an order is made under section 2 of this Act then for all purposes, including the purposes of the enactments relating to inheritance tax, the will or the law relating to intestacy, or both the will and the law relating to intestacy, as the case may be, shall have effect and be deemed to have had effect as from the deceased's death subject to the provisions of the order.

(2)   Any order made under section 2 or 5 of this Act in favour of –

    (a)   an applicant who was the former spouse or former civil partner of the deceased, or

    (b)   an applicant who was the husband or wife of the deceased in a case where the marriage with the deceased was the subject of a decree of judicial separation and at the date of death the decree was in force and the separation was continuing, or

    (c)   an applicant who was the civil partner of the deceased in a case where, at the date of death, a separation order under Chapter 2 of Part 2 of the Civil Partnership Act 2004 was in force in relation to their civil partnership and the separation was continuing,

shall, in so far as it provides for the making of periodical payments, cease to have effect on the formation by the applicant of a subsequent marriage or civil partnership, except in relation to any arrears due under the order on the date of the formation of the subsequent marriage or civil partnership.

(3)   A copy of every order made under this Act other than an order made under section 15(1) or 15ZA(1) of this Act shall be sent to the principal registry of the Family Division for entry and filing, and a memorandum of the order shall be endorsed on, or permanently annexed to, the probate or letters of administration under which the estate is being administered.

20   Provisions as to personal representatives

(1)   The provisions of this Act shall not render the personal representative of a deceased person liable for having distributed any part of the estate of the deceased, after the end of the period of six months from the date on which representation with respect to the estate of the deceased is first taken out, on the ground that he ought to have taken into account the possibility –

    (a)   that the court might permit the making of an application for an order under section 2 of this Act after the end of that period, or

(b)   that, where an order has been made under the said section 2, the court might exercise in relation thereto the powers conferred on it by section 6 of this Act,

but this subsection shall not prejudice any power to recover, by reason of the making of an order under this Act, any part of the estate so distributed.

(2)   Where the personal representative of a deceased person pays any sum directed by an order under section 5 of this Act to be paid out of the deceased's net estate, he shall not be under any liability by reason of that estate not being sufficient to make the payment, unless at the time of making the payment he has reasonable cause to believe that the estate is not sufficient.

(3)   Where a deceased person entered into a contract by which he agreed to leave by his will any sum of money or other property to any person or by which he agreed that a sum of money or other property would be paid or transferred to any person out of his estate, then, if the personal representative of the deceased has reason to believe that the deceased entered into the contract with the intention of defeating an application for financial provision under this Act, he may, notwithstanding anything in that contract, postpone the payment of that sum of money or the transfer of that property until the expiration of the period of six months from the date on which representation with respect to the estate of the deceased is first taken out or, if during that period an application is made for an order under section 2 of this Act, until the determination of the proceedings on that application.

21–22   [*Repealed*]

23   Determination of date on which representation was first taken out

In considering for the purposes of this Act when representation with respect to the estate of a deceased person was first taken out, a grant limited to settled land or to trust property shall be left out of account, and a grant limited to real estate or to personal estate shall be left out of account unless a grant limited to the remainder of the estate has previously been made or is made at the same time.

24   Effect of this Act on s.46(1)(vi)of Administration of Estates Act 1925

Section 46(1)(vi) of the Administration of Estates Act 1925, in so far as it provides for the devolution of property on the Crown, the Duchy of Lancaster or the Duke of Cornwall as *bona vacantia*, shall have effect subject to the provisions of this Act.

25   Interpretation

(1)   In this Act –
'beneficiary', in relation to the estate of a deceased person, means –

(a)   a person who under the will of the deceased or under the law relating to intestacy is beneficially interested in the estate or would be so interested if an order had not been made under this Act, and

(b)   a person who has received any sum of money or other property which by virtue of section 8(1) or 8(2) of this Act is treated as part of the net estate of the deceased or would have received that sum or other property if an order had not been made under this Act;

'child' includes an illegitimate child and a child *en ventre sa mere* at the death of the deceased;

'the court' unless the context otherwise requires means the High Court, or where a county court has jurisdiction by virtue of section 22 of this Act, a county court;

'former civil partner' means a person whose civil partnership with the deceased was during the lifetime of the deceased either –

(a) dissolved or annulled by an order made under the law of any part of the British Islands, or

(b) dissolved or annulled in any country or territory outside the British Islands by a dissolution or annulment which is entitled to be recognised as valid by the law of England and Wales;

'former spouse' means a person whose marriage with the deceased was during the lifetime of the deceased either –

(a) dissolved or annulled by a decree of divorce or a decree of nullity of marriage granted under the law of any part of the British Islands, or

(b) dissolved or annulled in any country or territory outside the British Islands by a divorce or annulment which is entitled to be recognised as valid by the law of England and Wales;

'net estate', in relation to a deceased person, means –

(a) all property of which the deceased had power to dispose by his will (otherwise than by virtue of a special power of appointment) less the amount of his funeral, testamentary and administration expenses, debts and liabilities, including any inheritance tax payable out of his estate on his death;

(b) any property in respect of which the deceased held a general power of appointment (not being a power exercisable by will) which has not been exercised;

(c) any sum of money or other property which is treated for the purposes of this Act as part of the net estate of the deceased by virtue of section 8(1) or (2) of this Act;

(d) any property which is treated for the purposes of this Act as part of the net estate of the deceased by virtue of an order made under section 9 of the Act;

(e) any sum of money or other property which is, by reason of a disposition or contract made by the deceased, ordered under section 10 or 11 of this Act to be provided for the purpose of the making of financial provision under this Act;

'property' includes any chose in action;

'reasonable financial provision' has the meaning assigned to it by section 1 of this Act;

'valuable consideration' does not include marriage or a promise of marriage;

'will' includes codicil.

(2) For the purposes of paragraph (a) of the definition of 'net estate' in subsection (1) above a person who is not of full age and capacity shall be treated as having power to dispose by will of all property of which he would have had power to dispose by will if he had been of full age and capacity.

(3) Any reference in this Act to provision out of the net estate of a deceased person includes a reference to provision extending to the whole of that estate.

(4) For the purposes of this Act any reference to a spouse, wife or husband shall be treated as including a reference to a person who in good faith entered into a void marriage with the deceased unless either –

(a) the marriage of the deceased and that person was dissolved or annulled during the lifetime of the deceased and the dissolution or annulment is recognised by the law of England and Wales, or

(b) that person has during the lifetime of the deceased formed a subsequent marriage or civil partnership.

(4A) For the purposes of this Act any reference to a civil partner shall be treated as including a reference to a person who in good faith formed a void civil partnership with the deceased unless either –

(a) the civil partnership between the deceased and that person was dissolved or annulled during the lifetime of the deceased and the dissolution or annulment is recognised by the law of England and Wales, or

(b) that person has during the lifetime of the deceased formed a subsequent civil partnership or marriage.

(5) Any reference in this Act to the formation of, or to a person who has formed, a subsequent marriage or civil partnership includes (as the case may be) a reference to the formation of, or to a person who has formed, a marriage or civil partnership which is by law void or voidable.

(5A) The formation of a marriage or civil partnership shall be treated for the purposes of this Act as the formation of a subsequent marriage or civil partnership, in relation to either of the spouses or civil partners, notwithstanding that the previous marriage or civil partnership of that spouse or civil partner was void or voidable.

(6) Any reference in this Act to an order or decree made under the Matrimonial Causes Act 1973 or under any section of that Act shall be construed as including a reference to an order or decree which is deemed to have been made under that Act or under that section thereof, as the case may be.

(6A) Any reference in this Act to an order made under, or under any provision of, the Civil Partnership Act 2004 shall be construed as including a reference to anything which is deemed to be an order made (as the case may be) under that Act or provision.

(7) Any reference in this Act to any enactment is a reference to that enactment as amended by or under any subsequent enactment.

26 Consequential amendments, repeals and transitional provisions

(1) . . .

(2) Subject to the provisions of this section, the enactments specified in the Schedule to this Act are hereby repealed to the extent specified in the third column of the Schedule; . . .

(3) The repeal of the said enactment shall not affect their operation in relation to any application made thereunder (whether before or after the commencement of this Act) with reference to the death of any person who died before the commencement of this Act.

(4) Without prejudice to the provisions of section 38 of the Interpretation Act 1889 (which relates to the effect of repeals) nothing in any repeal made by this Act shall affect any order made or direction given under any enactment repealed by this Act, and, subject to the provisions of this Act, every such order or direction (other than an order made under section 4A of the Inheritance (Family Provision) Act 1938 or section 28A of the Matrimonial Causes Act 1965) shall, if it is in force at the commencement of this Act or is made by virtue of subsection (2) above, continue in force as if it had been made under section 2(1)(a) of

this Act, and for the purposes of section 6(7) of this Act the court in exercising its powers under that section in relation to an order continued in force by this subsection shall be required to have regard to any change in any of the circumstances to which the court would have been required to have regard when making that order if the order had been made with reference to the death of any person who died after the commencement of this Act.

27 Short title, commencement and extent

(1) This Act may be cited as the Inheritance (Provision for Family and Dependants) Act 1975.

(2) This Act does not extend to Scotland or Northern Ireland.

(3) This Act shall come into force on 1st April 1976.

SCHEDULE

ENACTMENTS REPEALED

Section 26

Chapter	Short Title	Extent of Repeal
1938 c 72	The Inheritance (Family Provision) Act 1938	The whole Act.
1952 c 64	The Intestates' Estates Act 1952	Section 7 and Schedule 3.
1965 c 72	The Matrimonial Causes Act 1965	Section 26 to 28(A) and section 25(4) and (5) as applied by section 28(2).
1966 c 35	The Family Provision Act 1966	The whole Act, except section 1 and subsections (1) and (3) of section 10.
1969 c 46	The Family Law Reform Act 1969	Sections 5(1) and 18.
1970 c 31	The Administration of Justice Act 1970	In Schedule 2, paragraph 16.
1970 c 33	The Law Reform (Miscellaneous Provisions) Act 1970	Section 6.
1970 c 45	The Matrimonial Proceedings and Property Act 1970	Section 36.
1971 c 23	The Courts Act 1971	Section 45(1)(a).
1973 c 18	The Matrimonial Causes Act 1973	In section 50, in sub-section (1)(a) the words from 'and sections 26' to the end of the paragraph, in sub-section (1)(d) the words 'or sections 26 to 28A of the Matrimonial Causes Act 1965' and in subsection (2)(a) the words 'or under section 26 or 27 of the Matrimonial Causes Act 1965'. In Schedule 2, paragraph 5(1) and in paragraph 12 the words '(a) sections 26 to 28A of the Matrimonial Causes Act 1965'.
1975 c 7	The Finance Act 1975	In Schedule 12, paragraph 6.

157

Intestate Succession (Interest and Capitalisation) Order 1977, SI 1977/1491

1   Citation and Interpretation

(1)   This Order may be cited as the Intestate Succession (Interest and Capitalisation) Order 1977 and shall come into operation on 15th September 1977.

(2)   The Interpretation Act 1889 shall apply to the interpretation of this Order as it applies to the interpretation of an Act of Parliament.

2   Interest of Statutory Legacy

For the purposes of section 46(1)(i) of the Administration of Estates Act 1925, as it applies both in respect of persons dying before 1953 and in respect of persons dying after 1952, the specified rate of interest shall be 6 per cent, per annum.

3   Capitalisation of Life Interests

(1)   Where after the coming into operation of this Order an election is exercised in accordance with subsection (6) or (7) of section 47A of the Administration of Estates Act 1925, the capital value of the life interest of the surviving spouse or civil partner shall be reckoned in accordance with the following provisions of this article.

(2)   There shall be ascertained, by reference to the index compiled by the Financial Times, The Institute of Actuaries and the Faculty of Actuaries, the average gross redemption yield on medium coupon fifteen-year Government Stocks at the date on which the election was exercised or, if the index was not compiled on that date, by reference to the index on the last date before that date on which it was compiled; and the column which corresponds to that yield in whichever of the Tables set out in the Schedule hereto is applicable to the sex of the surviving spouse or civil partner shall be the appropriate column for the purposes of paragraph (3) of this article.

(3)   The capital value for the purposes of paragraph (1) of this article is the product of the part of the residuary estate (whether or not yielding income) in respect of which the election was exercised and the multiplier shown in the appropriate column opposite the age which the surviving spouse or civil partner had attained at the date on which the election was exercised.

SCHEDULE

Table 1 (see pages 160–2)

Multiplier to be applied to the part of the residuary estate in respect of which the election is exercised to obtain the capital value of the life interest of a surviving husband or a surviving male civil partner, when the average gross redemption yield on medium coupon fifteen-year Government Stocks is at the rate shown.

Age last birthday of husband or civil partner	Less than 8.5%	8.5% or between 8.5% and 9.5%	9.5% or between 9.5% and 10.5%	10.5% or between 10.5% and 11.5%	11.5% or between 11.5% and 12.5%	12.5% or between 12.5% and 13.5%	13.5% or between 13.5% and 14.5%	14.5% or between 14.5% and 15.5%	15.5% or more
16	0.882	0.897	0.908	0.917	0.923	0.927	0.931	0.934	0.936
17	0.879	0.895	0.906	0.915	0.921	0.926	0.930	0.933	0.935
18	0.876	0.892	0.904	0.913	0.920	0.925	0.929	0.932	0.934
19	0.873	0.890	0.902	0.911	0.918	0.923	0.928	0.931	0.933
20	0.870	0.887	0.900	0.909	0.917	0.922	0.926	0.930	0.933
21	0.866	0.884	0.897	0.907	0.915	0.921	0.925	0.929	0.932
22	0.863	0.881	0.895	0.905	0.913	0.919	0.924	0.928	0.931
23	0.859	0.878	0.892	0.903	0.911	0.918	0.923	0.927	0.930
24	0.855	0.875	0.890	0.901	0.909	0.916	0.921	0.925	0.929
25	0.852	0.872	0.887	0.898	0.907	0.914	0.920	0.924	0.928
26	0.847	0.868	0.884	0.896	0.905	0.912	0.918	0.923	0.926
27	0.843	0.864	0.880	0.893	0.903	0.910	0.916	0.921	0.925
28	0.838	0.860	0.877	0.890	0.900	0.908	0.914	0.919	0.923
29	0.834	0.856	0.873	0.887	0.897	0.905	0.912	0.917	0.922
30	0.828	0.851	0.869	0.883	0.894	0.903	0.910	0.915	0.920
31	0.823	0.847	0.865	0.879	0.891	0.900	0.907	0.913	0.918
32	0.818	0.842	0.861	0.876	0.887	0.897	0.904	0.911	0.916
33	0.812	0.837	0.856	0.871	0.884	0.893	0.901	0.908	0.913
34	0.806	0.831	0.851	0.867	0.880	0.890	0.898	0.905	0.911
35	0.799	0.825	0.846	0.862	0.875	0.886	0.895	0.902	0.908
36	0.792	0.819	0.840	0.857	0.871	0.882	0.891	0.899	0.905
37	0.785	0.813	0.834	0.852	0.866	0.878	0.887	0.895	0.902
38	0.778	0.806	0.828	0.846	0.861	0.873	0.883	0.891	0.898
39	0.771	0.799	0.822	0.840	0.856	0.868	0.879	0.887	0.894
40	0.763	0.792	0.815	0.834	0.850	0.863	0.874	0.883	0.890
41	0.755	0.784	0.808	0.828	0.844	0.857	0.869	0.878	0.886
42	0.746	0.776	0.801	0.821	0.838	0.852	0.863	0.873	0.881
43	0.737	0.768	0.793	0.814	0.831	0.845	0.857	0.868	0.876
44	0.728	0.759	0.785	0.806	0.824	0.839	0.851	0.862	0.871
45	0.719	0.750	0.776	0.798	0.816	0.832	0.845	0.856	0.866

Age last birthday of husband or civil partner	Less than 8.5%	8.5% or between 8.5% and 9.5%	9.5% or between 9.5% and 10.5%	10.5% or between 10.5% and 11.5%	11.5% or between 11.5% and 12.5%	12.5% or between 12.5% and 13.5%	13.5% or between 13.5% and 14.5%	14.5% or between 14.5% and 15.5	15.5% or more
46	0.709	0.741	0.768	0.790	0.809	0.825	0.838	0.850	0.860
47	0.699	0.731	0.758	0.781	0.801	0.817	0.831	0.843	0.853
48	0.688	0.721	0.749	0.772	0.792	0.809	0.823	0.836	0.847
49	0.678	0.711	0.739	0.763	0.783	0.800	0.815	0.828	0.839
50	0.666	0.700	0.729	0.753	0.774	0.791	0.807	0.820	0.832
51	0.655	0.689	0.718	0.743	0.764	0.782	0.798	0.812	0.824
52	0.613	0.678	0.707	0.732	0.754	0.772	0.789	0.803	0.815
53	0.631	0.666	0.695	0.721	0.743	0.762	0.779	0.794	0.807
54	0.619	0.654	0.684	0.710	0.732	0.752	0.769	0.784	0.797
55	0.606	0.641	0.671	0.698	0.721	0.741	0.758	0.774	0.787
56	0.594	0.628	0.659	0.685	0.709	0.729	0.747	0.763	0.777
57	0.580	0.615	0.646	0.673	0.696	0.717	0.735	0.752	0.766
58	0.567	0.602	0.633	0.660	0.683	0.705	0.723	0.740	0.755
59	0.553	0.588	0.619	0.646	0.670	0.692	0.711	0.728	0.743
60	0.539	0.574	0.605	0.632	0.657	0.678	0.698	0.715	0.731
61	0.525	0.560	0.590	0.618	0.642	0.664	0.684	0.702	0.718
62	0.510	0.545	0.576	0.603	0.628	0.650	0.670	0.688	0.704
63	0.496	0.530	0.561	0.588	0.613	0.636	0.656	0.674	0.691
64	0.481	0.515	0.546	0.573	0.598	0.621	0.641	0.659	0.676
65	0.466	0.500	0.530	0.558	0.583	0.605	0.626	0.644	0.661
66	0.451	0.485	0.515	0.542	0.567	0.590	0.610	0.629	0.646
67	0.436	0.469	0.499	0.526	0.551	0.574	0.594	0.613	0.631
68	0.421	0.454	0.483	0.510	0.535	0.557	0.578	0.597	0.615
69	0.407	0.438	0.467	0.494	0.518	0.541	0.562	0.581	0.598
70	0.392	0.423	0.452	0.478	0.502	0.524	0.545	0.564	0.582
71	0.377	0.407	0.436	0.462	0.485	0.508	0.528	0.547	0.565
72	0.362	0.392	0.420	0.445	0.469	0.491	0.511	0.530	0.548
73	0.348	0.377	0.404	0.429	0.452	0.474	0.494	0.513	0.531
74	0.333	0.362	0.388	0.413	0.436	0.457	0.477	0.496	0.513
75	0.319	0.347	0.373	0.397	0.419	0.441	0.460	0.479	0.496

Age last birthday of husband or civil partner	Less than 8.5%	8.5% or between 8.5% and 9.5%	9.5% or between 9.5% and 10.5%	10.5% or between 10.5% and 11.5%	11.5% or between 11.5% and 12.5%	12.5% or between 12.5% and 13.5%	13.5% or between 13.5% and 14.5%	14.5% or between 14.5% and 15.5	15.5% or more
76	0.305	0.332	0.357	0.381	0.403	0.424	0.443	0.461	0.479
77	0.292	0.318	0.342	0.365	0.387	0.407	0.426	0.444	0.461
78	0.278	0.304	0.328	0.350	0.371	0.391	0.410	0.427	0.444
79	0.265	0.290	0.313	0.335	0.355	0.375	0.393	0.410	0.427
80	0.253	0.277	0.299	0.320	0.340	0.359	0.377	0.394	0.410
81	0.241	0.264	0.285	0.306	0.325	0.343	0.361	0.377	0.393
82	0.229	0.251	0.272	0.292	0.310	0.328	0.345	0.361	0.377
83	0.218	0.239	0.259	0.278	0.296	0.313	0.330	0.346	0.361
84	0.207	0.227	0.246	0.265	0.282	0.299	0.315	0.331	0.345
85	0.196	0.216	0.234	0.252	0.269	0.285	0.301	0.316	0.330
86	0.186	0.205	0.223	0.240	0.256	0.272	0.287	0.302	0.315
87	0.177	0.195	0.212	0.228	0.244	0.259	0.274	0.288	0.301
88	0.168	0.185	0.201	0.217	0.232	0.247	0.261	0.275	0.288
89	0.159	0.176	0.191	0.207	0.221	0.235	0.249	0.262	0.275
90	0.151	0.167	0.182	0.197	0.211	0.224	0.237	0.250	0.262
91	0.144	0.159	0.173	0.187	0.201	0.214	0.227	0.239	0.251
92	0.137	0.151	0.165	0.179	0.192	0.205	0.217	0.229	0.240
93	0.130	0.144	0.158	0.171	0.183	0.196	0.208	0.219	0.230
94	0.124	0.138	0.151	0.163	0.175	0.187	0.199	0.210	0.221
95	0.119	0.132	0.144	0.156	0.168	0.179	0.190	0.201	0.212
96	0.113	0.126	0.138	0.149	0.161	0.172	0.182	0.193	0.203
97	0.108	0.120	0.132	0.143	0.154	0.164	0.175	0.185	0.195
98	0.103	0.115	0.126	0.137	0.147	0.157	0.167	0.177	0.187
99	0.098	0.109	0.119	0.130	0.140	0.150	0.159	0.169	0.178
100 and over	0.093	0.103	0.112	0.123	0.133	0.143	0.151	0.161	0.169

Table 2 (see pages 164–6)

Multiplier to be applied to the part of the residuary estate in respect of which the election is exercised to obtain the capital value of the life interest of a surviving wife or a surviving female civil partner, when the average gross redemption yield on medium coupon fifteen-year Government Stocks is at the rate shown.

Age last birthday of wife or civil partner	Less than 8.5%	8.5% or between 8.5% and 9.5%	9.5% or between 9.5% and 10.5%	10.5% or between 10.5% and 11.5%	11.5% or between 11.5% and 12.5%	12.5% or between 12.5% and 13.5%	13.5% or between 13.5% and 14.5%	14.5% or between 14.5% and 15.5	15.5% or more
16	0.892	0.905	0.915	0.922	0.927	0.930	0.933	0.936	0.937
17	0.889	0.903	0.913	0.920	0.925	0.929	0.933	0.935	0.937
18	0.887	0.901	0.911	0.919	0.924	0.929	0.932	0.934	0.936
19	0.884	0.899	0.910	0.917	0.923	0.928	0.931	0.934	0.936
20	0.882	0.897	0.908	0.916	0.922	0.927	0.930	0.933	0.935
21	0.879	0.895	0.906	0.915	0.921	0.926	0.929	0.932	0.934
22	0.877	0.893	0.904	0.913	0.920	0.925	0.928	0.931	0.934
23	0.874	0.890	0.902	0.911	0.918	0.923	0.927	0.931	0.933
24	0.871	0.888	0.900	0.910	0.917	0.922	0.926	0.930	0.932
25	0.868	0.885	0.898	0.908	0.915	0.921	0.925	0.929	0.932
26	0.864	0.882	0.896	0.906	0.914	0.920	0.924	0.928	0.931
27	0.861	0.879	0.893	0.904	0.912	0.918	0.923	0.927	0.930
28	0.857	0.876	0.891	0.901	0.910	0.916	0.921	0.925	0.929
29	0.853	0.873	0.888	0.899	0.908	0.915	0.920	0.924	0.928
30	0.849	0.869	0.885	0.896	0.906	0.913	0.918	0.923	0.926
31	0.845	0.866	0.882	0.894	0.903	0.911	0.916	0.921	0.925
32	0.840	0.862	0.878	0.891	0.901	0.908	0.914	0.919	0.923
33	0.836	0.858	0.875	0.888	0.898	0.906	0.912	0.918	0.922
34	0.831	0.853	0.871	0.884	0.895	0.903	0.910	0.916	0.920
35	0.826	0.849	0.867	0.881	0.892	0.901	0.908	0.913	0.918
36	0.820	0.844	0.863	0.877	0.889	0.898	0.905	0.911	0.916
37	0.815	0.839	0.858	0.873	0.885	0.895	0.902	0.909	0.914
38	0.809	0.834	0.853	0.869	0.881	0.891	0.899	0.906	0.911
39	0.803	0.828	0.848	0.864	0.877	0.888	0.896	0.903	0.909
40	0.796	0.822	0.843	0.860	0.873	0.884	0.893	0.900	0.906
41	0.790	0.816	0.838	0.855	0.869	0.880	0.889	0.897	0.903
42	0.783	0.810	0.832	0.850	0.864	0.876	0.885	0.893	0.900
43	0.775	0.803	0.826	0.844	0.859	0.871	0.881	0.889	0.896
44	0.768	0.796	0.820	0.838	0.854	0.866	0.877	0.885	0.893
45	0.760	0.789	0.813	0.832	0.848	0.861	0.872	0.881	0.889

Age last birthday of wife or civil partner	Less than 8.5%	8.5% or between 8.5% and 9.5%	9.5% or between 9.5% and 10.5%	10.5% or between 10.5% and 11.5%	11.5% or between 11.5% and 12.5%	12.5% or between 12.5% and 13.5%	13.5% or between 13.5% and 14.5%	14.5% or between 14.5% and 15.5%	15.5% or more
46	0.752	0.782	0.806	0.826	0.842	0.856	0.867	0.876	0.885
47	0.744	0.774	0.799	0.819	0.836	0.850	0.862	0.872	0.880
48	0.735	0.766	0.791	0.812	0.829	0.844	0.856	0.866	0.875
49	0.726	0.757	0.783	0.804	0.822	0.837	0.850	0.861	0.870
50	0.716	0.748	0.775	0.797	0.815	0.831	0.844	0.855	0.865
51	0.707	0.739	0.766	0.788	0.807	0.823	0.837	0.849	0.859
52	0.697	0.729	0.757	0.780	0.799	0.816	0.830	0.842	0.853
53	0.686	0.719	0.747	0.771	0.791	0.808	0.822	0.835	0.846
54	0.676	0.709	0.737	0.761	0.782	0.799	0.814	0.827	0.839
55	0.664	0.698	0.727	0.751	0.772	0.790	0.806	0.820	0.831
56	0.653	0.687	0.716	0.741	0.763	0.781	0.797	0.811	0.823
57	0.641	0.676	0.705	0.730	0.752	0.771	0.788	0.802	0.815
58	0.629	0.664	0.693	0.719	0.741	0.761	0.778	0.793	0.806
59	0.616	0.651	0.681	0.707	0.730	0.750	0.767	0.783	0.796
60	0.603	0.638	0.669	0.695	0.718	0.739	0.757	0.772	0.786
61	0.590	0.625	0.656	0.683	0.706	0.727	0.745	0.761	0.776
62	0.577	0.612	0.643	0.670	0.693	0.715	0.733	0.750	0.764
63	0.563	0.598	0.629	0.656	0.680	0.702	0.721	0.738	0.753
64	0.549	0.584	0.615	0.642	0.667	0.688	0.708	0.725	0.740
65	0.534	0.569	0.600	0.628	0.653	0.674	0.694	0.712	0.728
66	0.520	0.555	0.586	0.613	0.638	0.660	0.680	0.698	0.714
67	0.505	0.540	0.570	0.598	0.623	0.645	0.666	0.684	0.700
68	0.490	0.524	0.555	0.583	0.608	0.630	0.651	0.669	0.686
69	0.475	0.509	0.539	0.567	0.592	0.615	0.635	0.654	0.671
70	0.459	0.493	0.523	0.551	0.576	0.599	0.619	0.638	0.655
71	0.444	0.477	0.507	0.535	0.560	0.582	0.603	0.622	0.640
72	0.428	0.461	0.491	0.518	0.543	0.566	0.586	0.606	0.623
73	0.413	0.445	0.475	0.501	0.526	0.549	0.570	0.589	0.606
74	0.398	0.429	0.458	0.485	0.509	0.532	0.552	0.572	0.589
75	0.382	0.413	0.442	0.468	0.492	0.514	0.535	0.554	0.572

Age last birthday of wife or civil partner	Less than 8.5%	8.5% or between 8.5% and 9.5%	9.5% or between 9.5% and 10.5%	10.5% or between 10.5% and 11.5%	11.5% or between 11.5% and 12.5%	12.5% or between 12.5% and 13.5%	13.5% or between 13.5% and 14.5%	14.5% or between 14.5% and 15.5%	15.5% or more
76	0.367	0.397	0.425	0.451	0.475	0.497	0.517	0.536	0.554
77	0.352	0.381	0.408	0.434	0.457	0.479	0.499	0.518	0.536
78	0.337	0.365	0.392	0.417	0.440	0.461	0.482	0.500	0.518
79	0.322	0.350	0.376	0.400	0.423	0.444	0.464	0.482	0.500
80	0.307	0.334	0.360	0.393	0.406	0.426	0.446	0.464	0.482
81	0.293	0.319	0.344	0.367	0.389	0.409	0.428	0.446	0.463
82	0.279	0.304	0.328	0.351	0.372	0.392	0.410	0.428	0.445
83	0.265	0.290	0.313	0.335	0.355	0.375	0.393	0.410	0.427
84	0.252	0.276	0.298	0.319	0.339	0.358	0.376	0.393	0.409
85	0.239	0.262	0.284	0.304	0.323	0.342	0.359	0.376	0.392
86	0.227	0.249	0.269	0.289	0.308	0.326	0.343	0.359	0.374
87	0.215	0.236	0.256	0.275	0.293	0.310	0.327	0.342	0.357
88	0.204	0.224	0.243	0.261	0.279	0.295	0.311	0.327	0.341
89	0.193	0.212	0.230	0.248	0.265	0.281	0.296	0.311	0.325
90	0.182	0.201	0.218	0.235	0.251	0.267	0.282	0.296	0.310
91	0.173	0.190	0.207	0.223	0.239	0.254	0.268	0.282	0.296
92	0.164	0.180	0.197	0.212	0.227	0.242	0.256	0.269	0.282
93	0.155	0.171	0.187	0.202	0.216	0.230	0.243	0.256	0.269
94	0.147	0.162	0.177	0.192	0.205	0.219	0.232	0.244	0.256
95	0.139	0.154	0.168	0.182	0.195	0.208	0.221	0.233	0.244
96	0.132	0.146	0.159	0.173	0.185	0.198	0.210	0.222	0.233
97	0.125	0.138	0.151	0.164	0.176	0.188	0.199	0.211	0.222
98	0.118	0.130	0.143	0.155	0.167	0.178	0.189	0.200	0.210
99	0.110	0.122	0.134	0.146	0.157	0.168	0.178	0.189	0.199
100 and over	0.102	0.114	0.125	0.137	0.147	0.158	0.167	0.178	0.188

APPENDIX A5

Inheritance Tax Act 1984, ss.49, 49A–E, 142 and 146

CHAPTER II   INTERESTS IN POSSESSION, REVERSIONARY INTERESTS AND SETTLEMENT POWERS

49   Treatment of interests in possession

(1)   A person beneficially entitled to an interest in possession in settled property shall be treated for the purposes of this Act as beneficially entitled to the property in which the interest subsists.

(1A)   Where the interest in possession mentioned in subsection (1) above is one to which the person becomes beneficially entitled on or after 22nd March 2006, subsection (1) above applies in relation to that interest only if, and for so long as, it is –

    (a)   an immediate post-death interest,

    (b)   a disabled person's interest, or

    (c)   a transitional serial interest.

(1B)   Where the interest in possession mentioned in subsection (1) above is one to which the person became beneficially entitled before 22nd March, subsection (1) above does not apply in relation to that interest at any time when section 71A below applies to the property in which the interest subsists.

(2)   Where a person becomes entitled to an interest in possession in settled property as a result of a disposition for a consideration in money or money's worth, any question whether and to what extent the giving of the consideration is a transfer of value or chargeable transfer shall be determined without regard to subsection (1) above.

(3)   . . .

49A   Immediate post-death interest

(1)   Where a person ('L') is beneficially entitled to an interest in possession in settled property, for the purposes of this Chapter that interest is an 'immediate post-death interest' only if the following conditions are satisfied.

(2)   Condition 1 is that the settlement was effected by will or under the law relating to intestacy.

(3)   Condition 2 is that L became beneficially entitled to the interest in possession on the death of the testator or intestate.

(4)   Condition 3 is that –

    (a)   section 71A below does not apply to the property in which the interest subsists, and

    (b)   the interest is not a disabled person's interest.

(5)   Condition 4 is that Condition 3 has been satisfied at all times since L became beneficially entitled to the interest in possession.

49B   Transitional serial interests

Where a person is beneficially entitled to an interest in possession in settled property, for the purposes of this Chapter that interest is a 'transitional serial interest' only –

(a)   if section 49C or 49D below so provides, or
(b)   if, and to the extent that, section 49E below so provides.

49C   Transitional serial interest: interest to which person becomes entitled during period 22nd March 2006 to 5th April 2008

(1)   Where a person ('B') is beneficially entitled to an interest in possession in settled property ('the current interest'), that interest is a transitional serial interest for the purposes of this Chapter if the following conditions are met.
(2)   Condition 1 is that –

(a)   the settlement commenced before 22nd March 2006, and
(b)   immediately before 22nd March 2006, the property then comprised in the settlement was property in which B, or some other person, was beneficially entitled to an interest in possession ('the prior interest').

(3)   Condition 2 is that the prior interest came to an end at a time on or after 22nd March 2006 but before 6th April 2008.
(4)   Condition 3 is that B became beneficially entitled to the current interest at that time.
(5)   Condition 4 is that –

(a)   section 71A below does not apply to the property in which the interest subsists, and
(b)   the interest is not a disabled person's interest.

49D   Transitional serial interest: interest to which person becomes entitled on death of spouse or civil partner on or after 6th April 2008

(1)   Where a person ('E') is beneficially entitled to an interest in possession in settled property ('the successor interest'), that interest is a transitional serial interest for the purposes of this Chapter if the following conditions are met.
(2)   Condition 1 is that –

(a)   the settlement commenced before 22nd March 2006, and
(b)   immediately before 22nd March 2006, the property then comprised in the settlement was property in which a person other than E was beneficially entitled to an interest in possession ('the previous interest').

(3)   Condition 2 is that the previous interest came to an end on or after 6th April 2008 on the death of that other person ('F').
(4)   Condition 3 is that, immediately before F died, F was the spouse or civil partner of E.
(5)   Condition 4 is that E became beneficially entitled to the successor interest on F's death.
(6)   Condition 5 is that –

(a) section 71A below does not apply to the property in which the successor interest subsists, and

(b) the successor interest is not a disabled person's interest.

49E Transitional serial interest: contracts of life insurance

(1) Where –

(a) a person ('C') is beneficially entitled to an interest in possession in settled property ('the present interest'), and

(b) on C's becoming beneficially entitled to the present interest, the settled property consisted of, or included, rights under a contract of life insurance entered into before 22nd March 2006,

the present interest so far as subsisting in rights under the contract, or in property comprised in the settlement that directly or indirectly represents rights under the contract, is a 'transitional serial interest' for the purposes of this Chapter if the following conditions are met.

(2) Condition 1 is that –

(a) the settlement commenced before 22nd March 2006, and

(b) immediately before 22nd March 2006 –

(i) the property then comprised in the settlement consisted of, or included, rights under the contract, and

(ii) those rights were property in which C, or some other person, was beneficially entitled to an interest in possession ('the earlier interest').

(3) Condition 2 is that –

(a) the earlier interest came to an end at a time on or after 6th April 2008 ('the earlier-interest end-time') on the death of the person beneficially entitled to it and C became beneficially entitled to the present interest –

(i) at the earlier-interest end-time, or

(ii) on the coming to an end, on the death of the person beneficially entitled to it, of an interest in possession to which that person became beneficially entitled at the earlier-interest end-time, or

(iii) on the coming to an end of the second or last in an unbroken sequence of two or more consecutive interests in possession to the first of which a person became beneficially entitled at the earlier-interest end-time and each of which ended on the death of the person beneficially entitled to it, or

(b) C became beneficially entitled to the present interest –

(i) on the coming to an end, on the death of the person entitled to it, of an interest in possession that is a transitional serial interest under section 49C above, or

(ii) on the coming to an end of the second or last in an unbroken sequence of two or more consecutive interests in possession the first of which was a transitional serial interest under section 49C above and each of which ended on the death of the person beneficially entitled to it.

(4)   Condition 3 is that rights under the contract were comprised in the settlement throughout the period beginning with 22nd March 2006 and ending with C's becoming beneficially entitled to the present interest.

(5)   Condition 4 is that –

(a)   section 71A below does not apply to the property in which the present interest subsists, and

(b)   the present interest is not a disabled person's interest.

PART V MISCELLANEOUS RELIEFS

Changes in distribution of deceased's estate, etc.

142   Alteration of dispositions taking effect on death

(1)   Where within the period of two years after a person's death –

(a)   any of the dispositions (whether effected by will, under the law relating to intestacy or otherwise) of the property comprised in his estate immediately before his death are varied, or

(b)   the benefit conferred by any of those dispositions is disclaimed,

by an instrument in writing made by the persons or any of the persons who benefit or would benefit under the dispositions, this Act shall apply as if the variation had been effected by the deceased or, as the case may be, the disclaimed benefit had never been conferred.

(2)   Subsection (1) above shall not apply to a variation unless the instrument contains a statement, made by all the relevant persons, to the effect that they intend the subsection to apply to the variation.

(2A) For the purposes of subsection (2) above the relevant persons are –

(a)   the person or persons making the instrument, and

(b)   where the variation results in additional tax being payable, the personal representatives.

Personal representatives may decline to make a statement under subsection (2) above only if no, or no sufficient, assets are held by them in that capacity for discharging the additional tax.

(3)   Subsection (1) above shall not apply to a variation or disclaimer made for any consideration in money or money's worth other than consideration consisting of the making, in respect of another of the dispositions, of a variation or disclaimer to which that subsection applies.

(4)   Where a variation to which subsection (1) above applies results in property being held in trust for a person for a period which ends not more than two years after the death, this Act shall apply as if the disposition of the property that takes effect at the end of the period had had effect from the beginning of the period; but this subsection shall not affect the application of this Act in relation to any distribution or application of property occurring before that disposition takes effect.

(5)   For the purposes of subsection (1) above the property comprised in a person's estate includes any excluded property but not any property to which he is treated as entitled by virtue of section 49(1) above or section 102 of the Finance Act 1986.

(6)   Subsection (1) above applies whether or not the administration of the estate is complete or the property concerned has been distributed in accordance with the original dispositions.

(7) In the application of subsection (4) above to Scotland, property which is subject to a proper liferent shall be deemed to be held in trust for the liferenter.

146 Inheritance (Provision for Family and Dependants) Act 1975

(1) Where an order is made under section 2 of the Inheritance (Provision for Family and Dependants) Act 1975 ('the 1975 Act') in relation to any property forming part of the net estate of a deceased person, then, without prejudice to section 19(1) of that Act, the property shall for the purposes of this Act be treated as if it had on his death devolved subject to the provisions of the order.

(2) Where an order is made under section 10 of the 1975 Act requiring a person to provide any money or other property by reason of a disposition made by the deceased, then –

(a) if that disposition was a chargeable transfer and the personal representatives of the deceased make a claim for the purpose –

  (i) tax paid or payable on the value transferred by that chargeable transfer (whether or not by the claimants) shall be repaid to them by the Board or, as the case may be, shall not be payable, and

  (ii) the rate or rates of tax applicable to the transfer of value made by the deceased on his death shall be determined as if the values previously transferred by chargeable transfers made by him were reduced by that value;

(b) the money or property shall be included in the deceased's estate for the purpose of the transfer of value made by him on his death.

(3) Where the money or other property ordered to be provided under section 10 of the 1975 Act is less than the maximum permitted by that section, subsection (2)(a) above shall have effect in relation to such part of the value there mentioned as is appropriate.

(4) The adjustment in consequence of the provisions of this section or of section 19(1) of the 1975 Act of the tax payable in respect of the transfer of value made by the deceased on his death shall not affect –

(a) the amount of any deduction to be made under section 8 of that Act in respect of tax borne by the person mentioned in subsection (3) of that section, or

(b) the amount of tax to which regard is to be had under section 9(2) of that Act;

and where a person is ordered under that Act to make a payment or transfer property by reason of his holding property treated as part of the deceased's net estate under section 8 or 9 and tax borne by him is taken into account for the purposes of the order, any repayment of that tax shall be made to the personal representatives of the deceased and not to that person.

(5) Tax repaid under paragraph (a)(i) of subsection (2) above shall be included in the deceased's estate for the purposes of the transfer of value made by him on his death; and tax repaid under that paragraph or under subsection (4) above shall form part of the deceased's net estate for the purposes of the 1975 Act.

(6) Anything which is done in compliance with an order under the 1975 Act or occurs on the coming into force of such an order, and which would (apart from this subsection) constitute an occasion on which tax is chargeable under any provision, other than section 79, of Chapter III of Part III of this Act, shall not constitute such an occasion; and where an order under the 1975 Act provides for

property to be settled or for the variation of a settlement, and (apart from this subsection) tax would be charged under section 52(1) above on the coming into force of the order, section 52(1) shall not apply.

(7)   In subsections (2)(a) and (5) above references to tax include references to interest on tax.

(8)   Where an order is made staying or dismissing proceedings under the 1975 Act on terms set out in or scheduled to the order, this section shall have effect as if any of those terms which could have been included in an order under section 2 or 10 of that Act were provisions of such an order.

(9)   In this section any reference to, or to any provision of, the 1975 Act includes a reference to, or to the corresponding provision of, the Inheritance (Provision for Family and Dependants) (Northern Ireland) Order 1979.

APPENDIX A6

Taxation of Chargeable Gains Act 1992, s.62

62 Death: general provisions

(1) For the purposes of this Act the assets of which a deceased person was competent to dispose –

   (a) shall be deemed to be acquired on his death by the personal representatives or other person on whom they devolve for a consideration equal to their market value at the date of the death, but

   (b) shall not be deemed to be disposed of by him on his death (whether or not they were the subject of a testamentary disposition).

(2) Allowable losses sustained by an individual in the year of assessment in which he dies may, so far as they cannot be deducted from chargeable gains accruing in that year, be deducted from chargeable gains accruing to the deceased in the 3 years of assessment preceding the year of assessment in which the death occurs, taking chargeable gains accruing in a later year before those accruing in an earlier year.

(2A) Amounts deductible from chargeable gains for any year in accordance with subsection (2) above shall not be so deductible from any such gains so far as they are gains that are brought into account for that year by virtue of section 2(5)(b).

(2B) Where deductions under subsection (2) above fall to be made from the chargeable gains for any year, the provisions of this Act relating to taper relief shall have effect as if those deductions were deductions under section 2(2)(a) and (b) and, accordingly, as if –

   (a) those deductions were to be made (before the application of the relief) in computing for that year the excess (if any) mentioned in section 2A(1); and

   (b) for the purpose of determining the gains represented in that excess, the gains for that year from which those deductions are treated as made were to be ascertained in accordance with section 2A(6).

(3) In relation to property forming part of the estate of a deceased person the personal representatives shall for the purposes of this Act be treated as being a single and continuing body of persons (distinct from the persons who may from time to time be the personal representatives), and that body shall be treated as having the deceased's residence, ordinary residence, and domicile at the date of death.

(4) On a person acquiring any asset as legatee (as defined in section 64) –

   (a) no chargeable gain shall accrue to the personal representatives, and

   (b) the legatee shall be treated as if the personal representatives' acquisition of the asset had been his acquisition of it.

(5) Notwithstanding section 17(1) no chargeable gain shall accrue to any person on his making a disposal by way of donatio mortis causa.

(6) Subject to subsections (7) and (8) below, where within the period of 2 years after a person's death any of the dispositions (whether effected by will, under the law relating to intestacy or otherwise) of the property of which he was competent to dispose are varied, or the benefit conferred by any of those dispositions is disclaimed, by an instrument in writing made by the persons or any of the persons who benefit or would benefit under the dispositions –

    (a)   the variation or disclaimer shall not constitute a disposal for the purposes of this Act, and

    (b)   this section shall apply as if the variation had been effected by the deceased or, as the case may be, the disclaimed benefit had never been conferred.

(7) Subsection (6) above does not apply to a variation unless the instrument contains a statement by the persons making the instrument to the effect that they intend the subsection to apply to the variation.

(8) Subsection (6) above does not apply to a variation or disclaimer made for any consideration in money or money's worth other than consideration consisting of the making of a variation or disclaimer in respect of another of the dispositions.

(9) Subsection (6) above applies whether or not the administration of the estate is complete or the property has been distributed in accordance with the original dispositions.

(10) In this section references to assets of which a deceased person was competent to dispose are references to assets of the deceased which (otherwise than in right of a power of appointment or of the testamentary power conferred by statute to dispose of entailed interests) he could, if of full age and capacity, have disposed of by his will, assuming that all the assets were situated in England and, if he was not domiciled in the United Kingdom, that he was domiciled in England, and include references to his severable share in any assets to which, immediately before his death, he was beneficially entitled as a joint tenant.

Civil Procedure Rules 1998, SI 1998/3132, Parts 21, 57 and 64 with Practice Directions

PART 21   CHILDREN AND PATIENTS

Scope of this Part

21.1   (1)   This Part –

(a)   contains special provisions which apply in proceedings involving children and patients; and

(b)   sets out how a person becomes a litigation friend.

(2)   In this Part –

(a)   'child' means a person under 18; and

(b)   'patient' means a person who by reason of mental disorder within the meaning of the Mental Health Act 1983 is incapable of managing and administering his property and affairs.

(Rule 6.6 contains provisions about the service of documents on children and patients)
(Rule 48.5 deals with costs where money is payable by or to a child or patient)

Requirement for litigation friend in proceedings by or against children and patients

21.2   (1)   A patient must have a litigation friend to conduct proceedings on his behalf.

(2)   A child must have a litigation friend to conduct proceedings on his behalf unless the court makes an order under paragraph (3).

(3)   The court may make an order permitting the child to conduct proceedings without a litigation friend.

(4)   An application for an order under paragraph (3) –

(a)   may be made by the child;

(b)   if the child already has a litigation friend, must be made on notice to the litigation friend; and

(c)   if the child has no litigation friend, may be made without notice.

(5)   Where –

(a)   the court has made an order under paragraph (3); and

(b)   it subsequently appears to the court that it is desirable for a litigation friend to conduct the proceedings on behalf of the child,

the court may appoint a person to be the child's litigation friend.

Stage of proceedings at which a litigation friend becomes necessary

21.3   (1)   This rule does not apply where the court has made an order under rule 21.2(3).

        (2)   A person may not, without the permission of the court –

               (a)   make an application against a child or patient before proceedings have started; or

               (b)   take any step in proceedings except –

                      (i)   issuing and serving a claim form; or

                      (ii)   applying for the appointment of a litigation friend under rule 21.6,

               until the child or patient has a litigation friend.

        (3)   If a party becomes a patient during proceedings, no party may take any step in the proceedings without the permission of the court until the patient has a litigation friend.

        (4)   Any step taken before a child or patient has a litigation friend shall be of no effect unless the court otherwise orders.

Who may be a litigation friend without a court order

21.4   (1)   This rule does not apply if the court has appointed a person to be a litigation friend.

        (2)   A person authorised under Part VII of the Mental Health Act 1983 to conduct legal proceedings in the name of a patient or on his behalf is entitled to be the litigation friend of the patient in any proceedings to which his authority extends.

        (3)   If nobody has been appointed by the court or, in the case of a patient, authorised under Part VII, a person may act as a litigation friend if he –

               (a)   can fairly and competently conduct proceedings on behalf of the child or patient;

               (b)   has no interest adverse to that of the child or patient; and

               (c)   where the child or patient is a claimant, undertakes to pay any costs which the child or patient may be ordered to pay in relation to the proceedings, subject to any right he may have to be repaid from the assets of the child or patient.

How a person becomes a litigation friend without a court order

21.5   (1)   If the court has not appointed a litigation friend, a person who wishes to act as a litigation friend must follow the procedure set out in this rule.

        (2)   A person authorised under Part VII of the Mental Health Act 1983 must file an official copy of the order or other document which constitutes his authorisation to act.

        (3)   Any other person must file a certificate of suitability stating that he satisfies the conditions specified in rule 21.4(3).

        (4)   A person who is to act as a litigation friend for a claimant must file –

        (a)   the authorisation; or

        (b)   the certificate of suitability,

        at the time when the claim is made.

(5)   A person who is to act as a litigation friend for a defendant must file –

        (a)   the authorisation; or

        (b)   the certificate of suitability,

        at the time when he first takes a step in the proceedings on behalf of the defendant.

(6)   The litigation friend must –

        (a)   serve the certificate of suitability on every person on whom, in accordance with rule 6.6 (service on parent, guardian etc.), the claim form should be served; and

        (b)   file a certificate of service when he files the certificate of suitability.

(Rule 6.10 sets out the details to be contained in a certificate of service)

How a person becomes a litigation friend by court order

21.6   (1)   The court may make an order appointing a litigation friend.

       (2)   An application for an order appointing a litigation friend may be made by –

          (a)   a person who wishes to be the litigation friend; or

          (b)   a party.

       (3)   Where –

          (a)   a person makes a claim against a child or patient;

          (b)   the child or patient has no litigation friend;

          (c)   the court has not made an order under rule 21.2(3) (order that a child can act without a litigation friend); and

          (d)   either –

             (i)   someone who is not entitled to be a litigation friend files a defence; or

             (ii)   the claimant wishes to take some step in the proceedings,

        the claimant must apply to the court for an order appointing a litigation friend for the child or patient.

       (4)   An application for an order appointing a litigation friend must be supported by evidence.

       (5)   The court may not appoint a litigation friend under this rule unless it is satisfied that the person to be appointed complies with the conditions specified in rule 21.4(3).

Court's power to change litigation friend and to prevent person acting as litigation friend

21.7   (1)   The court may –

          (a)   direct that a person may not act as a litigation friend;

          (b)   terminate a litigation friend's appointment;

(c)   appoint a new litigation friend in substitution for an existing one.

(2)   An application for an order under paragraph (1) must be supported by evidence.

(3)   The court may not appoint a litigation friend under this rule unless it is satisfied that the person to be appointed complies with the conditions specified in rule 21.4(3).

Appointment of litigation friend by court order – supplementary

21.8   (1)   An application for an order under rule 21.6 or 21.7 must be served on every person on whom, in accordance with rule 6.6 (service on parent, guardian etc.), the claim form should be served.

(2)   Where an application for an order under rule 21.6 is in respect of a patient, the application must also be served on the patient unless the court orders otherwise.

(3)   An application for an order under rule 21.7 must also be served on –

(a)   the person who is the litigation friend, or who is purporting to act as the litigation friend, when the application is made; and

(b)   the person who it is proposed should be the litigation friend, if he is not the applicant.

(4)   On an application for an order under rule 21.6 or 21.7, the court may appoint the person proposed or any other person who complies with the conditions specified in rule 21.4(3).

Procedure where appointment of litigation friend ceases

21.9   (1)   When a child who is not a patient reaches the age of 18, a litigation friend's appointment ceases.

(2)   When a party ceases to be a patient, the litigation friend's appointment continues until it is ended by a court order.

(3)   An application for an order under paragraph (2) may be made by –

(a)   the former patient;

(b)   the litigation friend; or

(c)   a party.

(4)   The child or patient in respect of whom the appointment to act has ceased must serve notice on the other parties –

(a)   stating that the appointment of his litigation friend to act has ceased;

(b)   giving his address for service; and

(c)   stating whether or not he intends to carry on the proceedings.

(5)   If he does not do so within 28 days after the day on which the appointment of the litigation friend ceases the court may, on application, strike out any claim or defence brought by him.

(6)   The liability of a litigation friend for costs continues until –

(a)   the person in respect of whom his appointment to act has ceased serves the notice referred to in paragraph (4); or

(b) the litigation friend serves notice on the parties that his appointment to act has ceased.

Compromise etc. by or on behalf of child or patient

21.10   (1)   Where a claim is made –

    (a)   by or on behalf of a child or patient; or

    (b)   against a child or patient,

no settlement, compromise or payment and no acceptance of money paid into court shall be valid, so far as it relates to the claim by, on behalf of or against the child or patient, without the approval of the court.

    (2)   Where –

    (a)   before proceedings in which a claim is made by or on behalf of, or against a child or patient (whether alone or with any other person) are begun, an agreement is reached for the settlement of the claim; and

    (b)   the sole purpose of proceedings on that claim is to obtain the approval of the court to a settlement or compromise of the claim,

the claim must –

    (i)   be made using the procedure set out in Part 8 (alternative procedure for claims); and

    (ii)   include a request to the court for approval of the settlement or compromise.

    (3)   In proceedings to which Section II of Part 45 applies, the court shall not make an order for detailed assessment of the costs payable to the child or patient but shall assess the costs in the manner set out in that Section.

(Rule 48.5 contains provisions about costs where money is payable to a child or patient)

Control of money recovered by or on behalf of child or patient

21.11   (1)   Where in any proceedings –

    (a)   money is recovered by or on behalf of or for the benefit of a child or patient; or

    (b)   money paid into court is accepted by or on behalf of a child or patient, the money shall be dealt with in accordance with directions given by the court under this rule and not otherwise.

    (2)   Directions given under this rule may provide that the money shall be wholly or partly paid into court and invested or otherwise dealt with.

Expenses incurred by a litigation friend

21.11A   (1)   In proceedings to which rule 21.11 applies, a litigation friend who incurs expenses on behalf of a child or patient in any proceedings is entitled to recover the amount paid or payable out of any money recovered or paid into court to the extent that it –

(a) has been reasonably incurred; and
(b) is reasonable in amount.

(2) Expenses may include all or part of –

(a) an insurance premium, as defined by rule 43.2(1)(m); or
(b) interest on a loan taken out to pay an insurance premium or other recoverable disbursement.

(3) No application may be made under this rule for expenses that –

(a) are of a type that may be recoverable on an assessment of costs payable by or out of money belonging to a child or patient; but
(b) are disallowed in whole or in part on such an assessment.

(Expenses which are also 'costs' as defined in rule 43.2(1)(a) are dealt with under rule 48.5(2)).

(4) In deciding whether the expense was reasonably incurred and reasonable in amount, the court must have regard to all the circumstances of the case including the factors set out in rule 44.5(3).
(5) When the court is considering the factors to be taken into account in assessing the reasonableness of expenses incurred by the litigation friend on behalf of a child or patient, it will have regard to the facts and circumstances as they reasonably appeared to the litigation friend or child's or patient's legal representative when the expense was incurred.
(6) Where the claim is settled or compromised, or judgment is given, on terms that an amount not exceeding £5,000 is paid to the child or patient, the total amount the litigation friend may recover under paragraph (1) of this rule shall not exceed 25% of the sum so agreed or awarded, unless the Court directs otherwise. Such total amount shall not exceed 50% of the sum so agreed or awarded.

Appointment of guardian of child's estate

21.12 (1) The court may appoint the Official Solicitor to be a guardian of a child's estate where –

(a) money is paid into court on behalf of the child in accordance with directions given under rule 21.11 (control of money received by a child or patient);
(b) the Criminal Injuries Compensation Board or the Criminal Injuries Compensation Authority notifies the court that it has made or intends to make an award to the child;
(c) a court or tribunal outside England and Wales notifies the court that it has ordered or intends to order that money be paid to the child;
(d) the child is absolutely entitled to the proceeds of a pension fund; or
(e) in any other case, such an appointment seems desirable to the court.

(2)   The court may not appoint the Official Solicitor under this rule
        unless –

   (a)   the persons with parental responsibility (within the meaning of
          section 3 of the Children Act 1989 agree; or
   (b)   the court considers that their agreement can be dispensed with.

(3)   The Official Solicitor's appointment may continue only until the child
        reaches 18.

PRACTICE DIRECTION – CHILDREN AND PATIENTS

THIS PRACTICE DIRECTION SUPPLEMENTS CPR PART 21

GENERAL

1.1   In this practice direction 'child' means a person under 18 years old and
        'patient' means a person who by reason of mental disorder within the
        meaning of the Mental Health Act 1983 is incapable of managing and
        administering his property and affairs.
1.2   A patient must bring or defend proceedings by a litigation friend (see
        paragraph 2 below for the definition of a litigation friend).
1.3   In the proceedings referred to in paragraph 1.2 above the patient should be
        referred to in the title as 'A.B. (by C.D. his litigation friend)'.
1.4   A child must bring or defend proceedings by a litigation friend unless the
        court has made an order permitting the child to do so on his own behalf.
1.5   Where:

   (1)   the child has a litigation friend, the child should be referred to in the
          title to proceedings as 'A.B. (a child by C.D. his litigation friend)', and
   (2)   the child is conducting proceedings on his own behalf, the child
          should be referred to in the title as 'A.B. (a child)'.

1.6   The approval of the court must be obtained if a settlement of a claim by or
        against a child or patient is to be valid. A settlement includes an agreement
        on a sum to be apportioned to a dependant child under the Fatal Accidents
        Act 1976.
1.7   The approval of the court must also be obtained before making a voluntary
        interim payment to a child or patient.

(Rule 39.2(3) provides for a hearing or part of a hearing to be in private)

THE LITIGATION FRIEND

2.1   It is the duty of a litigation friend fairly and competently to conduct
        proceedings on behalf of a child or patient. He must have no interest in the
        proceedings adverse to that of the child or patient and all steps and deci-
        sions he takes in the proceedings must be taken for the benefit of the child
        or patient.
2.2   A person may become a litigation friend:

   (1)   of a child –

      (a)   without a court order under the provisions of rule 21.5, or
      (b)   by a court order under rule 21.6, and

(2) of a patient –

    (a) by authorisation under Part VII of the Mental Health Act 1983, or

    (b) by a court order under rule 21.6.

2.3   In order to become a litigation friend without a court order the person who wishes to act as litigation friend must:

    (1) if he wishes to act on behalf of a patient, file an official copy of the order or other document which constitutes the authorisation referred to in paragraph 2.2(2)(a) above, or

    (2) if he wishes to act on behalf of a child, or on behalf of a patient without the authorisation referred to in (1) above, file a certificate of suitability –

        (a) stating that he consents to act,

        (b) stating that he knows or believes that the [claimant] [defendant] is a [child][patient],

        (c) in the case of a patient, stating the grounds of his belief and if his belief is based upon medical opinion attaching any relevant document to the certificate,

        (d) stating that he can fairly and competently conduct proceedings on behalf of the child or patient and has no interest adverse to that of the child or patient,

        (e) where the child or patient is a claimant, undertaking to pay any costs which the child or patient may be ordered to pay in relation to the proceedings, subject to any right he may have to be repaid from the assets of the child or patient, and

        (f) which he has signed in verification of its contents.

2.4   The litigation friend must serve a certificate of suitability:

    (1) in the case of a child (who is not also a patient) on one of the child's parents or guardians or if there is no parent or guardian, on the person with whom the child resides or in whose care the child is, and

    (2) in the case of a patient on the person authorised under Part VII of the Mental Health Act 1983 to conduct proceedings on behalf of the patient or if there is no person so authorised, on the person with whom the patient resides or in whose care the patient is.

2.4A   The litigation friend is not required to serve the documents referred to in paragraph 2.3(2)(c) when he serves a certificate of suitability on the person to be served under paragraph 2.4.

2.5   The litigation friend must file either the certificate of suitability together with a certificate of service of it, or the authorisation referred to in paragraph 2.3(1) above:

    (1) where the litigation friend is acting on behalf of a claimant, when the claim form is issued, and

    (2) where the litigation friend is acting on behalf of a defendant, when he first takes a step in the action.

APPLICATION FOR A COURT ORDER APPOINTING A LITIGATION FRIEND

3.1 Rule 21.6 sets out who may apply for an order appointing a litigation friend.

3.2 An application should be made in accordance with Part 23 and must be supported by evidence.

3.3 The application notice must be served:

(1) on the persons referred to in paragraph 2.4 above, and

(2) where the application is in respect of a patient, on the patient unless the court orders otherwise.

3.4 The evidence in support must satisfy the court that the proposed litigation friend:

(1) consents to act,

(2) can fairly and competently conduct proceedings on behalf of the child or patient,

(3) has no interest adverse to that of the child or patient, and

(4) where the child or patient is a claimant, undertakes to pay any costs which the child or patient may be ordered to pay in relation to the proceedings, subject to any right he may have to be repaid from the assets of the child or patient.

3.5 Where a claimant wishes to take a step in proceedings against a child or patient who does not have a litigation friend he must apply to the court for an order appointing a litigation friend.

3.6 The proposed litigation friend must satisfy the conditions in paragraph 3.4(1), (2) and (3) above and may be one of the persons referred to in paragraph 2.4 above where appropriate, or otherwise may be the Official Solicitor. Where it is sought to appoint the Official Solicitor, provision should be made for payment of his charges.

CHANGE OF LITIGATION FRIEND AND PREVENTION OF PERSON ACTING AS LITIGATION FRIEND

4.1 Rule 21.7(1) states that the court may:

(1) direct that a person may not act as a litigation friend,

(2) terminate a litigation friend's appointment,

(3) substitute a new litigation friend for an existing one.

4.2 Where an application is made for an order under rule 21.7(1), the application notice must set out the reasons for seeking it. The application must be supported by evidence.

4.3 If the order sought is the substitution of a new litigation friend for an existing one, the evidence must satisfy the court of the matters set out in paragraph 3.4 above.

4.4 The application notice must be served:

(1) on the persons referred to in paragraph 2.4 above, and

(2) on the litigation friend or person purporting to act as litigation friend.

PROCEDURE WHERE THE NEED FOR A LITIGATION FRIEND HAS COME TO AN END

5.1   Rule 21.9 deals with the situation where the need for a litigation friend comes to an end during the proceedings because either:

(1)   a child who is not also a patient reaches the age of 18 (full age) during the proceedings, or

(2)   a patient ceases to be a patient (recovers).

5.2   A child on reaching full age must serve on the other parties to the proceedings and file with the court a notice:

(1)   stating that he has reached full age,

(2)   stating that his litigation friend's appointment has ceased,

(3)   giving an address for service, and

(4)   stating whether or not he intends to carry on with or continue to defend the proceedings.

5.3   If the notice states that the child intends to carry on with or continue to defend the proceedings he shall subsequently be described in the proceedings as:

'A.B. (formerly a child but now of full age)'

5.4   Whether or not a child having reached full age serves a notice in accordance with rule 21.9(4)(a) and paragraph 5.2(2) above, a litigation friend may at any time after the child has reached full age serve a notice on the other parties that his appointment has ceased.

5.5   The liability of a litigation friend for costs continues until a notice that his appointment to act has ceased is served on the other parties.

5.6   Where a patient recovers, an application under rule 21.9(3) must be made for an order under rule 21.9(2) that the litigation friend's appointment has ceased.

5.7   The application must be supported by the following evidence:

(1)   a medical report indicating that the patient has recovered and that he is capable of managing and administering his property and affairs,

(2)   where the patient's affairs were under the control of the Court of Protection, a copy of the order or notice discharging the receiver, and

(3)   if the application is made by the patient, a statement whether or not he intends to carry on with or continue to defend the proceedings.

5.8   An order under rule 21.9(2) must be served on the other parties to the proceedings. The patient must file with the court a notice:

(1)   stating that his litigation friend's appointment has ceased,

(2)   giving an address for service, and

(3)   stating whether or not he intends to carry on with or continue to defend the proceedings.

SETTLEMENT OR COMPROMISE BY OR ON BEHALF OF A CHILD OR PATIENT PRIOR TO THE START OF PROCEEDINGS

6.1   Where a claim by or on behalf of a child or patient has been dealt with by agreement prior to the start of proceedings and only the approval of the court to the agreement is sought, the claim:

(1)   must be made using the Part 8 procedure,

(2)   must include a request for approval of the settlement or compromise, and

(3)   subject to paragraph 6.4 in addition to the details of the claim, must set out the terms of the settlement or compromise or have attached to it a draft consent order in practice form N292.

6.2   In order to approve the settlement or compromise, the information concerning the claim that the court will require will include:

(1)   whether and to what extent the defendant admits liability,

(2)   the age and occupation (if any) of the child or patient,

(3)   the litigation friend's approval of the proposed settlement or compromise, and

(4)   in a personal injury case arising from an accident –

    (a)   the circumstances of the accident,

    (b)   any medical reports,

    (c)   where appropriate, a schedule of any past and future expenses and losses claimed and any other relevant information relating to personal injury as set out in the practice direction which supplements Part 16 (statements of case), and

    (d)   where considerations of liability are raised –

        (i)   any evidence or police reports in any criminal proceedings or in an inquest, and

        (ii)   details of any prosecution brought.

6.3   (1)   An opinion on the merits of the settlement or compromise given by counsel or solicitor acting for the child or patient should, except in very clear cases, be obtained.

    (2)   A copy of the opinion and, unless the instructions on which it was given are sufficiently set out in it, a copy of the instructions, must also be supplied to the court.

    (3)   A copy or record of any financial advice must also be supplied to the court.

6.4   Where in any personal injury case a claim for damages for future pecuniary loss is settled, the provisions in paragraphs 6.4A and 6.4B must in addition be complied with.

6.4A   The court must be satisfied that the parties have considered whether the damages should wholly or partly take the form of periodical payments.

6.4B   Where the settlement includes provision for periodical payments, the claim must –

(1)   set out the terms of the settlement or compromise; or

(2)   have attached to it a draft consent order,

which must satisfy the requirements of rules 41.8 and 41.9 as appropriate.

6.5   Applications for the approval of a settlement or compromise will normally be heard by a Master or district judge.

(For information about provisional damages claims see Part 41 and the practice direction which supplements it)

SETTLEMENT OR COMPROMISE BY OR ON BEHALF OF A CHILD OR PATIENT AFTER PROCEEDINGS HAVE BEEN COMMENCED

6.6   Where in any personal injury case a claim for damages for future pecuniary loss, by or on behalf of a child or patient, is dealt with by agreement after proceedings have been commenced, an application should be made for the court's approval of the agreement.

6.7   The court must be satisfied that the parties have considered whether the damages should wholly or partly take the form of periodical payments.

6.8   Where the settlement includes provision for periodical payments, an application under paragraph 6.6 must –

(1)   set out the terms of the settlement or compromise; or

(2)   have attached to it a draft consent order,

which must include the requirements of rules 41.8 and 41.9 as appropriate.

6.9   The court must be supplied with –

(1)   an opinion on the merits of the settlement or compromise given by counsel or solicitor acting for the child or patient, except in very clear cases; and

(2)   a copy or record of any financial advice.

APPORTIONMENT UNDER THE FATAL ACCIDENTS ACT 1976

7.1   A judgment on or settlement in respect of a claim under the Fatal Accidents Act 1976 must be apportioned between the persons by or on whose behalf the claim has been brought.

7.2   Where a claim is brought on behalf of a dependent child or children, the money apportioned to any child must be invested on his behalf in accordance with rules 21.10 and 21.11 and paragraphs 8 and 9 below.

7.3   In order to approve an apportionment of money to a dependent child, the court will require the following information:

(1)   the matters set out in paragraph 6.2(1),(2) above, and

(2)   in respect of the deceased

(a)   where death was caused by an accident, the matters set out in paragraph 6.2(3)(a),(b) and (c) above, and

(b)   his future loss of earnings, and

(3)   the extent and nature of the dependency.

CONTROL OF MONEY RECOVERED BY OR ON BEHALF OF A CHILD OR PATIENT

8.1   Money recovered or paid into court on behalf of or for the benefit of a child or patient shall be dealt with in accordance with directions of the court under rule 21.11.

8.2   The court:

(1)   may direct the money to be paid into the High Court for investment,

(2)   may also direct that certain sums be paid direct to the child or patient, his litigation friend or his legal representative for the immediate benefit of the child or patient or for expenses incurred on his behalf, and

(3) may direct the applications in respect of the investment of the money be transferred to a local district registry.

8.3 The Master or district judge will consider the general aims to be achieved for the money in court (the fund) by investment and will give directions as to the type of investment.

8.4 Where a child is also a patient, and likely to remain so on reaching full age, his fund should be administered as a patient's fund.

8.5 Where a child or patient is legally aided the fund will be subject to a first charge under s. 16 of the Legal Aid Act 1988 (the legal aid charge) and an order for the investment of money on the child or patient's behalf must contain a direction to that effect.

EXPENSES INCURRED BY LITIGATION FRIEND

8A.1 A litigation friend may make a claim for expenses under rule 21.11A(1) –

(a) where the court has ordered an assessment of costs under rule 48.5(2), at the detailed assessment hearing;

(b) where the litigation friend's expenses are not of a type which would be recoverable as costs on an assessment of costs between the parties, to the Master or District Judge at the hearing to approve the settlement or compromise under Part 21 (the Master or District Judge may adjourn the matter to the Costs Judge); or

(c) where an assessment of costs under Part 48.5(2) is not required, and no approval under Part 21 is necessary, by a Part 23 application supported by a witness statement to a Costs Judge or District Judge as appropriate.

8A.2 In all circumstances, the litigation friend shall support a claim for expenses by filing a witness statement setting out –

(i) the nature and amount of the expense;

(ii) the reason the expense was incurred.

GUARDIAN'S ACCOUNTS

9 Paragraph 8 of the practice direction supplementing Part 40 (Judgments and Orders) deals with the approval of the accounts of a guardian of assets of a child.

INVESTMENT ON BEHALF OF A CHILD

10.1 At the hearing of the application for the approval of the agreement the litigation friend or his legal representative should provide a CFO form 320 (request for investment) for completion by the Master or district judge.

10.2 On receipt of that form in the Court Funds Office the investment managers of the Public Trust Office will make the appropriate investment.

10.3 Where an award of damages for a child is made at trial the trial judge may direct:

(1) the money to be paid into court and placed in the special investment account, and

(2) the litigation friend to make an application to a Master or district judge for further investment directions.

10.4   If the money to be invested is very small the court may order it to be paid direct to the litigation friend to be put into a building society account (or similar) for the child's use.

10.5   If the money is invested in court it must be paid out to the child when he reaches full age.

INVESTMENT ON BEHALF OF A PATIENT

11.1   The Court of Protection is responsible for protecting the property of patients and is given extensive powers to do so under the Mental Health Act 1983. Fees are charged for the administration of funds by the Court of Protection and these should be provided for in any settlement.

11.2   Where the sum to be administered is:

(1)   over £30,000, the order approving the settlement will contain a direction to the litigation friend to apply to the Court of Protection for the appointment of a receiver, after which the fund will be transferred to the Court of Protection,

(2)   under £20,000, it may be retained in court and invested in the same way as the fund of a child, or

(3)   in intermediate cases the advice of the Master of the Court of Protection should be sought.

11.3   A form of order transferring the fund to the Court of Protection is set out in practice form N292.

11.4   In order for the Court Funds Office to release a fund which is subject to the legal aid charge to the Court of Protection the litigation friend or his legal representative should provide the appropriate area office of the Legal Aid Board with an undertaking in respect of a sum to cover their costs, following which the area office will advise the Court Funds Office in writing of that sum, enabling them to transfer the balance to the Court of Protection on receipt of a CFO form 200 payment schedule authorised by the court.

11.5   The CFO form 200 should be completed and presented to the court where the settlement or trial took place for authorisation, subject to paragraphs 11.6 and 11.7 below.

11.6   Where the settlement took place in the Royal Courts of Justice the CFO form 200 should be completed and presented for authorisation:

(1)   on behalf of a child, in the Masters' Secretary's Office, Room E214, and

(2)   on behalf of a patient, in the Action Department, Room E15.

11.7   Where the trial took place in the Royal Courts of Justice the CFO form 200 is completed and authorised by the court officer.

PAYMENT OUT OF FUNDS IN COURT

12.1   Applications to a Master or district judge;

(1)   for payment out of money from the fund for the benefit of the child, or

(2)   to vary an investment strategy,

may be dealt with without a hearing unless the court directs otherwise.

12.2   When the child reaches full age, his fund in court:

(1)   where it is a sum of money will be paid out to him, and

(2)   where it is in the form of investments other than money (for example shares or unit trusts), will be transferred into his name.

12.3   An application for payment out of funds being administered by the Court of Protection must be made to the Court of Protection.

(For further information on payments into and out of court see the practice directions supplementing Parts 36 and 37.)

PART 57   PROBATE AND INHERITANCE

Scope of this Part and definitions

57.1   (1)   This Part contains rules about –

(a)   probate claims;

(b)   claims for the rectification of wills;

(c)   claims and applications to –

(i)   substitute another person for a personal representative; or

(ii)   remove a personal representative; and

(d)   claims under the Inheritance (Provision for Family and Dependants) Act 1975.

(2)   In this Part:

(a)   'probate claim' means a claim for –

(i)   the grant of probate of the will, or letters of administration of the estate, of a deceased person;

(ii)   the revocation of such a grant; or

(iii)   a decree pronouncing for or against the validity of an alleged will;

not being a claim which is non-contentious (or common form) probate business;

(Section 128 of the Supreme Court Act 1981 defines non-contentious (or common form) probate business.)

(b)   'relevant office' means –

(i)   in the case of High Court proceedings in a Chancery district registry, that registry;

(ii)   in the case of any other High Court proceedings, Chancery Chambers at the Royal Courts of Justice, Strand, London, WC2A 2LL; and

(iii)   in the case of county court proceedings, the office of the county court in question;

(c)   'testamentary document' means a will, a draft of a will, written instructions for a will made by or at the request of, or under the instructions of, the testator, and any document purporting to be evidence of the contents, or to be a copy, of a will which is alleged to have been lost or destroyed;

(d)   'will' includes a codicil.

189

I PROBATE CLAIMS

General

57.2   (1)   This Section contains rules about probate claims.

(2)   Probate claims in the High Court are assigned to the Chancery Division.

(3)   Probate claims in the county court must only be brought in –

(a)   a county court where there is also a Chancery district registry; or

(b)   the Central London County Court.

(4)   All probate claims are allocated to the multi-track.

How to start a probate claim

57.3   A probate claim must be commenced –

(a)   in the relevant office; and

(b)   using the procedure in Part 7.

Acknowledgment of Service and Defence

57.4   (1)   A defendant who is served with a claim form must file an acknowledgment of service.

(2)   Subject to paragraph (3), the period for filing an acknowledgment of service is –

(a)   if the defendant is served with a claim form which states that particulars of claim are to follow, 28 days after service of the particulars of claim; and

(b)   in any other case, 28 days after service of the claim form.

(3)   If the claim form is served out of the jurisdiction under rule 6.19, the period for filing an acknowledgment of service is 14 days longer than the relevant period specified in rule 6.22 or the practice direction supplementing Section 3 of Part 6.

(4)   Rule 15(4) (which provides the period for filing a defence) applies as if the words 'under Part 10' were omitted from rule 15.4(1)(b).

Lodging of testamentary documents and filing of evidence about testamentary documents

57.5   (1)   Any testamentary document of the deceased person in the possession or control of any party must be lodged with the court.

(2)   Unless the court directs otherwise, the testamentary documents must be lodged in the relevant office –

(a)   by the claimant when the claim form is issued; and

(b)   by a defendant when he acknowledges service.

(3)   The claimant and every defendant who acknowledges service of the claim form must in written evidence –

(a)   describe any testamentary document of the deceased of which he has any knowledge or, if he does not know of any such testamentary document, state that fact, and

(b) if any testamentary document of which he has knowledge is not in his possession or under his control, give the name and address of the person in whose possession or under whose control it is or, if he does not know the name or address of that person, state that fact.

(A specimen form for the written evidence about testamentary documents is annexed to the practice direction.)

(4) Unless the court directs otherwise, the written evidence required by paragraph (3) must be filed in the relevant office –

(a) by the claimant, when the claim form is issued; and
(b) by a defendant when he acknowledges service.

(5) Except with the permission of the court, a party shall not be allowed to inspect the testamentary documents or written evidence lodged or filed by any other party until he himself has lodged his testamentary documents and filed his evidence.

(6) The provisions of paragraphs (2) and (4) may be modified by a practice direction under this Part.

Revocation of existing grant

57.6 (1) In a probate claim which seeks the revocation of a grant of probate or letters of administration every person who is entitled, or claims to be entitled, to administer the estate under that grant must be made a party to the claim.

(2) If the claimant is the person to whom the grant was made, he must lodge the probate or letters of administration in the relevant office when the claim form is issued.

(3) If a defendant has the probate or letters of administration under his control, he must lodge it in the relevant office when he acknowledges service.

(4) Paragraphs (2) and (3) do not apply where the grant has already been lodged at the court, which in this paragraph includes the Principal Registry of the Family Division or a district probate registry.

Contents of statements of case

57.7 (1) The claim form must contain a statement of the nature of the interest of the claimant and of each defendant in the estate.

(2) If a party disputes another party's interest in the estate he must state this in his statement of case and set out his reasons.

(3) Any party who contends that at the time when a will was executed the testator did not know of and approve its contents must give particulars of the facts and matters relied on.

(4) Any party who wishes to contend that –

(a) a will was not duly executed;
(b) at the time of the execution of a will the testator was not of sound mind, memory and understanding; or
(c) the execution of a will was obtained by undue influence or fraud,

must set out the contention specifically and give particulars of the facts and matters relied on.

191

(5)   (a)   A defendant may give notice in his defence that he does not raise any positive case, but insists on the will being proved in solemn form and, for that purpose, will cross-examine the witnesses who attested the will.

        (b)   If a defendant gives such a notice, the court will not make an order for costs against him unless it considers that there was no reasonable ground for opposing the will.

Counterclaim

57.8   (1)   A defendant who contends that he has any claim or is entitled to any remedy relating to the grant of probate of the will, or letters of administration of the estate, of the deceased person must serve a counterclaim making that contention.

        (2)   If the claimant fails to serve particulars of claim within the time allowed, the defendant may, with the permission of the court, serve a counterclaim and the probate claim shall then proceed as if the counterclaim were the particulars of claim.

Probate counterclaim in other proceedings

57.9   (1)   In this rule 'probate counterclaim' means a counterclaim in any claim other than a probate claim by which the defendant claims any such remedy as is mentioned in rule 57.1(2)(a).

        (2)   Subject to the following paragraphs of this rule, this Part shall apply with the necessary modifications to a probate counterclaim as it applies to a probate claim.

        (3)   A probate counterclaim must contain a statement of the nature of the interest of each of the parties in the estate of the deceased to which the probate counterclaim relates.

        (4)   Unless an application notice is issued within 7 days after the service of a probate counterclaim for an order under rule 3.1(2)(e) or 3.4 for the probate counterclaim to be dealt with in separate proceedings or to be struck out, and the application is granted, the court shall order the transfer of the proceedings to either –

            (a)   the Chancery Division (if it is not already assigned to that Division) and to either the Royal Courts of Justice or a Chancery district registry (if it is not already proceeding in one of those places); or

            (b)   if the county court has jurisdiction, to a county court where there is also a Chancery district registry or the Central London County Court.

        (5)   If an order is made that a probate counterclaim be dealt with in separate proceedings, the order shall order the transfer of the probate counterclaim as required under paragraph (4).

Failure to acknowledge service or to file a defence

57.10   (1)   A default judgment cannot be obtained in a probate claim and rule 10.2 and Part 12 do not apply.

     (2)   If any of several defendants fails to acknowledge service the claimant may –

          (a)   after the time for acknowledging service has expired; and
          (b)   upon filing written evidence of service of the claim form and (if no particulars of claim were contained in or served with the claim form) the particulars of claim on that defendant;

          proceed with the probate claim as if that defendant had acknowledged service.

     (3)   If no defendant acknowledges service or files a defence then, unless on the application of the claimant the court orders the claim to be discontinued, the claimant may, after the time for acknowledging service or for filing a defence (as the case may be) has expired, apply to the court for an order that the claim is to proceed to trial.

     (4)   When making an application under paragraph (3) the claimant must file written evidence of service of the claim form and (if no particulars of claim were contained in or served with the claim form) the particulars of claim on each of the defendants.

     (5)   Where the court makes an order under paragraph (3), it may direct that the claim be tried on written evidence.

Discontinuance and dismissal

57.11   (1)   Part 38 does not apply to probate claims.

         (2)   At any stage of a probate claim the court, on the application of the claimant or of any defendant who has acknowledged service, may order that –

          (a)   the claim be discontinued or dismissed on such terms as to costs or otherwise as it thinks just; and
          (b)   a grant of probate of the will, or letters of administration of the estate, of the deceased person be made to the person entitled to the grant.

II RECTIFICATION OF WILLS

Rectification of Wills

57.12   (1)   This Section contains rules about claims for the rectification of a will.

(Section 20 of the Administration of Justice Act 1982 provides for rectification of a will. Additional provisions are contained in rule 55 of the Non-Contentious Probate Rules 1987.)

         (2)   Every personal representative of the estate shall be joined as a party.

         (3)   The practice direction makes provision for lodging the grant of probate or letters of administration with the will annexed in a claim under this Section.

III   SUBSTITUTION AND REMOVAL OF PERSONAL REPRESENTATIVES

Substitution and Removal of Personal Representatives

57.13   (1)   This Section contains rules about claims and applications for substitution or removal of a personal representative.

(2)   Claims under this Section must be brought in the High Court and are assigned to the Chancery Division.

(Section 50 of the Administration of Justice Act 1985 gives the High Court power to appoint a substitute for, or to remove, a personal representative.)

(3)   Every personal representative of the estate shall be joined as a party.

(4)   The practice direction makes provision for lodging the grant of probate or letters of administration in a claim under this Section.

(5)   If substitution or removal of a personal representative is sought by application in existing proceedings, this rule shall apply with references to claims being read as if they referred to applications.

IV   CLAIMS UNDER THE INHERITANCE (PROVISION FOR FAMILY AND DEPENDANTS) ACT 1975

Scope of this section

57.14   This Section contains rules about claims under the Inheritance (Provision for Family and Dependants) Act 1975 ('the Act').

Proceedings in the High Court

57.15   Proceedings in the High Court under the Act shall be issued in either –

(a)   the Chancery Division; or
(b)   the Family Division.

(2)   The Civil Procedure Rules apply to proceedings under the Act which are brought in the Family Division, except that the provisions of the Family Proceedings Rules 1991 relating to the drawing up and service of orders apply instead of the provisions in Part 40 and its practice direction.

Procedure for claims under section 1 of the Act

57.16   (1)   A claim under section 1 of the Act must be made by issuing a claim form in accordance with Part 8.

(2)   Rule 8.3 (acknowledgment of service) and rule 8.5 (filing and serving written evidence) apply as modified by paragraphs (3) to (5) of this rule.

(3)   The written evidence filed and served by the claimant with the claim form must have exhibited to it an official copy of –

(a)   the grant of probate or letters of administration in respect of the deceased's estate; and
(b)   every testamentary document in respect of which probate or letters of administration were granted.

(4) Subject to paragraph (4A), the time within which a defendant must file and serve –

    (a) an acknowledgment of service; and

    (b) any written evidence,

is not more than 21 days after service of the claim form on him.

(4A) If the claim form is served out of the jurisdiction under rule 6.19, the period for filing an acknowledgment of service and any written evidence is 7 days longer than the relevant period specified in rule 6.22 or the practice direction supplementing Section III of Part 6.

(5) A defendant who is a personal representative of the deceased must file and serve written evidence, which must include the information required by the practice direction.

PRACTICE DIRECTION – PROBATE

THIS PRACTICE DIRECTION SUPPLEMENTS PART 57

I PROBATE CLAIMS

General

1.1   This Section of this practice direction applies to contentious probate claims.

1.2   The rules and procedure relating to non-contentious probate proceedings (also known as 'common form') are the Non-Contentious Probate Rules 1987 as amended.

How to start a probate claim

2.1   A claim form and all subsequent court documents relating to a probate claim must be marked at the top 'In the estate of [name] deceased (Probate)'.

2.2   The claim form must be issued out of –

    (1) Chancery Chambers at the Royal Courts of Justice; or

    (2) one of the Chancery district registries; or

    (3) if the claim is suitable to be heard in the county court –

        (a) a county court in a place where there is also a Chancery district registry; or

        (b) the Central London County Court.

    There are Chancery district registries at Birmingham, Bristol, Cardiff, Leeds, Liverpool, Manchester, Newcastle upon Tyne and Preston.

(Section 32 of the County Courts Act 1984 identifies which probate claims may be heard in a county court.)

2.3   When the claim form is issued, the relevant office will send a notice to Leeds District Probate Registry, Coronet House, Queen Street, Leeds, LS1 2BA, DX 26451 Leeds (Park Square), telephone 0113 243 1505, requesting that all testamentary documents, grants of representation and other relevant documents currently held at any probate registry are sent to the relevant office.

2.4   The commencement of a probate claim will, unless a court otherwise directs, prevent any grant of probate or letters of administration being made until the probate claim has been disposed of.

(Rule 45 of the Non-Contentious Probate Rules 1987 makes provision for notice of the probate claim to be given, and section 117 of the Supreme Court Act 1981 for the grant of letters of administration pending the determination of a probate claim. Paragraph 8 of this practice direction makes provision about an application for such a grant.)

Testamentary documents and evidence about testamentary documents

3.1 Unless the court orders otherwise, if a testamentary document is held by the court (whether it was lodged by a party or it was previously held at a probate registry) when the claim has been disposed of the court will send it to the Leeds District Probate Registry.

3.2 The written evidence about testamentary documents required by this Part –

(1) should be in the form annexed to this practice direction; and

(2) must be signed by the party personally and not by his solicitor or other representative (except that if the party is a child or patient the written evidence must be signed by his litigation friend).

3.3 In a case in which there is urgent need to commence a probate claim (for example, in order to be able to apply immediately for the appointment of an administrator pending the determination of the claim) and it is not possible for the claimant to lodge the testamentary documents or to file the evidence about testamentary documents in the relevant office at the same time as the claim form is to be issued, the court may direct that the claimant shall be allowed to issue the claim form upon his giving an undertaking to the court to lodge the documents and file the evidence within such time as the court shall specify.

Case management

4 In giving case management directions in a probate claim the court will give consideration to the questions –

(1) whether any person who may be affected by the claim and who is not joined as a party should be joined as a party or given notice of the claim, whether under rule 19.8A or otherwise; and

(2) whether to make a representation order under rule 19.6 or rule 19.7.

Summary judgment

5.1 If an order pronouncing for a will in solemn form is sought on an application for summary judgment, the evidence in support of the application must include written evidence proving due execution of the will.

5.2 If a defendant has given notice in his defence under rule 57.7(5) that he raises no positive case but –

(1) he insists that the will be proved in solemn form; and

(2) for that purpose he will cross-examine the witnesses who attested the will;

any application by the claimant for summary judgment is subject to the right of that defendant to require those witnesses to attend court for cross-examination.

Settlement of a probate claim

6.1   If at any time the parties agree to settle a probate claim, the court may –

       (1)   order the trial of the claim on written evidence, which will lead to a grant in solemn form;

       (2)   order that the claim be discontinued or dismissed under rule 57.11, which will lead to a grant in common form; or

       (3)   pronounce for or against the validity of one or more wills under section 49 of the Administration of Justice Act 1985.

       (For a form of order which is also applicable to discontinuance and which may be adapted as appropriate, see Practice Form No. CH38)

(Section 49 of the Administration of Justice Act 1985 permits a probate claim to be compromised without a trial if every 'relevant beneficiary', as defined in that section, has consented to the proposed order. It is only available in the High Court.)

6.2   Applications under section 49 of the Administration of Justice Act 1985 may be heard by a master or district judge and must be supported by written evidence identifying the relevant beneficiaries and exhibiting the written consent of each of them. The written evidence of testamentary documents required by rule 57.5 will still be necessary.

Application for an order to bring in a will, etc.

7.1   Any party applying for an order under section 122 of the Supreme Court Act 1981 ('the 1981 Act') must serve the application notice on the person against whom the order is sought.

(Section 122 of the 1981 Act empowers the court to order a person to attend court for examination, and to answer questions and bring in documents, if there are reasonable grounds for believing that such person has knowledge of a testamentary document. Rule 50(1) of the Non-Contentious Probate Rules 1987 makes similar provision where a probate claim has not been commenced.)

7.2   An application for the issue of a witness summons under section 123 of the 1981 Act –

       (1)   may be made without notice; and

       (2)   must be supported by written evidence setting out the grounds of the application.

(Section 123 of the 1981 Act empowers the court, where it appears that any person has in his possession, custody or power a testamentary document, to issue a witness summons ordering such person to bring in that document. Rule 50(2) of the Non-Contentious Probate Rules makes similar provision where a probate claim has not been commenced.)

7.3   An application under section 122 or 123 of the 1981 Act should be made to a master or district judge.

7.4   A person against whom a witness summons is issued under section 123 of the 1981 Act who denies that the testamentary document referred to in the witness summons is in his possession or under his control may file written evidence to that effect.

Administration pending the determination of a probate claim

8.1 An application under section 117 of the Supreme Court Act 1981 for an order for the grant of administration pending the determination of a probate claim should be made by application notice in the probate claim.

8.2 If an order for a grant of administration is made under section 117 of the 1981 Act –

    (1) Rules 69.4 to 69.7 shall apply as if the administrator were a receiver appointed by the court;

    (2) if the court allows the administrator remuneration under rule 69.7, it may make an order under section 117(3) of the 1981 Act assigning the remuneration out of the estate of the deceased; and

    (3) every application relating to the conduct of the administration shall be made by application notice in the probate claim.

8.3 An order under section 117 may be made by a master or district judge.

8.4 If an order is made under section 117 an application for the grant of letters of administration should be made to the Principal Registry of the Family Division, First Avenue House, 42–49 High Holborn, London WC1V 6NP.

8.5 The appointment of an administrator to whom letters of administration are granted following an order under section 117 will cease automatically when a final order in the probate claim is made but will continue pending any appeal.

II RECTIFICATION OF WILLS

Scope of this Section

9. This Section of this practice direction applies to claims for the rectification of a will.

Lodging the grant

10.1 If the claimant is the person to whom the grant was made in respect of the will of which rectification is sought, he must, unless the court orders otherwise, lodge the probate or letters of administration with the will annexed with the court when the claim form is issued.

10.2 If a defendant has the probate or letters of administration in his possession or under his control, he must, unless the court orders otherwise, lodge it in the relevant office within 14 days after the service of the claim form on him.

Orders

11. A copy of every order made for the rectification of a will shall be sent to the Principal Registry of the Family Division for filing, and a memorandum of the order shall be endorsed on, or permanently annexed to, the grant under which the estate is administered.

III SUBSTITUTION AND REMOVAL OF PERSONAL REPRESENTATIVES

Scope of this Section

12.   This Section of this practice direction applies to claims and applications for substitution or removal of a personal representative. If substitution or removal of a personal representative is sought by application in existing proceedings, this Section shall apply with references to the claim, claim form and claimant being read as if they referred to the application, application notice and applicant respectively.

Starting the claim

13.1   The claim form must be accompanied by:

(1)   a sealed or certified copy of the grant of probate or letters of administration; and

(2)   written evidence containing the grounds of the claim and the following information so far as it is known to the claimant –

   (a)   brief details of the property comprised in the estate, with an approximate estimate of its capital value and any income that is received from it;
   (b)   brief details of the liabilities of the estate;
   (c)   the names and addresses of the persons who are in possession of the documents relating to the estate;
   (d)   the names of the beneficiaries and their respective interests in the estate; and
   (e)   the name, address and occupation of any proposed substituted personal representative.

13.2   If the claim is for the appointment of a substituted personal representative, the claim form must be accompanied by –

(1)   a signed or (in the case of the Public Trustee or a corporation) sealed consent to act; and

(2)   written evidence as to the fitness of the proposed substituted personal representative, if an individual, to act.

Production of the grant

14.1   On the hearing of the claim the personal representative must produce to the Court the grant of representation to the deceased's estate.

14.2   If an order is made substituting or removing the personal representative, the grant (together with a sealed copy of the order) must be sent to and remain in the custody of the Principal Registry of the Family Division until a memorandum of the order has been endorsed on or permanently annexed to the grant.

IV CLAIMS UNDER THE INHERITANCE (PROVISION FOR FAMILY AND DEPENDANTS) ACT 1975

Acknowledgment of service by personal representative – rule 57.16(4)

15   Where a defendant who is a personal representative wishes to remain neutral in relation to the claim, and agrees to abide by any decision which the court may make, he should state this in Section A of the acknowledgment of service form.

Written evidence of personal representative – rule 57.16(5)

16   The written evidence filed by a defendant who is a personal representative must state to the best of that person's ability –

   (1)   full details of the value of the deceased's net estate, as defined in section 25(1) of the Act;

   (2)   the person or classes of persons beneficially interested in the estate, and –

      (a)   the names and (unless they are parties to the claim) addresses of all living beneficiaries; and

      (b)   the value of their interests in the estate so far as they are known.

   (3)   whether any living beneficiary (and if so, naming him) is a child or patient within the meaning of rule 21.1(2); and

   (4)   any facts which might affect the exercise of the court's powers under the Act.

Separate representation of claimants

17   If a claim is made jointly by two or more claimants, and it later appears that any of the claimants have a conflict of interests –

   (1)   any claimant may choose to be represented at any hearing by separate solicitors or counsel, or may appear in person; and

   (2)   if the court considers that claimants who are represented by the same solicitors or counsel ought to be separately represented, it may adjourn the application until they are.

Production of the grant

18.1   On the hearing of a claim the personal representative must produce to the court the original grant of representation to the deceased's estate.

18.2   If the court makes an order under the Act, the original grant (together with a sealed copy of the order) must be sent to the Principal Registry of the Family Division for a memorandum of the order to be endorsed on or permanently annexed to the grant in accordance with section 19(3) of the Act.

18.3   Every final order embodying terms of compromise made in proceedings under the Act, whether made with or without a hearing, must contain a direction that a memorandum of the order shall be endorsed on or permanently annexed to the probate or letters of administration and a copy of the order shall be sent to the Principal Registry of the Family Division with the relevant grant of probate or letters of administration for endorsement.

ANNEX

A FORM OF WITNESS STATEMENT OR AFFIDAVIT ABOUT TESTAMENTARY DOCUMENTS

(CPR RULE 57.5)

(Title of the claim)

I [name and address] the claimant/defendant in this claim state [on oath] that I have no knowledge of any document –

(i) being or purported to be or having the form or effect of a will or codicil of [name of deceased] whose estate is the subject of this claim;
(ii) being or purporting to be a draft or written instructions for any such will or codicil made by or at the request of or under the instructions of the deceased;
(iii) being or purporting to be evidence of the contents or a copy of any such will or codicil which is alleged to have been lost or destroyed,

except . . . [describe any testamentary document of the deceased, and if any such document is not in your control, give the name and address of the person who you believe has possession or control of it, or state that you do not know the name and address of that person] . . .

[I believe that the facts stated in this witness statement are true] [or jurat for affidavit]

(NOTE: 'testamentary document' is defined in CPR rule 57.1)

PART 64   ESTATES, TRUSTS AND CHARITIES

General

64.1   (1)   This Part contains rules –

(a)   in Section I, about claims relating to –

(i)   the administration of estates of deceased persons, and
(ii)   trusts; and

(b)   in Section II, about charity proceedings.

(2)   In this Part and its practice directions, where appropriate, references to trustees include executors and administrators.
(3)   All proceedings in the High Court to which this Part applies must be brought in the Chancery Division.

I   CLAIMS RELATING TO THE ADMINISTRATION OF ESTATES AND TRUSTS

Scope of this Section

64.2   This Section of this Part applies to claims –

(a)   for the court to determine any question arising in –

(i)   the administration of the estate of a deceased person; or
(ii)   the execution of a trust;

(b)   for an order for the administration of the estate of a deceased person, or the execution of a trust, to be carried out under the direction of the court ('an administration order');

(c)   under the Variation of Trusts Act 1958; or

(d)   under section 48 of the Administration of Justice Act 1985.

Claim form

64.3   A claim to which this Section applies must be made by issuing a Part 8 claim form.

Parties

64.4   (1)   In a claim to which this Section applies, other than an application under section 48 of the Administration of Justice Act 1985 –

(a)   all the trustees must be parties;

(b)   if the claim is made by trustees, any of them who does not consent to being a claimant must be made a defendant; and

(c)   the claimant may make parties to the claim any persons with an interest in or claim against the estate, or an interest under the trust, who it is appropriate to make parties having regard to the nature of the order sought.

(2)   In addition, in a claim under the Variation of Trusts Act 1958, unless the court directs otherwise any person who –

(a)   created the trust; or

(b)   provided property for the purposes of the trust,

must, if still alive, be made a party to the claim.

(The court may, under rule 19.2, order additional persons to be made parties to a claim.)

II   CHARITY PROCEEDINGS

Scope of this Section and interpretation

64.5   (1)   This Section applies to charity proceedings.

(2)   In this Section –

(a)   'the Act' means the Charities Act 1993;

(b)   'charity proceedings' has the same meaning as in section 33(8) of the Act; and

(c)   'the Commissioners' means the Charity Commissioners for England and Wales.

Application for permission to take charity proceedings

64.6   (1)   An application to the High Court under section 33(5) of the Act for permission to start charity proceedings must be made within 21 days after the refusal by the Commissioners of an order authorising proceedings.

(2)   The application must be made by issuing a Part 8 claim form, which must contain the information specified in the practice direction.

(3)   The Commissioners must be made defendants to the claim, but the claim form need not be served on them or on any other person.

(4)   The judge considering the application may direct the Commissioners to file a written statement of their reasons for their decision.

(5)   The court will serve on the applicant a copy of any statement filed under paragraph (4).

(6)   The judge may either –

    (a)   give permission without a hearing; or

    (b)   fix a hearing.

PRACTICE DIRECTION – ESTATES, TRUSTS AND CHARITIES

THIS PRACTICE DIRECTION SUPPLEMENTS PART 64

I CLAIMS RELATING TO THE ADMINISTRATION OF ESTATES AND TRUSTS

Examples of claims under rule 64.2(a)

1   The following are examples of the types of claims which may be made under rule 64.2(a) –

(1)   a claim for the determination of any of the following questions –

    (a)   any question as to who is included in any class of persons having –

        (i)   a claim against the estate of a deceased person;

        (ii)   a beneficial interest in the estate of such a person; or

        (iii)   a beneficial interest in any property subject to a trust;

    (b)   any question as to the rights or interests of any person claiming –

        (i)   to be a creditor of the estate of a deceased person;

        (ii)   to be entitled under a will or on the intestacy of a deceased person; or

        (iii)   to be beneficially entitled under a trust;

(2)   a claim for any of the following remedies –

    (a)   an order requiring a trustee –

        (i)   to provide and, if necessary, verify accounts;

        (ii)   to pay into court money which he holds in that capacity; or

        (iii)   to do or not to do any particular act;

    (b)   an order approving any sale, purchase, compromise or other transaction by a trustee; or

    (c)   an order directing any act to be done which the court could order to be done if the estate or trust in question were being administered or executed under the direction of the court.

Applications by trustees for directions

2   A separate practice direction contains guidance about applications by trustees for directions.

Administration orders – rule 64.2(b)

3.1   The court will only make an administration order if it considers that the issues between the parties cannot properly be resolved in any other way.

3.2   If, in a claim for an administration order, the claimant alleges that the trustees have not provided proper accounts, the court may –

(1)   stay the proceedings for a specified period, and order them to file and serve proper accounts within that period; or

(2)   if necessary to prevent proceedings by other creditors or persons claiming to be entitled to the estate or fund, make an administration order and include in it an order that no such proceedings are to be taken without the court's permission.

3.3   Where an administration order has been made in relation to the estate of a deceased person, and a claim is made against the estate by any person who is not a party to the proceedings –

(1)   no party other than the executors or administrators of the estate may take part in any proceedings relating to the claim without the permission of the court; and

(2)   the court may direct or permit any other party to take part in the proceedings, on such terms as to costs or otherwise as it thinks fit.

3.4   Where an order is made for the sale of any property vested in trustees, those persons shall have the conduct of the sale unless the court directs otherwise.

Applications under the Variation of Trusts Act 1958 – rule 64.2(c)

4.1   Where children or unborn beneficiaries will be affected by a proposed arrangement under the Act, the evidence filed in support of the application must –

(1)   show that their litigation friends or the trustees support the arrangements as being in the interests of the children or unborn beneficiaries; and

(2)   unless paragraph 4.3 applies or the court orders otherwise, be accompanied by a written opinion to this effect by the advocate who will appear on the hearing of the application.

4.2   A written opinion filed under paragraph 4.1(2) must –

(1)   if it is given on formal instructions, be accompanied by a copy of those instructions; or

(2)   otherwise, state fully the basis on which it is given.

4.3   No written opinion needs to be filed in support of an application to approve an arrangement under section 1(1)(d) of the Act (discretionary interests under protective trusts).

4.4   Where the interests of two or more children, or two or more of the children and unborn beneficiaries, are similar, only a single written opinion needs to be filed.

Applications under section 48 of the Administration of Justice Act 1985 – rule 64.2(d)

5   A Part 8 claim form for an application by trustees under section 48 of the Administration of Justice Act 1985 (power of High Court to authorise action to be taken in reliance on legal opinion) may be issued without naming a defendant, under rule 8.2A. No separate application for permission under rule 8.2A need be made.

Prospective costs orders

6.1   These paragraphs are about the costs of applications under rule 64.2(a).

6.2   Where trustees have power to agree to pay the costs of a party to such an application, and exercise such a power, rule 48.3 applies. In such a case, an order is not required and the trustees are entitled to recover out of the trust fund any costs which they pay pursuant to the agreement made in the exercise of such power.

6.3   Where the trustees do not have, or decide not to exercise, a power to make such an agreement, the trustees or the party concerned may apply to the court at any stage of proceedings for an order that the costs of any party (including the costs of the trustees) shall be paid out of the fund (a 'prospective costs order').

6.4   The court, on an application for a prospective costs order, may –

(a)   in the case of the trustees' costs, authorise the trustees to raise and meet such costs out of the fund;

(b)   in the case of the costs of any other party, authorise or direct the trustees to pay such costs (or any part of them, or the costs incurred up to a particular time) out of the trust fund to be assessed, if not agreed by the trustees, on the indemnity basis or, if the court directs, on the standard basis, and to make payments from time to time on account of such costs. A model form of order is annexed to this Practice Direction.

6.5   The court will always consider whether it is possible to deal with the application for a prospective costs order on paper without a hearing and in an ordinary case would expect to be able to do so. The trustees must consider whether a hearing is needed for any reason. If they consider that it is they should say so and explain why in their evidence. If any party to the application referred to in paragraph 6.1 above (or any other person interested in the trust fund) considers that a hearing is necessary (for instance because he wishes to oppose the making of a prospective costs order) this should be stated, and the reasons explained, in his evidence, if any, or otherwise in a letter to the court.

6.6   If the court would be minded to refuse the application on a consideration of the papers alone, the parties will be notified and given the opportunity, within a stated time, to ask for a hearing.

6.7   The evidence in support of an application for a prospective costs order should be given by witness statement. The trustees and the applicant (if different) must ensure full disclosure of the relevant matters to show that the case is one which falls within the category of case where a prospective costs order can properly be made.

6.8   The model form of order is designed for use in the more straightforward cases, where a question needs to be determined which has arisen in the administration of the trust, whether the claimants are the trustees or a beneficiary. The form may be adapted for use in less straightforward cases, in particular where the proceedings are hostile, but special factors may also have to be reflected in the terms of the order in such a case.

II   CHARITY PROCEEDINGS

Role of Attorney-General

7   The Attorney-General is a necessary party to all charity proceedings, other than any commenced by the Charity Commissioners, and must be joined as a defendant if he is not a claimant.

Service on Charity Commissioners or Attorney-General

8   Any document required or authorised to be served on the Commissioners or the Attorney-General must be served on the Treasury Solicitor in accordance with paragraph 2.1 of the Practice Direction supplementing Part 66.

Applications for permission to take charity proceedings – rule 64.6

9.1   The claim form for an application under section 33(5) of the Act must state –

   (1)   the name, address and description of the applicant;
   (2)   details of the proceedings which he wishes to take;
   (3)   the date of the Commissioners' refusal to grant an order authorising the taking of proceedings;
   (4)   the grounds on which the applicant alleges that it is a proper case for taking proceedings; and
   (5)   if the application is made with the consent of any other party to the proposed proceedings, that fact.

9.2   If the Commissioners have given reasons for refusing to grant an order, a copy of their reasons must be filed with the claim form.

Appeals against orders of the Charity Commissioners

10   Part 52 applies to any appeal against an order of the Charity Commissioners. Section III of the practice direction supplementing Part 52 contains special provisions about such appeals.

APPENDIX

Model form of prospective costs order

UPON THE APPLICATION etc.

AND UPON HEARING etc.

AND UPON the Solicitors for the ... Defendant undertaking to make the repayments mentioned in paragraph 2 below in the circumstances there mentioned

IT IS [BY CONSENT] ORDERED THAT:

1. The Claimants as trustees of . . . ('the [Settlement/Scheme]') do –

    (a) pay from the assets of the [Settlement/Scheme] the costs of and incidental to these proceedings incurred by the . . . Defendant such costs to be subject to a detailed assessment on the indemnity basis if not agreed and (for the avoidance of doubt) to –

         (i) include costs incurred by the . . . Defendant from and after [date] in anticipation of being appointed to represent any class of persons presently or formerly beneficially interested under the trusts of the [Settlement/Scheme] irrespective of whether [he/she] is in fact so appointed; and
         (ii) exclude (in the absence of any further order) costs incurred in prosecuting any Part 20 claim or any appeal;

    (b) indemnify the . . . Defendant in respect of any costs which he may be ordered to pay to any other party to these proceedings in connection therewith.

2. Until the outcome of the detailed assessment (or the agreement regarding costs) contemplated in paragraph 1 above, the Claimants as trustees do pay from the assets of the [Settlement/Scheme] to the Solicitors for the . . . Defendant monthly (or at such other intervals as may be agreed) such sums on account of the costs referred to in paragraph 1(a) of this Order as the Solicitors for the . . . Defendant shall certify –

    (i) to have been reasonably and properly incurred and not to exceed such amount as is likely in their opinion to be allowed on a detailed assessment on the indemnity basis; and
    (ii) to have [accrued] on account of the present proceedings in the period prior to the date of such certificate and not to have been previously provided for under this Order.

PROVIDED ALWAYS that the Solicitors for the . . . Defendant shall repay such sums (if any) as, having been paid to them on account, are disallowed on a detailed assessment or are otherwise agreed to be repaid and any such sums shall be repaid together with interest at 1% above the base rate for the time being of [Barclays] Bank plc from and including the date of payment to those Solicitors up to and including the date of repayment, such interest to accrue daily.

3. Any party may apply to vary or discharge paragraphs 1 and 2 of this Order but only in respect of costs to be incurred after the date of such application.

Note: this form of order assumes that the trustees are the claimants. If the claimant is a beneficiary and the trustees are defendants, references to the parties need to be adapted accordingly.

PRACTICE DIRECTION – APPLICATIONS TO THE COURT FOR DIRECTIONS BY TRUSTEES IN RELATION TO THE ADMINISTRATION OF THE TRUST

THIS PRACTICE DIRECTION SUPPLEMENTS SECTION I OF PART 64.

1 This Practice Direction is about applications to the court for directions by trustees in relation to the administration of the trust.

Contents of the claim form

2   If confidentiality of the directions sought is important (for example, where the directions relate to actual or proposed litigation with a third party who could find out what directions the trustees are seeking through access to the claim form under CPR rule 5.4) the statement of the remedy sought, for the purposes of CPR rule 8.2(b), may be expressed in general terms. The trustees must, in that case, state specifically in the evidence what it is that they seek to be allowed to do.

Proceedings in private

3   The proceedings will in the first instance be listed in private (see paragraph 1.5 of the Practice Direction supplementing Part 39 and rule 39.2(3)(f)). Accordingly the order made, as well as the other documents among the court records (apart from a claim form which has been served), will not be open to inspection by third parties without the court's permission (rule 5.4(2)). If the matter is disposed of without a hearing, the order made will be expressed to have been made in private.

Joining defendants or giving notice to those interested

4.1   Rule 64.4(1)(c) deals with the joining of beneficiaries as defendants. Often, especially in the case of a private trust, it will be clear that some, and which, beneficiaries need to be joined as defendants. Sometimes, if there are only two views of the appropriate course, and one is advocated by one beneficiary who will be joined, it may not be necessary for other beneficiaries to be joined since the trustees may be able to present the other arguments. Equally, in the case of pension trust, it may not be necessary for a member of every possible different class of beneficiaries to be joined.

4.2   In some cases the court may be able to assess whether or not to give the directions sought, or what directions to give, without hearing from any party other than the trustees. If the trustees consider that their case is in that category they may apply to the court to issue the claim form without naming any defendants under rule 8.2A. They must apply to the court before the claim form is issued (rule 8.2A(2)) and include a copy of the claim form that they propose to issue (rule 8.2A(3)(b)).

4.3   In other cases the trustees may know that beneficiaries need to be joined as defendants, or to be given notice, but may be in doubt as to which. Examples could include a case concerning a pension scheme with many beneficiaries and a number of different categories of interest, especially if they may be differently affected by the action for which directions are sought, or a private trust with a large class of discretionary beneficiaries. In those cases the trustees may apply to issue the claim form without naming any defendants under rule 8.2A. The application may be combined with an application to the court for directions as to which persons to join as parties or to give notice to under rule 19.8A.

4.4   In the case of a charitable trust the Attorney-General is always the appropriate defendant, and almost always the only one.

Case management directions

5.1   The claim will be referred to the master or district judge once a defendant has acknowledged service, or otherwise on expiry of the period for acknowledgment of service, (or, if no defendant is named, as soon as the claimants' evidence has been filed) to consider directions for the management of the case. Such directions may be given without a hearing in some cases; these might include directions as to parties or as to notice of proceedings, as mentioned in paragraph 4 above.

Proceeding without a hearing

6.1   The court will always consider whether it is possible to deal with the application on paper without a hearing. The trustees must always consider whether a hearing is needed for any reason. If they consider that it is they should say so and explain why in their evidence. If a defendant considers that a hearing is needed, this should be stated, and the reasons explained, in his evidence, if any, or otherwise in a letter to the court.

6.2   If the court would be minded to refuse to give the directions asked for on a consideration of the papers alone, the parties will be notified and given the opportunity, within a stated time, to ask for a hearing.

6.3   In charity cases, the master or district judge may deal with the case without a hearing on the basis of a letter by or on behalf of the Attorney-General that sets out his attitude to the application.

Evidence

7.1   The trustees' evidence should be given by witness statement. In order to ensure that, if directions are given, the trustees are properly protected by the order, they must ensure full disclosure of relevant matters, even if the case is to proceed with the participation of beneficiaries as defendants.

7.2   Applications for directions whether or not to take or defend or pursue litigation should be supported by evidence including the advice of an appropriately qualified lawyer as to the prospects of success and other matters relevant to be taken into account, including a cost estimate for the proceedings and any known facts concerning the means of the opposite party to the proceedings, and a draft of any proposed statement of case. There are cases in which it is likely to be so clear that the trustees ought to proceed as they wish that the costs of making the application, even on a simplified procedure without a hearing and perhaps without defendants, are not justified in comparison with the size of the fund or the matters at issue.

7.3   References in this practice direction to an appropriately qualified lawyer mean one whose qualifications and experience are appropriate to the circumstances of the case. The qualifications should be stated. If the advice is given on formal instructions, the instructions should always be put in evidence as well, so that the court can see the basis on which the advice was given. If it is not, the advice must state fully the basis on which it is given.

7.4   All applications for directions should be supported by evidence showing the value of the trust assets, the significance of the proposed litigation or other course of action for the trust, and why the court's directions are needed. In the case of a pension trust the evidence should include the latest actuarial valuation, and should describe the membership profile and, if a deficit on winding up is likely, the priority provisions and their likely effect.

7.5   On an application for directions about actual or possible litigation the evidence should also state whether (i) any relevant Pre-Action Protocol has been followed; and (ii) the trustees have proposed or undertaken, or intend to propose, mediation by ADR, and (in each case) if not why not.

7.6   If a beneficiary of the trust is a party to the litigation about which directions are sought, with an interest opposed to that of the trustees, that beneficiary should be a defendant to the trustees' application, but any material which would be privileged as regards that beneficiary in the litigation should be put in evidence as exhibits to the trustees' witness statement, and should not be served on the beneficiary. However if the trustees' representatives consider that no harm would be done by the disclosure of all or some part of the material, then that material should be served on that defendant. That defendant may also be excluded from part of the hearing, including that which is devoted to discussion of the material withheld.

Consultation with beneficiaries

7.7   The evidence must explain what, if any, consultation there has been with beneficiaries, and with what result. In preparation for an application for directions in respect of litigation, the following guidance is to be followed:

     (1)   If the trust is a private trust where the beneficiaries principally concerned are not numerous and are all or mainly adult, identified and traceable, the trustees will be expected to have canvassed with all the adult beneficiaries the proposed or possible courses of action before applying for directions.

     (2)   If it is a private trust with a larger number of beneficiaries, including those not yet born or identified, or children, it is likely that there will nevertheless be some adult beneficiaries principally concerned, with whom the trustees must consult.

     (3)   In relation to a charitable trust the trustees must have consulted the Attorney-General, through the Treasury Solicitor, as well as the Charity Commissioners whose consent to the application will have been needed under section 33 of the Charities Act 1993.

     (4)   In relation to a pension trust, unless the members are very few in number, no particular steps by way of consultation with beneficiaries (including, where relevant, employers) or their representatives are required in preparation for the application, though the trustees' evidence should describe any consultation that has in fact taken place. If no consultation has taken place, the court could in some cases direct that meetings of one or more classes of beneficiaries be held to consider the subject matter of the application, possibly as a preliminary to deciding whether a member of a particular class ought to be joined as a defendant, though in a case concerning actual or proposed litigation, steps would need to be considered to protect privileged material from too wide disclosure.

7.8   (1)   If the court gives directions allowing the trustees to take, defend or pursue litigation it may do so up to a particular stage in the litigation, requiring the trustees, before they carry on beyond that point, to renew their application to the court. What stage that should be will depend on the likely management of the litigation under the CPR. If the application is to be renewed after disclosure of documents, and disclosed documents need to be shown to the court, it may be necessary to obtain permission to do this from the court in which the other litigation is proceeding.

(2) In such a case the court may sometimes direct that the case be dealt with at that stage without a hearing if the beneficiaries obtain and lodge the written advice of an appropriately qualified lawyer stating that he or they support the continuation of the directions. Any such advice will be considered by the court and, if thought fit, the trustees will be given a direction allowing them to continue pursuing the proceedings without a hearing.

7.9 In a case of urgency, such as where a limitation period or period for service of proceedings is about to expire, the court may be able to give directions on a summary consideration of the evidence to cover the steps which need to be taken urgently, but limiting those directions so that the application needs to be renewed on fuller consideration at an early stage.

7.10 In any application for directions where a child is a defendant, the court will expect to have put before it the instructions to and advice of an appropriately qualified lawyer as to the benefits and disadvantages of the proposed, and any other relevant, course of action from the point of view of the child beneficiary.

7.11 The master or district judge may give the directions sought though, if the directions relate to actual or proposed litigation, only if it is a plain case, and therefore the master or district judge may think it appropriate to give the directions without a hearing: see the Practice Direction supplementing Part 2: Allocation of Cases to Levels of the Judiciary, para 4.1 and para 5.1(e), and see also paragraph 6 above. Otherwise the case will be referred to the judge.

7.12 Where a hearing takes place, if the advice of a lawyer has been put in evidence in accordance with paragraph 7.2 or 7.10, that lawyer should if possible appear on the hearing.

B. Forms and Precedents

Letter of claim

Dear Sirs,

Re: [*name*] Deceased

Our client [*name*]

This is a formal letter of claim by which we give notice our client intends to make a claim under the Inheritance (Provision for Family and Dependants) Act 1975 for reasonable provision to be made for [him/her] from the estate of [*name deceased*]. Our client makes [his/her] claim as [*describe e.g. the deceased's spouse*] under section 1(1) [*complete*] of the Act.

[We enclose a statement from our client which will form the basis of his/her evidence in support of a claim. We also enclose a draft Part 8 claim form that will be issued in due course, unless the claim can be settled by agreement in the meantime.]

You are aware the court will consider the factors set out in section 3 of the Act in determining both the question whether there is reasonable provision for our client on the death of the deceased and the question what provision, if any, should be awarded by an order under section 2 of the Act. We will consider the relevant parts of section 3 further below, but would first comment as follows on the provision made for our client [on intestacy] [under the deceased's will dated . . .].

[*Complete description of provision made for client on deceased's death.*]

[Our client will rely on the following. . .*complete facts to describe basis of claim*]

SECTION 3 FACTORS

We consider below the factors in section 3 that we believe are relevant to our client's claim.

(a) The first of these is in section 3(1)(a) and concerns our client's present and future financial needs and resources. [You will see from our client's draft statement and Schedule of Assets that he/she has income [*complete*]. She has capital [*complete*]]. [*Describe client's income/expenditure/financial needs and resources, preferably by reference to schedules.*]

(b) We propose to consider the needs and resources of [the will/intestacy beneficiaries/other applicants] (section 3(1)(b) and (c)) as far as they are known to us [*complete*].

(c) The needs and resources of our client and the [will/intestacy beneficiaries] [other applicants] must be considered in the light of the size of the net estate (section 3(1)(e)) upon which we have the following observations [*complete*].

(d)   We now turn to section 3(1)(d) of the Act. The deceased owed an obligation to [*complete*]. The deceased owed a responsibility to [*complete*].

(e)   [*Refer to the mental and/or physical disability of any applicant/beneficiary under section 3(1)(d).*]

(f)   We would ask you to consider [*section 3(1)(g) – 'Other matters'- to be completed*].

(g)   [*If spouse applicant*] Finally, we refer to section 3(2) of the Act. Our client is [. . .] years of age. The marriage lasted [. . .]. Our client contributed to the welfare of the deceased and his family in the following respects [*complete*]. You will be aware that a spouse applicant under the Act is not limited to financial provision for maintenance but is entitled to such provision as is reasonable in all the circumstances. We consider [*go on to explain what would be reasonable in the circumstances and why*].

We enclose the following documents in support of our client's claim: [*list*].

We would ask you now to provide us with a formal letter of response within 21 days. We believe you have in your possession or control the following documents relevant to the claim [*list*] and request receipt of copies of the same from you with your letter of response. Included in this list are a number of documents marked with an asterisk. We invite you to provide copies of these to us within 14 days of your receipt of this letter or to give us your written authority, in the form enclosed, so that we may obtain them.

We have also sent this letter to [*complete*] and enclose a [copy/copies] of the same.

Yours faithfully

APPENDIX B2

Letter of response from personal representatives

Dear Sirs,

Re: [*name*] Deceased

Our Client: [*name*]

Your Client: [*name*]

We write in response to your letter of [*date*] by which you advised us formally of your client's intended application under the Inheritance (Provision for Family and Dependants) Act 1975 for provisions to be made for your client from the Deceased's estate. We act for the [executor(s)/person(s) entitled to a grant of letters of administration]. [As you are aware] a grant [has/has not] been issued [on [*date*] and a copy of the same is enclosed herewith [with the will].]

This letter is intended to address the matters relevant to personal representatives as parties to claims under the 1975 Act and therefore anticipates the requirements set out in CPR 1998 Part 57.16(5) and the Practice Direction paragraphs 15 and 16. This letter will not address the substantive merits of your client's claim, nor the defences that may be raised by the persons entitled to the Deceased's estate [under the will/on intestacy].

If proceedings are issued our client intends to acknowledge service and state that he/she/they will remain neutral and abide the outcome of the trial or the other parties' compromise of your claim.

The beneficiaries of the estate have been notified by us of your claim and we would suggest that you communicate directly with them. Please advise us if you need details of who they are and how to contact them. [The estimated gross value of the estate is £[. . .].] [We enclose copies of the Inland Revenue Account (and a corrective account)] [and a schedule of the capital assets in the estate, and its income. The values given are estimates where indicated.]

We note that the date for service of your claim form expires under section 4 of the 1975 Act [6 months after the issue of a grant of representation [which will be on [*date*]]. Please keep us advised of the progress of your claim.

[You have a caused a caveat to be entered to prevent the issue of a grant of representation for the estate. This is an inappropriate step to take and effectively prevents you proceeding with your client's claim, which cannot progress until a grant is made. We invite you to withdraw your caveat forthwith. The estate will not be distributed pending the expiry of 6 months from the date any grant is obtained and will then be held to await the outcome of your client's claim if he/she chooses to pursue it.]

Yours faithfully,

APPENDIX B3

Claim form for all applicants with claims for extension of time[1] and joint property to be treated as part of net estate[2]

[For insertion on Part 8 Claim Form]

In the High Court of Justice
Family or Chancery Division[3]

BETWEEN

AB   *Claimant*

AND

(1) CD

(2) EF(A child by his litigation friend)[4]   *Defendants*

Are there any Human rights issues involved in this application?   No

Brief details of Claim

1. Part 8 of the Civil Procedure Rules 1998 applies to this claim.
2. [*choose the description of the applicant from the following list*]

- The Claimant was the wife of the above-named deceased *or*
- The Claimant was the civil partner of the above-named deceased *or*
- The Claimant was the former wife of the above-named deceased *or*
- The Claimant was the former civil partner of the above-named deceased *or*
- The Claimant lived with the above-named deceased during the whole of the period of 2 years ending immediately before the date when the deceased died in the same household as the deceased and as the husband/wife of the deceased *or*

---

1 See **Chapter 8**.
2 Section 9 of the Inheritance (Provision for Family and Dependants) Act 1975 (1975 Act). See **Chapter 7**.
3 The claim can be brought in either Division. Claims by spouses are perhaps better brought in the Family Division because of the judges' experience in relation to divorce.
4 A child has to have a litigation friend (CPR rule 21.2).

- The Claimant lived with the above-named deceased during the whole of the period of 2 years ending immediately before the date when the deceased died in the same household as the deceased and as the civil partner of the deceased *or*
- The Claimant is a child of the above-named deceased *or*
- The Claimant was treated by the deceased as a child of the family in relation to his marriage to the Claimant's mother/father *or*
- The Claimant was treated by the deceased as a child of the family in relation to the deceased's civil partnership with the Claimant's mother/father *or*
- The Claimant was immediately before the death of the deceased being maintained, either wholly or partly, by the deceased.

3. The deceased died on [. . .] and a grant of letters of administration was issued to the First Defendant out of the [. . .] Probate Registry on [. . .] or a grant of probate issued to the First Defendants out of the [. . .] Probate Registry on [. . .]
4. The Second Defendant is the infant child of the deceased and entitled to share his estate on intestacy.
5. The Claimant seeks the following relief:

    (a) that provision be made for him/her out of the estate of the above-named deceased;
    (b) that permission be granted for bringing this application notwithstanding the fact that more than 6 months has elapsed since the making of the grant of probate;[5]
    (c) that the above-named deceased's severable share of [his] property known as *(insert details)*, at the value thereof immediately before his death, shall, to such extent as appears to the court to be just in all the circumstances of the case, be treated for the purposes of the Inheritance (Provision for Family and Dependants) Act 1975 as part of the net estate of the above-named deceased.[6]
    (d) That provision be made for the costs of this application.

(5) This application is made under sections 1, 4 and 9 of the Inheritance (Provision for Family and Dependants) Act 1975.

I believe that the contents of this Claim Form are true

Signed: Dated:

---

5   See 1975 Act, s.4 and Chapter 8.
6   See 1975 Act, s.9 and Chapter 8.

Witness statement in support of application by spouse for provision[1]

Claimant
Date
Exhibits

In the High Court of Justice

Chancery Division

In the Estate of XY Deceased

In the Matter of the Inheritance (Provision For Family And Dependants) Act 1975

BETWEEN

GH   *Claimant*

AND

(1) IJ
(2) KL   *Defendants*

**WITNESS STATEMENT IN SUPPORT OF APPLICATION FOR
REASONABLE FINANCIAL PROVISION**

I, GH of . . . WILL SAY as follows:

BACKGROUND

1. I am the Claimant herein and I make this statement in support of my application for reasonable financial provision to be made for me out of the estate of XY ('the Deceased') who died on 18 September 2005.

---

1   This is just an example of a witness statement in a particular case. It can be adapted for other classes of applicants.

2. The First and Second Defendants are the executors and trustees of the Will of the Deceased and a grant or probate was made to them out of the Principal Registry of the Family Division on 13 December 2005. I now refer to a copy of that grant and the Will marked 'GH1'.
3. By his Will the Deceased provided for a legacy to me of £50,000 but otherwise left his estate to his sons from his first marriage, the First and Second Defendants.

HISTORY OF THE RELATIONSHIP

4. I was born on 13 June 1951. I met the Deceased in 1981 and we started living together in December 1982. I moved into a house which he owned known as Dunromin, sold my own flat and used the monies to buy furniture for our new home. We were married on 14 April 1991 and I now refer to a copy of our marriage certificate marked 'GH2'. At that date I was aged 40 and the Deceased 53. There were no children of the marriage but the Defendants came to stay at weekends and holidays from the age of 5 and 9 and I cared for them.
5. At the date when I started living with the Deceased I worked as a librarian. However once we married he suggested that I give up work. He supported me financially. He worked as a city accountant and was very successful. We had a very good lifestyle. We ate out at least twice a week. We had two cars and a housekeeper. We had a holiday home which we purchased near Sienna and we spent at least five weeks a year there.
6. Shortly before he died, I discovered that the Deceased had been having an affair with his secretary and was planning to leave me. It was when I confronted him with this that he suffered the heart attack which proved fatal.

CURRENT FINANCIAL NEEDS AND RESOURCES

7. I am now aged 55. Although I used to work as a librarian, I have not worked since my marriage in 1991.
8. At page . . . of 'GH3' is a schedule[2] I have prepared which shows my outgoings. There are other needs which I will have in the future. I suffer from arthritis and my mobility may become restricted as I get older. I anticipate that I may need to go into residential care earlier than might otherwise be expected.

SIZE OF THE ESTATE

9. I do not have a complete picture of the estate and what it consists of and I refer to a bundle of correspondence marked 'GH4' between my solicitors and the solicitors acting for the estate. This indicates that the estate is worth in the region of £3.2million and Dunromin is worth about £700,000 of that sum. There is no valuation as yet of the house in Sienna.

THE BENEFICIARIES OF THE ESTATE

10. As set out above the Deceased left his estate to the Defendants apart from the legacy of £50,000 to me. The First Defendant is aged 33 and is a criminal

---

2   This should set out outgoings in detail, income and capital, see the following sample schedule for a suggestion.

barrister and unmarried. The Second Defendant is aged 29 and is a drummer in a rock band which has had some success. He is unmarried but has a child aged 2 whom he supports. I have no details of their financial position but both appear to be comfortable and were not dependent on their father.

EXTENSION OF TIME

11. I appreciate that this claim has been brought just outside the 6 month time limit provided for in the 1975 Act and I seek permission of the Court to bring this claim notwithstanding the effluxion of time. I understand that the date for making this claim was recorded incorrectly on the computer at my solicitors, Messrs Sue Grabit and Run. Mr. Sue of that firm has signed a statement explaining the circumstances. My solicitors and I erroneously believed that we had until the end of December to make the claim. Solicitors for the administrators, Messrs Clueless & Co., have always been aware that this claim was to be made and I refer to correspondence passing between my solicitors and them marked 'GH5'. I do not believe that there has been any prejudice caused as a result of the short delay in issuing proceedings for which I apologise.[3]

STATEMENT OF TRUTH

12. I believe that the facts set out in this statement are true.

Signed etc.

SCHEDULE OF FINANCIAL POSITION[4]

[name]

SUMMARY OF SCHEDULES OF ANNUAL INCOME NEEDS

Schedule		Schedule A	Schedule B
1	Housing	0.00	0.00
2	Housekeeping	0.00	0.00
3	Clothes and footwear	0.00	0.00
4	Cars	0.00	0.00
5	Personal expenditure	0.00	0.00
6	Holidays, entertainment, sports, hobbies	0.00	0.00
7	Miscellaneous	0.00	0.00
TOTAL		**£0.00**	**£0.00**

Schedule A represents estimated income needs at [current property]
Schedule B represents estimated income needs at [new property]

---

3 This statement sets out circumstances which are almost an inadvertent failure to comply with the time limits. In cases where there has been a long delay the circumstances should be explained to the court in as much detail as possible by the claimant and/or her solicitor.
4 This schedule will need to be adapted depending on client circumstances.

SCHEDULE 1

Housing

Schedule A (£)		Schedule B (£)
0.00	Road maintenance	0.00
0.00	Council tax	0.00
0.00	Water rates	0.00
0.00	Insurance – buildings and contents	0.00
0.00	Gas	0.00
0.00	Electricity	0.00
0.00	Other fuel	0.00
0.00	Telephone – landline	0.00
0.00	Telephone – Internet	0.00
0.00	Telephone – fax	0.00
0.00	Telephone – mobile	0.00
0.00	TV – licence	0.00
0.00	TV – cable/satellite	0.00
0.00	Burglar alarm	0.00
0.00	Interior/exterior decoration	0.00
0.00	Maintenance of domestic machines/ central heating	0.00
0.00	Equipment insurance (including water and sewage pipes)	0.00
0.00	Repairs, cleaning, replacement of furniture/machines/carpets/curtains (average over [5] years)	0.00
0.00	Sweep	0.00
0.00	Window cleaner	0.00
0.00	Garden (plants, seeds, sundries)	0.00
0.00	House plants and cut flowers	0.00
TOTAL	**£0.00**	**£0.00**

SCHEDULE 2

Housekeeping

Schedule A (£)		Schedule B (£)
0.00	Food, wine and household goods	0.00
0.00	Chemist	0.00
0.00	Laundry/dry cleaning	0.00
0.00	Shoe repairs	0.00
0.00	Newspapers and magazines	0.00
0.00	Stationery and postage	0.00
0.00	Domestic help ([frequency])	0.00
0.00	Cleaner ([frequency])	0.00
0.00	Gardener ([frequency])	0.00
0.00	Wages: other ([description])	0.00
0.00	Pets ([description])	0.00
0.00	Food	0.00
0.00	Vet	0.00

0.00	Insurance	0.00
0.00	Kennels	0.00
TOTAL	**£0.00**	**£0.00**

SCHEDULE 3

Clothes and footwear

Schedule A (£)		Schedule B (£)
0.00	Clothes (average over [5] years)	0.00
0.00	Footwear (average over [5] years)	0.00
0.00	Accessories (average over [5] years)	0.00
TOTAL	**£0.00**	**£0.00**

SCHEDULE 4

Cars

Schedule A (£)		Schedule B (£)
	[Description of car]	
	[Description of car]	
0.00	Road tax	0.00
0.00	Insurance	0.00
0.00	Servicing	0.00
0.00	Maintenance and repairs	0.00
0.00	MOT	0.00
0.00	Tyres	0.00
0.00	Petrol	0.00
0.00	Oil	0.00
0.00	Car wash/valet service	0.00
0.00	Parking expenses	0.00
0.00	AA or RAC subscriptions (or other)	0.00
0.00	Depreciation	0.00
TOTAL	**£0.00**	**£0.00**

SCHEDULE 5

Personal expenses

Schedule A (£)		Schedule B (£)
0.00	Hairdressing	0.00
0.00	Cosmetics and toiletries	0.00
0.00	Optician	0.00
0.00	Dentist	0.00
0.00	Beautician	0.00
0.00	Health clubs and equipment	0.00
0.00	Tobacco	0.00
0.00	Taxis	0.00
0.00	Train fares/bus fares/underground	0.00
TOTAL	**£0.00**	**£0.00**

SCHEDULE 6

Holidays, entertainment, sports and hobbies

Schedule A (£)		Schedule B (£)
0.00	Restaurants	0.00
0.00	Theatre, cinema, concerts	0.00
0.00	Other spectator events (e.g. sporting events)	0.00
0.00	Books	0.00
0.00	Videos, compact discs, DVDs	0.00
0.00	Subscriptions for clubs and societies	0.00
0.00	Holidays (average for past [5] years)	0.00
0.00	Weekend breaks (average for the past [5] years)	0.00
0.00	Christmas expenses	0.00
0.00	Birthday and other gifts, parties, etc.	0.00
0.00	Film developing	0.00
0.00	Sport ([description])	0.00
TOTAL	**£0.00**	**£0.00**

225

SCHEDULE 7

Miscellaneous

Schedule A (£)		Schedule B (£)
0.00	Annual accountancy charges	0.00
0.00	Donations (e.g. to charities)	0.00
0.00	Covenants	0.00
0.00	Other items of expenditure not set out elsewhere (tips, etc.)	0.00
TOTAL	**£0.00**	**£0.00**

Witness statement by personal representative setting out matters required by paragraph 16 of the Practice Direction to CPR Part 57[1]

First Defendant
Date
Exhibits

In the High Court of Justice Chancery division

In the Estate Of XY Deceased

In the Matter of the Inheritance (Provision For Family And Dependants) Act 1975

BETWEEN

GH   *Claimant*

AND

(1) IJ

(2) KL   *Defendants*

WITNESS STATEMENT OF FIRST DEFENDANT

I, IJ of . . . WILL SAY as follows:

1. I am the First Defendant herein and one of the executors of the estate of XY ('the Deceased') who was my father. I make this statement in respect of the claim which has been made under the Inheritance (Provision for Family and Dependants) Act 1975 by the Claimant who is my stepmother. I make this statement in my capacity as one of the executors of XY and I am duly authorised by the Second Defendant who is the other executor to provide the information in this statement in accordance with paragraph 57.16 to the Practice Direction to Part 57 of the Civil Procedure Rules 1998 on his behalf too.

---

1 CPR rule 57.16 deals with the contents required in the personal representatives' statement and para. 16 of the Practice Direction expands that.

DETAILS OF THE NET ESTATE

2.   There are now produced to me marked 'IJ1' interim estate accounts [*or a schedule of assets in estate*] which show that the net estate after the payment of inheritance tax is worth £3.2million. The estate comprises the house in which the Deceased lived with the Claimant worth £700,000 and a property near Sienna which we have had valued at £200,000. The rest of the estate comprises a portfolio of stocks and shares.

NAMES AND ADDRESSES OF BENEFICIARIES OF THE ESTATE.

3.   As the Claimant states in her statement the Deceased left a legacy of £50,000 to her and the residue of his estate to be divided between the Second Defendant and me. There is also a small legacy to the Deceased's secretary not mentioned in the Claimant's statement which amounts to £5,000. She is called MN and lives at [address].[2]

OTHER MATTERS[3]

4.   I take issue with the amount of outgoings which the Claimant provides for in her schedule of needs and resources. It seems very high. Also she paints a picture of an extravagant life led with the Deceased whereas in fact he was rather mean with his money. I do not recall them eating out regularly or taking expensive holidays.
5.   The Deceased confided in me on many occasions during the last ten years that his marriage to the Claimant was an unhappy one. Certainly as a child I found the Claimant to be very uncaring towards me when I went to stay with the Deceased. She certainly did not look after me as she suggests.

MY FINANCIAL POSITION[4]

6.   I am a barrister practising in criminal work and I have been greatly affected financially by the cuts in legal aid. I am engaged to be married and expect to marry next year. My fiancée works for the Crown Prosecution Service. My income is £50,000 per annum. I own a flat worth £450,000 which is subject to a mortgage amounting to £350,000. My outgoings exceed my income considerably and I have an overdraft of £30,000.
7.   My father assisted me financially while I was establishing my career at the bar and he has contributed £2,000 to help clear my overdraft every year at Christmas. Apart from my flat I have no other capital.

---

2   There is only a need to include addresses of beneficiaries who are not parties.
3   In cases where the personal representatives are not beneficiaries, their role is to remain neutral in the dispute. Where as envisaged here, the defendants are also the major beneficiaries, the statement can deal with other matters which the parties would like the court to take into account. If the parties can avoid conduct becoming an issue in the proceedings that is a good thing.
4   If the beneficiaries of the estate want their financial position to weigh against the claim then they need to disclose it. Sometimes beneficiaries may be reluctant to do so. In that case the court will assume against them that they are comfortable financially.

EXTENSION OF TIME

8. I accept that the delay in bringing these proceedings was only one week. However the Claimant was fully aware that the claim had to be brought within 6 months and I urge the Court not to extend time.

9. I believe that the facts set out in this statement are true.

Signed: Dated:

Tomlin order settling claim of spouse taking advantage of spouse exemption[1]

In the High Court of Justice

Chancery Division

[Name of Judge]

[Date]

In the Estate of XY Deceased

In the Matter of the Inheritance (Provision For Family And Dependants) Act 1975

BETWEEN

GH   *Claimant*

AND

(1) IJ

(2) KL   *Defendants*

MINUTE OF ORDER

UPON the application of the Claimant for provision from the estate of the above mentioned Deceased under the Inheritance (Provision for Family and Dependants) Act 1975.

AND UPON the Claimant and the First and Second Defendants agreeing the terms set forth in the Schedule hereto.

AND THE Court being satisfied that the disposition of the Deceased's estate effected by the Will is not such as to make reasonable financial provision for the Claimant.

---

1   For tax considerations in respect of compromise of these claims see **Chapter 9**. The aim of this order is to provide the spouse with a lump sum which will be exempt from tax, to utilise the nil-rate band for inheritance tax to direct money to the children and then to create a short-term life interest in favour of the spouse which will attract spouse relief (even after the changes made in the Finance Act 2006 – it is an immediate post-death interest in possession within s.49(1A)(iii) of the Inheritance Tax Act 1984).

BY CONSENT IT IS ORDERED THAT:

1. The original Grant in this Estate together with a sealed copy of this Order be sent to the Principal Registry of the Family Division by the Claimant and the Defendants for a memorandum of this Order to be endorsed on or permanently annexed to the Grant in accordance with section 19(3) of the Inheritance (Provision for Family and Dependants) Act 1975.[2]
2. The Claimant and the Defendants having agreed to the terms set out in the Schedule hereto all further proceedings herein be stayed except for the purpose of carrying into effect the terms set out in the said Schedule. Liberty to apply as to carrying such terms into effect.
3. The costs of these proceedings (including costs of mediation) of the Claimant be subject to a detailed assessment on the standard basis[3] if not agreed and the costs of the Defendants be subject to a detailed assessment on the indemnity basis if not agreed and the said costs be raised and paid out of the estate.

SCHEDULE

(1) The Terms of the Will be varied to make provision for the Claimant under section 2 of the Inheritance (Provision for Family and Dependants) Act 1975 by the substitution of the following provisions marked (A), (B) and (C) for clauses 2, 3 and 4 of the Will and the Claimant and the Defendants (as executors of the Deceased) do carry the terms of this Schedule into effect.

    (A) I GIVE to my children IJ and KL in equal shares such sum of money as is equal in value to the largest sum of cash which I can give without any inheritance tax becoming due in respect of the transfer of my estate which I am deemed to make immediately before my death[4].

    (B) I GIVE the sum of £1,000,000 to my wife GH.

    (C) I GIVE all the residue of my estate (out of which shall be paid my funeral and testamentary expenses and my debts) and any property over which I have at my death any general power of appointment to my trustees to pay the income to my wife for her life or until 1 March 2008 whichever is the shorter period[5] and subject thereto for my children IJ and KL in equal shares absolutely.

(2) The Claimant agrees to co-operate with the Defendants or either of them in providing information and undertaking any medical examination required for the purpose of effecting insurance on her life against any inheritance tax which may become due on the gift set out in clause (C) above.[6]

(3) The above terms are in full and final settlement of all claims which any party may have arising out of these proceedings.

---

2   This should be included in the order as a reminder to the personal representatives to comply with s.19(3) of the Act.
3   That would be the usual basis of assessment for parties not acting as personal representatives although it is not uncommon for parties to agree that assessment should be on the indemnity basis.
4   Depending on the tax position of the deceased this is likely to be equal to the nil-rate band for inheritance tax at the date of his death.
5   While HMRC looks suspiciously at any interest less than five years, any interest which terminates more than two years after the date of death should work.
6   Provided that the trust comes to an end on the termination of the interest in possession during the lifetime of the spouse she will make a PET. The possibility she might not survive seven years thereafter and additional inheritance tax would become payable can be insured against.

Tomlin order settling claim by spouse: approval of court on behalf of her infant children[1]

In the High Court of Justice

Chancery Division

[Judge]

[Date]

In the Estate of OP Deceased

In the Matter of the Inheritance (Provision For Family And Dependants) Act 1975

BETWEEN

QR *Claimant*

AND

(1) ST

(2) UV

(3) WX (a child by his litigation friend)

(4) YZ (a child by her litigation friend) *Defendants*

MINUTE OF ORDER

ON the application of the Claimant as the widow of the above named Deceased for reasonable financial provision from his estate under the Inheritance (Provision for Family and Dependants) Act 1975 ('the 1975 Act').

AND the Claimant agreeing to the terms of compromise set forth in a Schedule hereto and the First and Second Defendants as administrators of the estate agreeing to carry the said terms into effect.[2]

AND the Court being satisfied that the disposition of the Deceased's estate on intestacy is not such as to make reasonable financial provision for the Claimant.

---

1   Under Part 21 of the CPR.

AND the Court being satisfied that the said terms of compromise are for the benefit of the Third and Fourth Defendants **HEREBY APPROVES** the said terms of compromise and requires the First and Second Defendants to carry the said terms into effect.

IT IS ORDERED THAT:

In the High Court of Justice Chancery Division

1. The original grant together with the sealed copy of this Order be sent to the Principal Registry of the Family Division by the First and Second Defendants for a memorandum of this Order to be endorsed on or permanently annexed to the Grant in accordance with Section 19(3) of the 1975 Act.
2. All further proceedings in this action except for the purpose of carrying this Order and the said terms into effect be stayed, and for that purpose the parties are to be at liberty to apply.
3. That there be assessed on an indemnity basis[3] all parties' costs of and incidental to the said application of the Claimant (including the costs of and incidental to the application pursuant to CPR 21.10), in the event of such costs not being agreed and such costs be raised and paid out of the estate in the course of administration.
4. That the litigation friend of the Third and Fourth Defendants be authorised to make agreement on behalf of the Third and Fourth Defendants in relation to all parties' costs.[4]

SCHEDULE

(1) These terms shall be in full and final settlement of all claims which the Claimant may have against the estate of the said Deceased.
(2) The disposition of the Deceased's estate on intestacy be varied to make provision for the Claimant under Section 2 of the Inheritance (Provision for Family and Dependants) Act 1975 by the substitution of the following provisions in place of the intestacy rules.
(3) The First and Second Defendants as the personal representatives of the Deceased shall hold the Deceased's net estate:

  (a) as to one half thereof for the Claimant absolutely;
  (b) as to the other half thereof on trust for the Third and Fourth Defendants to hold the same UPON TRUST for them upon their attaining the age of [18][5]

---

2 The children cannot, of course, agree.
3 There is no reason why the parties cannot agree this even though most parties' costs would be assessed on the standard basis and the personal representatives' costs on the indemnity basis.
4 It is useful to include this provision as there is some doubt otherwise as to whether they have authority.
5 Parents often wish their children to have capital at a later age than 18. There are two possible problems. It is perhaps doubtful whether the court has power to approve a settlement which postpones the vesting of capital in a child who would otherwise be entitled at 18, although in practice judges often are prepared to approve on that basis. Secondly, the Finance Act 2006 introduced changes to the way in which accumulation and maintenance trusts are taxed. If children do not attain an absolute interest in capital at 18 there is an inheritance tax charge (albeit quite limited) between then and 25. However, sometimes the reasons for an 18-year-old not inheriting a substantial sum of capital if they inherit from their parent can outweigh the tax disadvantages.

in equal shares absolutely **PROVIDED** always that if either **WX** or **YZ** shall die before attaining the age of 18 leaving a child or children living who shall attain the age of 18 such child or children shall take if more than one in equal shares absolutely the interest in the residuary estate which his or her parent would have taken at 18 and subject thereto for the Claimant absolutely.

APPENDICES

C. ACTAPS Guidance

ACTAPS Code – preliminary note[1]

Preliminary note regarding the interaction between the ACTAPS Practice Guidance and Notes regarding pre-action behaviour in other cases

In general terms, the ACTAPS Practice Guidance Notes (hereafter referred to as 'The ACTAPS Code') are designed to promote the resolution of trust and probate disputes without the need for what are often bitter and very expensive court proceedings by encouraging careful use at an early stage of mediation processes and explaining how best to manage the difficulty, so often present in these cases, that not all parties can speak for themselves.

The ACTAPS Code is not part of the CPR but it is hoped that judicial regard will be given to appropriate attempts to comply with the Code in the spirit of the CPR.

The Code is designed to make specific provision for particular aspects of trust and probate disputes which have been found in practice to call for special care.

The Code lists a wide variety of disputes to which the Code may apply, and mentioning some to which it does not –

- by recommending and providing a precedent for a letter of claim encompassing and adaptable to various types of dispute or claim (e.g. Inheritance Act claims)
- by providing lists of evidential documents to be produced in different types of disputes
- by promoting the early production of medical and social security records and evidence and providing precedent letters to that end (including a letter to a testator's GP agreed with the BMA)
- by providing for early production of evidence of testamentary capacity and a precedent *Larke* v. *Nugus* letter to the testator's solicitor
- by suggesting reasonable time limits
- by providing for cooperation in obtaining joint and third party letters of authority to disclose evidence
- by reproducing the new CPR covering the representation of unborn, minor, unascertained and incapable parties
- by encouraging mediation on the footing that the outcome will be subject to the approval of the Court in those cases where such approval is indispensable, and
- by providing for those cases where Revenue considerations arise.

---

1 © ACTAPS 2006.

ACTAPS Practice Guidance for the Resolution of Probate and Trust Disputes ('the ACTAPS Code')[1]

Paragraph 4 of the Practice Direction on Protocols has been substantially amended. It states that 'in cases not covered by any protocol, the court will expect the parties to act reasonably in exchanging information and documents relevant to their claim and in trying to avoid the necessity for the start of proceedings'.

Moreover, with effect from 1 April 2003, the 30th update to the CPR imposes on all parties to a dispute (whatever its nature) an obligation to comply with specified procedures designed to avoid litigation commencing.

Practitioners will no doubt remember the dicta of the Court of Appeal in *Carlson* v. *Townsend* [2001] 3 All ER 663 where it stated the use of the protocol was not limited to fast track cases. The spirit if not the letter of the protocol was equally appropriate to some higher value claims. In accordance with the aims of the civil justice reforms, the courts expected to see the spirit of reasonable pre-action behaviour applied in all cases regardless of the existence of a specific protocol.

The Association of Contentious Trust and Probate Specialists 'ACTAPS' and the Trust Law Committee have, as many practitioners will be aware, given much thought to the possibility that a special pre-action protocol ought to be developed for disputes within their area of expertise. Indeed a draft has for some time been on the ACTAPS website (**www.actaps.com**) and has since been the subject of extensive discussions with representatives of the judiciary concerned.

It is now clear that no special protocol will be adopted, despite a recognition that the draft contains useful elements. It will be seen that it deals in particular with the following matters:

(a) appointment of a representative to act on behalf of beneficiaries who cannot be ascertained or traced;
(b) requirement for a letter of claim setting out the basis of claim;
(c) early disclosure of documents;
(d) use of joint experts where possible;
(e) a joint letter of request for medical records;
(f) a joint *Larke* v. *Nugus* letter; and
(g) a joint letter requesting details of deceased's capacity.

In these circumstances the committee of ACTAPS has concluded that it would be useful to encourage members to have regard to The ACTAPS Code as a means of developing best practices in areas where special problems may arise, for example the need to have representatives for persons who cannot speak for themselves in a context where others may feel that mediation would be desirable.

---

1 © ACTAPS 2006.

It is understood that the judges who have considered The ACTAPS Code have expressed no concerns that it is out of line with the CPR objectives or that to follow its principles would give rise to unnecessary problems in practice. In particular it is thought that CPR Rule 19.7(3)(b) gives the necessary scope for securing the appointment of representatives of those who are absent, unborn, or members of a large class, as well before as after the commencement of proceedings.

It is also hoped that in the context of probate issues the common difficulty of medical practitioners considering that they may as a matter of professional confidence be restricted in releasing records can be overcome by joint application (and following discussions between ACTAPS and the BMA the latter has confirmed that its future guidance will facilitate disclosure in accordance with The ACTAPS Code). The ACTAPS Code contains an outline for such a letter.

In these circumstances it is suggested that practitioners in the areas of trust and probate law should seek to follow the approaches indicated in The ACTAPS Code, approved by the Trust Law Committee and ACTAPS, on the basis that it may serve to amplify the basic principles of the general protocols and indicate considered methods of carrying the objectives of the general protocols into effect in areas which may be found to give rise to special difficulties with which the general protocols do not grapple. In putting forward this suggestion the committee of ACTAPS believes that it has the support of all who have been concerned to consider the draft protocol; the rejection of the proposal that it be adopted as a special protocol owes nothing (so far as is known) to any perception of defects and merely reflects the belief that the public interest is best served by seeking, where possible, to avoid specific protocols and to develop best practices in areas where general protocols have to be supplemented to meet the needs of special situations.

With that in mind the committee of ACTAPS encourages members and other users to help move the search for best practices forward by commenting on any defects, inadequacies or other difficulties which may be found to arise in carrying the terms of The ACTAPS Code into effect. Please make any such comments to the ACTAPS Chairman's or the ACTAPS Secretary's e-mail address.

Practitioners will wish to bear in mind the need for trustees and executors to consider the adequacy of their powers to enter into any particular course of conduct and the possibility that they may need e.g. Beddoes type directions if they propose a course of conduct to which their beneficiaries might wish to raise objection (as for example where the trustees wish voluntarily to disclose confidential documents to third parties) or which may involve material burdens of costs (as for example the institution of a lengthy mediation). But of course in circumstances where the aim is to explore ways of reaching agreement or otherwise saving costs any necessary order might be expected to be forthcoming (within the appropriate limits) without difficulty on the basis that the Court would be being asked to facilitate a course of action essentially in accordance with the overriding objective.

1.   INTRODUCTION

The Scope of The Code

1.1   This Code is intended to apply to disputes about:

- the devolution and administration of estates of deceased persons
- the devolution and administration of trust funds ('probate and trust disputes'). It is not intended to displace other protocols if in the circumstances of the case they can be seen to be more appropriate.

The main types of disputes within the ambit of this Code can be expected to be:

- challenges to the validity of a will, for example on grounds of want of capacity or knowledge and approval, undue influence or forgery
- claims under the Inheritance (Provision for Family and Dependants) Act 1975 ('the Inheritance Act')
- actions for the removal of an administrator or executor or trustee or the appointment of a judicial trustee
- actions for the rectification of a will or other document
- disputes as to the meanings of provisions in a will or a trust
- administration actions
- allegations of breach of trust.

The ACTAPS Code may also apply to certain types of dispute where the provisions of a trust or the devolution of an estate are of the essence, for example where a claimant seeks in the alternative to set aside or overturn a trust or to take advantage of rights under a trust.

The Code has two aims; to encourage the resolution of disputes without hostile litigation; and even where litigation may be necessary to ensure that it is simplified as far as possible by maximizing the scope for the exchange of relevant information before the litigation process has commenced.

The Code is in general terms unlikely to be appropriate for disputes which involve:

- disputes as to the rights appertaining under rules of forced heirships under the law of some foreign jurisdiction
- the need for emergency injunctions
- (except in so far as concerns pre-action exchange of information) the need for a binding precedent or a declaration by the Court as to the true construction of some trust instrument or testamentary disposition.

The Code is formed in general terms to cover the broad range of trust and probate disputes; but it is recognised that the appropriate investigations and exchange of information will vary according to the circumstances of the dispute. However one of its primary purposes is to provide for a special feature of disputes in this area, namely that there may be beneficiaries who cannot speak for themselves but whose interests must be protected.

1.2   In cases where the express terms of The Code are not appropriate parties will be expected to follow the spirit of The Code and seek to achieve its aims so far as practicable in the particular case.

1.3   It is also to be borne in mind that there are certain cases in which a trust or probate dispute seeks to fulfil some non-contentious purpose, as for example where a question of difficulty is identified to which the parties are agreed that the best solution lies in inviting the Court to approve constructive proposals by way of compromise or where the objective is simply to find the cheapest way of protecting trustees or personal representatives against the risks involved in the existence of some theoretical doubt. In such cases The Code is unlikely to have any role to play.

1.4 One of the principal features of trust and probate disputes is that they may affect the interests of persons not of full capacity, as yet unborn or unascertained, or interested as members of a large class of persons who have similar beneficial interests. The Code is thus designed to make express provision for the need to find mechanisms that assist despite the absence of such persons (providing in particular an expedited process for Court approval of agreements reached in mediation). It is thus wrong in principle to regard a dispute as not amenable to the use of The Code just because there are persons concerned who cannot speak for themselves.

2. PRINCIPAL GUIDELINES

Parties

2.1 The parties to the probate or trust dispute will usually be trustees (or personal representatives or persons claiming to be entitled as such) and beneficiaries of the trust or estate who are of full capacity, though The Code is designed also to be capable of being used in exterior/third party disputes where appropriate.

2.2 In the case where interests of unascertained persons, minors, unborns, mentally incapacitated persons or members of a large class (such that it is not appropriate for all members of the class to be made parties to the dispute) will be affected, the procedure to be adopted will be an application to the Court (see Annex A) whether or not a claim has yet been instituted before the Court.

Status of Letters of Claim and Response

2.3 A letter of claim or of response is not intended to have the same status as pleadings. Matters may come to light as a result of investigation after the letter of claim has been sent or after the defendant has responded. These investigations could result in the pleaded case of a party differing in some respects from the case outlined in that party's letter of claim or response. It would not be consistent with the spirit of The Code for a party to complain about this difference provided that there was no indication of any intention to mislead.

Disclosure of Documents

2.4 The aim of the early disclosure of documents by the defendant is not to encourage 'fishing expeditions' by the claimant, but to promote an early exchange of relevant information to help in clarifying or resolving issues in dispute. The claimant's solicitors can assist by identifying in the letter of claim or in a subsequent letter the particular documents or categories of documents which they consider are relevant, and by providing copies of these where appropriate.

2.5 All documents are disclosed on the basis that they are not to be disclosed to third parties (other than legal advisers) or used for any purpose other than the resolution of the dispute, unless otherwise agreed in writing or permitted by the court.

Experts

2.6 Expert evidence appropriate to probate and trust disputes may include in particular medical evidence, handwriting evidence, valuation evidence, tax-related or
actuarial evidence.

2.7 The Code encourages joint selection of, and access to, experts. However, it main-
tains the flexibility for each party to obtain their own expert's report. It is for the
court to decide whether the costs of more than one expert's report should be
recoverable.

Costs

2.8 Where The Code provides for the initial cost of obtaining information or reports
to be borne by one party, it shall not restrict the court's discretion in relation to
ultimate liability for such costs.

Negotiations/Mediation

2.9 Parties and their legal representatives are encouraged to enter into discussions
and/or negotiations prior to starting proceedings. The parties should bear in
mind that the courts increasingly take the view that litigation should be a last
resort, and that claims should not be issued prematurely when a settlement is in
reasonable prospect. Mediation of probate and trust disputes may assist in
achieving a compromise, particularly in relation to disputes between family
members. The form of the mediation will be set out in the mediation agreement
between the mediator and the parties.

2.10 Mediation can be used to try to achieve a compromise whenever negotiation is
appropriate and can be used at any stage in a trust dispute. Typically mediation
may be considered:

(i) before proceedings have commenced but once the issues are fairly well
defined and the parties affected by them are known;
(ii) even after proceedings have commenced and the statements of case have
been served so that the parties have a better appreciation of the issues;
(iii) at any critical stage in the litigation such as after disclosure of documents,
exchange of experts' reports, exchange of witness statements and in the lead
up to the trial.

The parties should seek to conclude a mediation within 42 days of the appointment of the mediator.

2.11 Since mediation negotiations are treated by the Courts as without prejudice,
points disclosed during an attempt to reach a settlement will be confidential
between the parties and cannot be used as evidence in subsequent Court
proceedings unless expressly agreed by the party who made the disclosure. The
mediator will not divulge information without consent. Also he will not pass
on such information to outside parties or act for either party to the dispute in
subsequent proceedings.

2.12 A settlement reached pursuant to a mediation should be recorded in writing and
signed by the parties or their authorised representative. In probate and trust
disputes, if and insofar as the subject matter of the dispute requires the sanction
and approval of the Court, any agreement achieved as a result of the mediation
should be expressed to be subject to the approval of the Court.

2.13 In a probate or trust dispute where the position of the Inland Revenue may have some bearing on any compromise solution which may be reached, any agreement may be made conditional upon indications of the Inland Revenue's position or adjourned to enable clarification of its position to be sought.

3. THE CODE

Letters of Claim

3.1 The Claimant shall send a letter of claim to each of the deceased's personal representatives or to the trustees, as the case may be and, unless it is impractical (e.g. because there is a large class of beneficiaries or the beneficiaries are minors) to each beneficiary or potential beneficiary of the estate or trust fund likely to be adversely affected by the claim (referred to as 'the proposed Defendants'), as soon as sufficient information is available to substantiate a realistic claim which the Claimant has decided he is prepared to pursue.

3.2 The letter shall contain a clear summary of the claim and the facts upon which it is based and state the remedy sought by the claimant.

3.3 Solicitors are recommended to use a standard format for the claim letter. A sample letter is set out at Annex B; this can be amended to suit the particular case.

3.4 In claims under the Inheritance Act the claimant should give details to the best of his ability of the matters set out in Section 3 of the Inheritance Act as relevant to the exercise of the Court's discretion (see Annex B).

3.5 Copies of documents in the claimant's possession which he wishes to rely upon or which any other party is likely to wish to rely upon should be enclosed with the letter of claim. Examples of documents likely to be relevant in different types of dispute are set out at Annex C. These lists are not exhaustive. The letter of claim may specify classes of document considered relevant for early disclosure by the proposed defendants.

Letter of Response

3.6 Each of the proposed defendants should respond to the letter of claim within 21 days stating whether he admits or denies the claim, responding in outline to the matters of fact relied upon by the claimant and setting out any particular matters of fact upon which he relies. If a proposed defendant intends to make an answering claim on his own behalf, the letter of response should contain the same information and documents as a letter of claim in relation to the Part 20 claim. If a proposed defendant is unable to respond within the time limit on any particular matter, the letter of response should give the reasons for the absence of a full response and state when it will be available.

3.7 In claims under the Inheritance Act each proposed defendant should give details to the best of his ability of the matters set out in Section 3 of the Inheritance Act as relevant to the exercise of the Court's discretion (and set out in Annex B).

3.8 Copies of documents in the proposed defendant's possession which he wishes to rely upon or which any other party is likely to wish to rely upon should be enclosed with the letter of response. Examples of relevant documents in relation to different categories of disputes are set out at Annex C. These lists are not exhaustive.

Documents

3.9 In relation to the documents in Annex C, the personal representatives of the deceased (including executors named in the last alleged will of the deceased) or trustees as appropriate should provide copies of such documents (if available) to a party requesting a copy within 14 days of the date of a letter of request (or such other reasonable time as may be agreed between the parties) or, if a copy is only available from a third party with the consent of the personal representatives or trustees, provide to the party making the request written authority to the third party to provide a copy of the document to that party.

3.10 Trustees or personal representatives should not be inhibited from making full disclosure by the absence of litigation.

Applications for documents or information in control of third parties

3.11 In a probate dispute the release of medical notes may cast much light on the likely outcome and it should be assumed for the purposes of The Code that they ought to be disclosed at the outset absent special reason.

3.12 If so requested in writing by any party all parties shall (in the absence of good reason to withhold the relevant items) within 14 days of any such request (or such longer period as shall reasonably be agreed):

   (1) Sign and return to the party making the request, a joint application for the provision of copies of the deceased's medical notes or social worker's reports to all parties. The notes and/or reports should be sent separately and directly to each party. A specimen joint application is at Annex D.

   (2) Sign, and return to the party making the request, a joint application for a statement by the solicitor who prepared the will of the deceased setting out all the circumstances leading up to the preparation and making of the will. A specimen joint application is at Annex E.

3.13 The party making the request for a joint application for information or documents from a third party shall:

   (1) Submit it to the third party within 7 days of receipt of the joint application completed by the other parties.

   (2) On receipt of the information or documents from the third party check that they have been received by all other parties and, if not, provide them with copies within 7 days of receipt.

3.14 In cases where the mental capacity of a deceased at the date of a testamentary instrument is in issue, the party seeking to uphold the testamentary instrument should obtain a report as to the deceased's mental capacity from his GP as soon as possible after the issue is identified and send it to all other parties within 7 days of receipt. A specimen letter of request is at Annex F.

Experts

3.15 Parties should consider the use of jointly instructed experts so far as possible. Accordingly before any prospective party (the first party) instructs an expert he should (unless of the opinion that another party will want to instruct his own expert) give the other (second) party a list of the name(s) of one or more experts in the relevant discipline whom he considers are suitable to instruct.

3.16 Within 14 days the second party may indicate an objection to one or more of such experts and suggest alternatives. The first party should then instruct a mutually acceptable expert.

3.17 If an expert to be jointly instructed is not agreed, the parties may then instruct experts of their own choice. It would be for the court to decide subsequently, if proceedings are issued, whether either party had acted unreasonably. No party shall be entitled to instruct an expert proposed in a list of experts for joint instructions until it is clear that joint instructions cannot be agreed and thereafter the party who submitted the list of experts shall be entitled to nominate one of the experts on this list as his own chosen expert and no other party shall instruct any expert named on the list until such nomination has taken place.

3.18 If the second party does not object to an expert nominated, he shall not be entitled to rely on his own expert evidence within that particular discipline unless:

(1) the court so directs, or

(2) the first party's expert report has been amended and the first party is not prepared to disclose the original report.

3.19 Either party may send to the expert written questions on the report, relevant to the issues, via the first party's solicitors. The expert should send answers to the question separately and directly to each party.

3.20 The cost of the report from an agreed expert will usually be paid by the party first proposing that a joint expert be instructed. The costs of the expert replying to questions will usually be borne by the party asking the questions. The ultimate liability for costs will be determined by the Court.

ANNEX A

Representation in Estate or Trust Disputes of interested persons who cannot be ascertained etc.

(1) In any estate or trust dispute concerning:

(a) property comprised in an estate or subject to a trust or alleged to be subject to a trust; or

(b) the construction of a written instrument; or

(c) a situation where the interests of beneficiaries may require separate representation

the Court, if satisfied that it is expedient to do so, and that one or more of the conditions specified in paragraph (2) are satisfied, may appoint one or more persons to represent any person (including a person under a disability, a minor or an unborn person) or class who is or may be interested (whether presently or for any future, contingent or unascertained interest) in or affected by the dispute.

(2) The conditions for the exercise of the power conferred by paragraph (1) are as follows:

(a) that the person, the class or some member of the class cannot be ascertained or cannot be readily ascertained, or is not of full capacity; or

(b) that the person, the class or some member of the class, though ascertained, cannot be found; or

(c) that, though the person or the class and members thereof can be ascertained and found, it appears to the Court expedient (regard being had to all the circumstances, including the amount at stake and the degree of difficulty of the point to be determined) to exercise the power for the purposes of saving expense or for any other reason.

(3) Where, in any case to which paragraph 1 applies, the Court exercises the power conferred by that paragraph, a judgment or order of the Court given or made when the person or persons appointed in exercise of that power are before the Court shall be binding on the person or class represented by the person or persons so appointed.

(4) Where, in any such case, a compromise is proposed and some of the persons who are interested in, or who may be affected by the compromise have not been consulted (including persons under a disability, minors or unborn or unascertained persons) but

    (a)   there is some other person in the same interest before the Court who assents to the compromise or on whose behalf the Court sanctions the compromise; or

    (b)   the absent persons are represented by a person appointed under paragraph (1) who so assents,

the Court, if satisfied that the compromise will be for the benefit of the absent persons and that it is expedient to exercise this power, may approve the compromise and order that it shall be binding on absent persons, and they shall be bound accordingly except where the order has been obtained by fraud or non-disclosure of material facts.

ANNEX B

To
Defendant
Dear
Re:

The estate of [*name of deceased*]
The Settlement made by [*Settlor*] on [*date*]

We are instructed on behalf of [*claimant*] [*give details of relief sought, e.g.* to seek reasonable provision out of the estate of the above-named deceased; to set aside probate of the will of the above-named deceased dated [*date*]; to seek a declaration that upon a proper construction of the above settlement our client is entitled to . . .]

The basis of our client's claim is: [*brief outline*]

The facts upon which our client relies are as follows: [*set out material facts with suffi-cient clarity and detail for the proposed defendants to make a preliminary assessment of the claim*]

The details of matters to which the Court would have regard under Section 3 of the Inheritance (Provision for Family and Dependants) Act 1975 insofar as they are known to our client are:

(a)   Financial resources and needs of claimant;
(b)   Financial resources and needs of any other claimant;
(c)   Financial resources and needs of beneficiaries;
(d)   Obligations and responsibilities of deceased towards claimants and beneficiaries;
(e)   Size and nature of estate;
(f)   Disabilities of claimants and beneficiaries;
(g)   Any other matter; and if claimant spouse or co-habitee,

(h)   age of claimant, length of marriage/co-habitation and contribution to family welfare.

We enclose the following documents which are relevant to the claim:

[*list documents*]

In accordance with The ACTAPS Code for probate and trust disputes, we look forward to receiving a letter of response, enclosing the documents in your possession and relevant to the claim within [21] days. We believe that the following documents relevant to the claim are likely to be in your possession: [*list documents*]

Pursuant to The ACTAPS Code as [personal representatives of the deceased/trustees of the settlement] we invite you to furnish us within 14 days of the date of this letter with copies of the following documents or written authority, in the form enclosed, to obtain copies of such document(s): [*list asterisked documents required*]

We have also sent a letter of claim to [*name and address*] and a copy of that letter is enclosed.

Yours faithfully

ANNEX C

All documents upon which you rely or upon which the other party is likely to wish to rely including but not limited to the following categories:

1.   In disputes in which the assets of an estate/trust fund or the financial resources of an individual are relevant; e.g. claims under the Inheritance Act, breach of trust claims:

  –   The Inland Revenue Account and any Corrective Account;
  –   A schedule of the capital assets (with values, estimated where appropriate) and income of the estate, trust fund or individual as appropriate;
  –   Trust or Estate Accounts.

2.   In disputes in which the mental capacity or medical condition of an individual is relevant, e.g. challenges to testamentary capacity, Inheritance Act claims where disability is alleged:

  –   A copy of the medical records of the individual or, if appropriate, the written authority of the personal representatives of a deceased to obtain his medical records together with an office copy of the grant of probate or letters of administration or other proof of their status.

3.   In disputes as to the validity, construction or rectification of a will or other testamentary instrument of the deceased:

  –   A statement setting out details of any testamentary script (now in CPR called testamentary document) within the knowledge of the claimant or proposed defendant and details of the name and address of the person who, to the best of his knowledge, has possession or control of such script.

Nb1: The provision of the statement in 3 above is of vital importance to all parties in a dispute since it ensures that the correct testamentary documents are being considered. This will prevent the problem of a dispute over a later testamentary document being allowed to overshadow the existence of an intermediate testamentary document which would be upheld if the later testamentary document fails.

Also it helps identify the correct parties to the existing disputes.

Nb2: Following from Nb1 above, it is most important that the fullest and most exhaustive search for all testamentary documents is made. Accordingly while the following list is not exhaustive it is incumbent upon all parties to check:

(i)   with all known solicitors of the deceased as to the existence of a testamentary document;

(ii)   with all attesting witnesses to testamentary documents as to the existence of testamentary documents;

(iii) with all named executors of testamentary documents as to the existence of testamentary documents;

(iv) with immediate family members (brothers, sisters, parents and children of the deceased) as to the existence of testamentary documents.

Nb3: *Definition of Testamentary Script (now in CPR called Testamentary document)*

A will, a draft of a will, written instructions for a will made by or at the request of, or under the instructions of, the testator, and any document purporting to be evidence of the contents, or to be a copy, of a will which is alleged to have been lost or destroyed. The word 'will' includes a codicil.

ANNEX D

JOINT APPLICATION FOR MEDICAL NOTES OR SOCIAL WORKER'S REPORTS

To: The medical records officer/social services

Dear Sir

Re: [*Name*] Deceased of [address], [*date of birth*]

We the undersigned Messrs [*firm's name*] [*ref.*] of [*firm's address*], Solicitors for the Executors named in the Will of the late [*deceased's name*] of [*deceased's address*] who died on [*date of death*] and we, the undersigned Messrs [*firm's name*] of [*firm's address*], Solicitors for parties interested in his/her estate, hereby authorise you to forward [a full set of copies of the deceased's Medical Records] [all social worker's reports and notes relating to the deceased] to each of the aforementioned firms.

We confirm that we will be responsible for your reasonable photocopying charges and your invoice in this regard should be sent to [*firm's name*] and marked for the attention of [*ref.*].

Dated [...] 200[...]

Signed

....

Signed

....

ANNEX E

JOINT APPLICATION LETTER TO SOLICITORS WHO PREPARED WILL REQUESTING *LARKE* V. *NUGUS* STATEMENT

Dear Sirs

[Name of Deceased] deceased

We, the undersigned Messrs [*firm's name*] [*ref.*] of [*firm's address*], solicitors for the Executors named in the Will of [*deceased's name*] of [*deceased's address*] and we, the undersigned Messrs [*firm's name*] [*ref.*] of [*firm's address*], solicitors for parties interested in his/her estate regret to inform you that [*deceased's name*] died on [*date of death*].

We understand that you drafted the deceased's last will dated [...].

You may be aware that in 1959 the Law Society recommended that in circumstances such as this the testator's solicitor should make available a statement of his or her evidence regarding instructions for the preparation and execution of the will and surrounding circumstances. This recommendation was endorsed by the Court of Appeal on 21st February 1979 in *Larke* v. *Nugus*.

The practice is also recommended at paragraph 24.02 of the Law Society's *Guide to the Professional Conduct of Solicitors* [1999, 8th edition, p.450].

Accordingly, we hereby request and authorise you to forward to each of the aforementioned firms statements from all appropriate members of your firm on the following points:

- How long had you known the deceased?
- Who introduced you to the deceased?
- On what date did you receive instructions from the deceased?
- Did you receive instructions by letter? If so, please provide copies of any correspondence.
- If instructions were taken at a meeting, please provide copies of your contemporaneous notes of the meeting including an indication of where the meeting took place and who else was present at the meeting.
- How were the instructions expressed?
- What indication did the deceased give to you that he knew he was making a will?
- Were you informed or otherwise aware of any medical history of the deceased that might bear upon the issue of his capacity?
- Did the deceased exhibit any signs of confusion or loss of memory? If so, please give details.
- To what extent were earlier wills discussed and what attempts were made to discuss departures from his earlier will-making pattern? What reasons, if any, did the testator give for making any such departures?
- When the will had been drafted, how were the provisions of the will explained to the deceased?
- Who, apart from the attesting witnesses, was present at the execution of the will? Where, when and how did this take place?
- Please provide copies of any other documents relating to your instructions for the preparation and execution of the will and surrounding circumstances or confirm that you have no objection to us inspecting your relevant file(s) on reasonable notice.

We confirm that we will be responsible for your reasonable photocopying charges in this connection and your invoice in this regard should be sent to [*each firm's name etc.*] and marked for the attention of [*each firm's ref.*].

Dated this [...] day of [...] 200[...]

Signed

....

Signed

....

ANNEX F

LETTER TO DECEASED'S GP REQUESTING REPORT AS TO MENTAL CAPACITY

To: Deceased's GP

Dear Dr . . ...

Re: [*Name*] Deceased of [*address*], [*date of birth*]

We the undersigned Messrs [*firm's name*] [*ref.*] of [*firm's address*] are Solicitors for the Executors named in the Will of the late [*deceased's name*] of [*deceased's address*] who died on [*date of death*] and we, the undersigned Messrs [*firm's name*] of [*firm's address*], are Solicitors for parties interested in his/her estate.

We enclose a photocopy of the deceased's last Will. The clauses in the Will which cause particular concern are [*clause numbers*].

The question of the deceased's mental capacity at the time of the making of his/her last Will dated has now been raised.

The test of testamentary capacity remains that established in the case of *Banks* v. *Goodfellow* where it was said:

'It is essential that a testator (1) shall understand the nature of the act and its effects; (2) shall understand the extent of the property of which he is disposing; and (3) shall be able to comprehend and appreciate the claims to which he ought to give effect, and; with a view to the latter object, (4) that no disorder of mind shall poison his affections, pervert his sense of right or pervert the exercise of his natural faculties; (5) that no insane delusions shall influence his mind in disposing of his property and bring about a disposal of it which if his mind had been sound, would not have been made.' [We have added numbers for convenience].

[*Set out the nature of the Estate if complex.*]

We would therefore be grateful if you would kindly provide us with a report setting out:

1. Your medical qualifications and your experience in assessing mental states and capacity
2. For how long you were the deceased's GP, how well you knew the deceased and a summary of his/her medical condition, insofar as it may have bearing upon the deceased's mental capacity.
3. Your findings as to the deceased's mental capacity at and around the time of the date of his/her last will.

4. Please also deal with any mental disorder from which the deceased may have been suffering at the relevant time, and any medication which could have affected his/her capacity as detailed above.
5. Please also consider any issues of vulnerability or suggestibility at or around the date of the deceased's last Will

We confirm that we will be responsible for your reasonable fees in the preparation of your report which we look forward to receiving as soon as possible.

Dated this [...] day of [...] 200[...]

Signed

.... [ref: ...]

Signed

.... [ref: ...]

Index